The Importance of Governance in
Regional Labour Market Monitoring for
Evidence-based Policy-making

Christa Larsen, Sigrid Rand, Alfons Schmid,
Tilman Nagel*, Heike Hoess* (Eds.)

The Importance of Governance in Regional Labour Market Monitoring for Evidence-based Policy-making

Rainer Hampp Verlag

Augsburg, München 2017

* Deutsche Gesellschaft für Internationale Zusammenarbeit

Bibliographic information published by the Deutsche Nationalbibliothek

Deutsche Nationalbibliothek lists this publication in the Deutsche Nationalbibliografie; detailed bibliographic data are available in the Internet at http://dnb.d-nb.de.

ISBN 978-3-95710-200-3 (print)
ISBN 978-3-95710-300-0 (e-book)
ISBN-A/DOI 10.978.395710/3000
First published in 2017

© 2017   Rainer Hampp Verlag   Augsburg, München
         Vorderer Lech 35   86150 Augsburg, Germany
         www.Hampp-Verlag.de

All rights preserved. No part of this publication may be reprinted or reproduced or utilized in any form or by any electronic, mechanical, or other means, now known or hereafter invented, including photocopying and recording, or in any information storage or retrieval system, without permission in writing from the publisher.

In case of complaints please contact Rainer Hampp Verlag.

FOREWORD

It is clear that the labour market world is dramatically changing and that we are facing a real revolution pushed in particular by the digitalisation. This is and will be for the next future our main priority as Workers' Group of the Economic and Social Committee, in particular from the perspective of the governance of this new process. Digitalisation transforms all segments of society and the economy and thus logically affects work and employment as well. Our duty is to protect the quality, the skills and competences of this generation of workers. We really need a deep analysis on the impact of these developments on skills, life-long training and we have to avoid any negative effect of these dramatic changes on jobs and workers. Local and regional examples are fundamental to understand obstacles and/or best solutions; but no solution can be realistic at local or regional level. In many opinions, the EESC has underlined the importance to have a European employment strategy, a European vision for the future of work. In our opinion on the European Pillar of Social Rights (G. Bischoff – EESC SOC), we underline that "Social partners have a specific role to play in the elaboration and implementation of policies directly or indirectly affecting employment and labour markets". Pro-active policy-makers at the EU and national levels can and must ensure that the evident potentials of digitalisation can be unlocked while its pitfalls are avoided. With its Digital Agenda for Europe and the Digital Single Market initiative, the EU is an active player in the field of digital policy. However, most of the employment effects of digitalisation remain unacknowledged and thus are poorly addressed by relevant policies. As we say in the opinion on "Effects of digitalisation on service industries and employment" (W. Greif – EESC CCMI), the employment effects of digitalisation warrant political attention and management. We would like for these reasons to thank all actors involved in this extremely interesting work – institutes, universities, regional and local social partners that have contributed to such a valid result.

Gabriele Bischoff
President of the Workers' Group
European Economic and Social Committee (EESC)

Brussels, 4 September 2017

CONTENTS

INTRODUCTION

Christa Larsen and Sigrid Rand   11

1. HIERARCHY AND MARKET AS DOMINANT GOVERNANCE MODES

The Governance Process in the Swiss Regional Labour Market Observatories
Moreno Baruffini and Luzius Stricker   25

Labour Market, Economic Policy and Economic Growth Perspectives in Russia
Nina Oding   41

Precarious Employment Governance in Russia: Challenges, Practice, Scientific Validity
Vyacheslav Bobkov, Vadim Kvachev and Irina Novikova   63

A Conceptual Model of Collaborative Support System for Labour Market Governance
Ciprian Pânzaru and Claudiu Brândaş   81

Labour Market Governance in England: Devolution and Localism
Andrew Dean   95

The Reaction of Social Partners to the Application of the "Jobs Act": A Comparison Between Digital Communication Strategies

Renato Fontana, Vera D'Antonio, Martina Ferrucci and Carmine Piscopo **115**

The Best Offer: Monitoring and Analysis of Best Practices of the Centres for Public and Private Employment and University Orientation and Placement Services

Patrizio Di Nicola, Alessandra Fasano, Piera Rella and Ludovica Rossotti **147**

2. HIERACHY AND NETWORK AS DOMINANT GOVERNANCE MODES

The Importance of Governance in the Regional Labour Market Monitoring for Evidence-based Policy-making: Basque Country Case

Javier Ramos Salazar **185**

Employment Support Project in Bosnia and Herzegovina

Željko Tepavčević, Siniša Veselinović and Zvjezdana Jelić **199**

Modelling Scenarios for Securing Skilled Healthcare Personnel: Confronting Shortages in Skilled Personnel with Data-driven, Participatory Strategies

Lisa Schäfer, Oliver Lauxen and Melanie Castello **217**

Challenges for Albania Regrading Improving the Labour Market Information System and Labour Market Governance from Hierarchy to Market to Network Governance

Neshat Zeneli **241**

The Provision of Skills Information in Scotland and Its Governance – Skills Investment Plans and Regional Skills Assessments

Ronald McQuaid **263**

3. NETWORK RELATED TO MARKET AND HIERARCHY

(Regional) Labour Market Monitoring - Experience from Developing and Transition Countries

Sara Ennya, Heike Hoess, Uwe Kühnert, Pierre Lucante, Laura Schmid and Etleva Vertopi **277**

4. PERSPECTIVES

Government – Governance: The Quality of the Regulatory Systems to Improve the Performances of Labour Market Services

Marco Ricceri **323**

INFORMATION ON AUTHORS **333**

INTRODUCTION

Christa Larsen and Sigrid Rand

1. Point of departure

Information on regional and local labour markets is an essential precondition for evidence-based policy decisions in the field of labour markets. In Europe, there are over 560 regional and local labour market observatories (RLMO), which provide reliable and targeted information of the current and future developments of the labour markets in their region or locality. If this information is made available to policy-makers, it finds its way into the processes of decision-making, strategy development, policy-making and policy implementation on the regional and local level (Dean et al. 2015, Martini et al. 2016).

For several years, the members of the European Network on Regional Labour Market Monitoring (EN RLMM) have been discussing how to address political decision-makers more effectively. Supply-oriented information provided on websites or disseminated through printed reports often does not reach the desired impact, thus demonstrating the limits of the information function of the monitoring approach. We assume that further impact can be reached by applying the communication and decision-making functions of the monitoring approach (Larsen et al. 2013). As a result, increasing the demand-orientation of information will facilitate its incorporation into the regional or local policy context and create a solid basis for adequate interpretation and decision-making processes. The configuration of these processes depends to a large extent on regional and local (and sometimes national) conditions.

From an analytical perspective, the decision-making structures and processes constitute elements of governance. So far, however the members of the EN RLMM have not discussed thoroughly, which modes of governance in the provision and use of labour market information are particularly functional for evidence-based labour market politics. Also, the issue of formats most suitable for presenting the information needs to be re-addressed. Therefore, it would be important to start such a conceptually oriented reflection of (successful) strategies at the regional and local level in order to understand better why certain regional/local strategies work well and others do not. First and foremost, these insights could help the observatories to enhance their own strategies. Moreover, other data providers who aim to close the gap between their data and the political process could profit from this work as well.

To begin with, our understanding of governance is based on the definition of Lynn (2010: 67) as the "directing, guiding or regulating individuals, organizations, or nations in conduct or actions". Therefore, the study of governance is concerned with the structure of decision-making and policy implementation in a distinct system (Greer et al. 2016: 3). Over the past years, several typologies of governance modes have been developed, exploring the rationalities, most common mechanisms of control and the focus of policy development characteristic for every mode. Based on the approach of Considine and Lewis (2003), we adopt a threefold typology of governance modes and elaborate them based on Meulemann (2008):

- **Hierarchy**: The government designs and implements policies on the basis of a system of fixed rules and statutes, which are applied by bureaucratic organisations. This renders the legislation the primary source of rationality, which is applied in a centralised and top-down manner. The functionality of this mode is based on authority, legality and accountability.
- **Market:** The role of the government is seen as providing a framework for competition efficiency and performance-based rewards. Here, the private sector is commonly assigned a major role.
- **Network**: Interests between different actors (stakeholders) are negotiated within collaborative structures. This is based on mutual trust, empathy, acceptance of interdependency and consensus. This can allow stakeholders to be involved in the development of policies.

Since these governance modes are implemented in combinations (Meuleman 2008, Saltman et al. 2011, Tuohy 2012, Newman 2005, Kuhlmann et al. 2016), this year's Anthology focuses on exploring specific connections between these modes through presenting examples from eleven countries. The case examples selected for the Anthology illustrate not only the different combinations of governance modes, but also demonstrate that there are different degrees of connections between the modes. The contributions show how information, i.e. evidence, can be placed in different constellations and processes and describe the challenges occurring in this process.

2. Which structural combinations of and connections between governance modes exist?

In all case examples, it becomes clear that labour markets and the VET system are in the first place governed through a strongly top-down hierarchical structure, in which the relevant ministries and subordinate entities are located. In federalist states, this mode is applied also at the regional level in combination with the governance modes of market and network.

2.1 Combination of hierarchy and market as governance modes

In several case examples presented in the Anthology, regional labour markets are considered to be liberalised. The balancing of interests between employers and employees is described to take place through deliberation and negotiation between social partners. Consequently, this renders the hierarchic governance of the state as a co-ordination mechanism not effective. Rather, the state actors are involved merely as intermediaries, facilitators or mediators in the market mechanism responsible for balancing the interests of the social partners. Here, competition and performance are essential elements. The case example of Switzerland in this Anthology shows how the governments of the cantons established the framework for the functioning of the market mechanism that led to concurrently functional, practice-oriented and efficient results. Along the same lines, also the two case examples from Russia show how the co-operation of market actors sets impulses for the modernisation of the Russian labour market. In contrast, the hierarchical state governance is considered not very conducive of information and susceptible of corruption.

In all examples is becomes clear that the exchange between market actors needs to be incorporated into regional and local processes by feeding existing data and studies into that dialogue. These can be interpreted, as far as necessary, with the help of experts and connected to new information from the praxis, so that the evidence can be produced even better. Experts from universities and research institutes or from regional observatories can assume this function. In order to use the evidence created through market mechanism for the process of policy-making, it needs to be connected to the hierarchical structure. This can take place through so-called hybrid organisations, which are created on the boundary of market and hierarchy. These can, considering the example of Switzerland, be observatories, through which the governments of the cantons feed data and information into the exchange of social partners. The results of the discourse are then fed through the hierarchical line of public administration to the policy-makers in the cantonal government. The self-governance of market partners in hybrid institutions can also be supported through the use of IT. Whether the labour administration is a suitable location for such hybrid institutions or can fulfil their functions, is only implied in the case studies as there seems to be no implementation yet. It becomes clear, however, that especially in countries with strong social partners no hybrid organisations are considered desirable and the dialogues of social partners do not always follow the balancing of interests in the sense of competition as shown in the case examples from Italy.

Reconnecting to policy-making seems to be considerably easier within a structure, which does not necessitate the combining of two separate system logics with each other. This is demonstrated through further case examples.

2.2 Connections of Hierarchy and Network

For networks connected to a hierarchical public structure we can observe two different patterns. In the first case, the network is constituted through the public labour administration representing the government or the relevant ministry. It involves representatives of different stakeholders such as representatives of trade unions, sectoral associations, chambers and employers from the corporate sector as well as representatives from the public VET area, universities and to some extent also the civil society. To a greater or lesser extent, the public labour administration defines the rules of the game in the networks and feeds partly also the data and information into the cooperative exchange within the network. In the next step, the results produced in the network move in a bottom-up process along the hierarchical structure back into the policy-making. Thereby, the networks assume not only the function of impulse givers in the policy process, but also the role of the evaluators in the newly implemented policies as well as labour market and VET programmes. Also, the scientifically produced evaluation results are often interpreted and validated in networks. Moreover, in the case example from the Basque Country it is shown, that the network can work as the multiplier for the information that is provided by the public labour administration. Through that, a higher level of transparency can be reached locally so that the regional and local labour market can function more efficiently. Also in Bosnia and Herzegovina the installation of such a network is promoted.

The second pattern for establishing a connection between hierarchy and network is presented in the case examples from Albania and the Federal State of Rhineland-Palatinate in Germany. The starting point in both cases is the political will in the relevant ministries for developing innovative labour market programmes as well as initiating innovations in the labour market or the VET politics. For reaching this goal, project funds are made available for a longer period of time and a network affiliated with the project is established. Similarly to the examples mentioned above, the network is chaired by a ministry or its representatives, who also have decision-making powers, and brings together stakeholders from many different areas. The functions within the network and the project are clearly defined: the data experts bring in the necessary information and moderate the process and the representatives of the ministries accompany the discourses, where necessary steering them hierarchically. In the project, data for creating transparency are first collected and then completed and interpreted within the network. Based on that, cooperative concepts, drafts or suggestions for the policy process are developed. After the development and implementation of the programme or the initiatives, the network assumes the function of monitoring and evaluation and develops suggestions for readjustments. The stakeholders in the network bring in their interests, which are voiced in a co-operative manner. Also here, the stakeholders in the network partially work as multipliers concerning the produced data and can so contribute to the transparency in the regional and local labour market as well as support the process of matching.

2.3 Network with Hierarchy or Market

Analysing the case examples from Morocco and Egypt and comparing them to the patterns sketched above, it becomes clear that a regional network that is connected to hierarchical, participative as well as market-based structures can be set up as a centrepiece of planned activities. However, it seems to be considerably more difficult to influence the political decision-making process than in the examples where a network is built and steered along a hierarchical structure.

The three patterns of connecting different modes of governance show that they are responsible for the different preconditions for the processes of information generation and dissemination and their engagement in the policy process.

3. Which configuration of networks is conducive of evidence-based policy-making?

In most case examples included in this Anthology, the central role of networks is underlined. However, it also becomes clear that the existence of a network does not automatically lead to an enhanced state of information and a better connection to the policy process. To a greater degree, it is important how the network is set up. Different criteria can be identified, which support the co-operative deliberation processes within the network. The criterion of **transparency** seems to be central. This means, for example, that all network members know with which purpose and goal the network has been installed and which expectations are directed towards the members. As a second principle **accountability** needs to be listed. This involves clarity about the roles of single members, the rules for collaboration and the forms of decision-making. Furthermore, **participation** is of importance, to make sure that all those who are affected by the policy process are included in the network. This way, they can bring their needs and reservations into the process or can make suggestions for the suitable implementation. In most case examples, this criterion proves very difficult to implement, because institutionalised interest representation through associations, for example, can follow other interests and can have little connection to the praxis. Closely connected to this bloc is **integrity**. Here, it should be ensured that the process is organised in a manner that rules out corruption. This is particularly difficult in countries, where corruption is widespread. But also the corporatist structures in the Western European democracies can produce a similar effect. Furthermore, networks can function well if those involved have enough **capacities** in the sense of possessing the necessary expertise, understanding the structures and processes, being able to communicate as well as understanding different rationalities of businesses, politics, public administration, etc. Depending on the network, necessary competencies can also include the ability to formulate policies or to accompany implementation processes and evaluations.

Two more aspects can be crucial for successful governance in networks: the moderator needs the right skills in order to facilitate the process as neutrally as possible as well as to build up trust and reliability. Moderators from politics or the labour administration often have to manifest the credibility of their "neutral" role first, before they are fully accepted by the network members. Representatives of research organisations or professional supporters of such processes like coaches can eventually build up trust easier. Several case examples in the Anthology show that it is beneficial if networks are subjected to an internal differentiation. This includes the installation of a steering group at the strategic and decision-making level. This group receives its thematic input from content-oriented working groups, in which operative actors collaborate. In this constellation it is important that the translation from the operative to the strategic level can be ensured and that the function of the strategic group and the tasks and responsibilities of single members are unequivocally stated and adhered to.

4. In which forms are data and information embedded into governance structures?

Data and information, which constitute the basis for evidence-based politics, are embedded into governance structures and processes in a different manner. Several case examples show that specific data are generated as a starting point of all activities. After that, they are validated within the governance processes, fine-tuned and specified in a way that creates the foundation for policy-making. In this case, the validation and the policy-making often blend into each other. Depending on the combinations of and connections between governance modes, the information can constitute an important engine in the whole process. Nevertheless, the precondition is that at the beginning there is a clear political will for generating data and bringing public data from labour administration, the statistical offices and other sources into the exchange of social partners or networks. This creates the basis for an improved information situation through the interpretation and supplementation of original data. In these cases, the dialogue of the partners or the exchange in the network are prominently placed so that the information function is easily marginalised. If there is a clear connection to the hierarchical structure, the ascertained information can be brought into the policy-making. If the connections are weak, the chances of this happening are considerably worse, especially if the political decision-makers have not issued a declaration of will for the producing this evidence. Judging from the submitted case examples, the ensuring of the feedback of information, which is created in the market-based constellations of social partners, proves even more difficult. They demonstrate that if this structure is rather weakly connected to the hierarchy, conveying information into the policy-making process can be difficult.

5. How can the sustainability of evidence-based policy-making be reached?

Situations of high modernisation and innovation pressures constitute a favourable precondition for evidence-based policy-making, as they initiate high motivation levels of those involved in the process: there is awareness that the regional economy cannot grow any more, young people leave the region and the regions decline. Alternatively, changes are tied to the payment of subsidies or project funds. Furthermore, it becomes clear in the case examples that the EU-accession or the membership in a regional entity can be an important incentive. Furthermore, in many European and non-European countries decentralisation and regionalisation processes take effect, where competences and tasks are decentralised and need constituting. Hereby, the example from England shows that the configuration can be complex if the decision-making power is not systematically delegated and implemented de-centrally. In some case examples several of the listed factors cumulate and reinforce each other.

The chances of a sustainable anchoring of an evidence-based policy process appear better in the case examples when the communication processes are systematically and professionally initiated and the missing competencies are conveyed to those involved. The exact specification of the different functions and tasks seems to be important. Furthermore, the functional connection of the governance modes of network and market with hierarchy are essential for transferring evidence into the policy process. Institutionalisation and standardisation can help, but remain ambivalent, since it is possible that the participants get caught up in routines or engage themselves in interest politics.

Furthermore, constituting an evidence-based policy-making needs time. For example, if after the implementation of an evidence-base labour market programme for the stakeholders and politicians tangible and measurable successes take place, then it is highly probable that this process can be continued as the readiness can be activated more easily. The long-term examples in this Anthology also show that over the time a specific communication culture is established and those who are involved go through learning processes. Sincerity and appreciation are also important parameters for keeping up the motivation of the participants.

Finally, planning towards end results or products, meaning that processes are anchored in long-term structures, stabilise the whole process. Especially in the areas of information generation and communication significant facilitation through the involvement of information technology can be reached. Furthermore, data generation starting with monitoring and ending with evaluation can be implemented in a continuous cyclical process, so that transparency and evidence can be created continuously.

6. How is the Anthology structured?

The structure of the Anthology is oriented towards the three structural patterns of connections between the governance modes. The first three chapters of the Anthology are concerned with the identified patters, while the fourth chapter summarises the perspectives that can be derived from the changes in the governance structures depicted in the case examples.

In Chapter 1, the focus is on case examples, in which the governance mode of hierarchy is combined with the market. In the first example, Moreno Baruffini und Luzius Stricker describe the governance process into which the labour market observatories of the Swiss cantons are embedded. This process is clearly defined and structured. In contrast, structurally similar processes in Russia are far more open. This is shown by the case example provided by Nina Oding, describing the hierarchical public governance and arguing that the involvement of business actors in the policy process is necessary for achieving innovative impulses for the modernisation of the Russian labour market and economy. Along a similar line, Vyacheslav Bobkov, Vadim Kvachev and Irina Novikova focus on the area of precarious employment and the necessary labour market reforms. Also they see essential impulses for this process in the exchange with market actors, whereby in their opinion essential inputs for the discourses of experts should come from research. Ciprian Pânzaru and Claudiu Brândaș show in their contribution how the discourses of market actors can be tied in with the hierarchical structure of public administration. They develop a model by creating a connection through a hybrid structure, which can essentially support the governance process. Furthermore, they refer to the usefulness of IT in these processes.

The three following articles are concerned with the challenges to the governance structure and processes as a result of change processes. Andrew Dean addresses the important aspect of decentralisation and regionalisation, which in many countries is the starting point for changes in governance and can lead to the establishment of regional networks and dialogues of social partners. Following the example of England he shows that the transfer of competences to regional entities is not enough. Rather, a new governance structure needs to be set up, which among other things is endowed with central decision-making powers. The steering through hierarchies quickly reaches its limits in such processes. Renato Fontana, Vera D'Antonio, Martina Ferrucci and Carmine Piscopo describe by the example of the introduction of the Jobs Act in Italy that next to hierarchy the dialogue of social partners is installed as a second mode. However, this is not filled with life in the sense of an actual participation. They show clearly that decentral governance is no guarantee for participation and bottom-up processes. Patrizio Di Nicola, Alessandra Fasano, Piera Rella and Ludovica Rossotti consider a case where the hierarchical and market-based modes run parallel and analyse the dysfunctionality of their coexistence. Along the example of job centres of the public labour administration and private labour agencies the complementary advantages are revealed. They plead for connecting both organisation structures, in order to meet the real needs of the clients who are to be consulted and placed.

In Chapter 2, case examples are presented in which the connection of hierarchy and networks is described. The first contributions are concerned with networks, which are connected to the hierarchically organised public labour administrations and as a result are close to policy-making. Javier Ramos Salazar describes in great detail for Lanbide - The Basque Employment Service how a highly specialised and well-functioning network is installed. Željko Tepavčević, Siniša Veselinović and Zvjezdana Jelić describe the case of Bosnia and Herzegovina. They also show how the public labour administration can install corresponding network structures. The three following articles are concerned with relevant ministries, which already have the readiness for evidence-based politics and start a project with a concrete need for information. They initiate projects, where information is de-centrally validated and supplemented and fed into the policy-making process. Lisa Schäfer, Oliver Lauxen and Melanie Castello show for the health and elderly care sector in the Federal State of Rhineland-Palatinate in Germany how such a process is set up and implemented. They demonstrate how learning processes are established, which contribute to the continuation and stabilisation of the initiative. Neshat Zeneli describes for Albania the starting point for a process, which is thematically oriented towards the improvement of matching between qualification and the needs of businesses. The same case example is presented from a different perspective also in the last article in this section. In his contribution, Ronald McQuaid describes and analyses the complex governance system in Scotland, which integrates various stakeholders through different modes of governance. Following the example of skills he demonstrates how data are created, interpreted and used for action in the sophisticated system involving bottom-up processes.

In Chapter 3, there are three case examples, which are concerned with the central factors influencing governance processes in the developing and emerging countries. Sara Ennya, Heike Hoess, Uwe Kühnert, Pierre Lucante, Laura Schmid and Etleva Vertopi show in their examples very clearly that the basic topics, which have been addressed in the previous chapters, are highly relevant also for the starting points in the developing and emerging countries. Especially interesting are the case examples for Morocco and Egypt showing how regional, i.e. decentral networks are established. Their loose coupling with the hierarchical development structures as well as market-based fields enables the feeding of data and information into the policy-making process on regional level.

The case examples of this Anthology will constitute the basis for the discussions at the Annual Meeting of the EN RLMM in Tirana, Albania on 5-6 October 2017. There, the structures presented in this introduction will be specified and the concepts developed further in the process of mutual learning. Recommendations can be derived also from the Chapter 4 of the Anthology. There, Marco Ricceri shows that the further development of governance can lead to the improvement of the performance of labour market services.

We are very glad that so many of the Network members approached the topic that so far has hardly been discussed in the EN RLMM and would like to thank the authors for their interesting contributions. We hope, that our analysis has contributed to the localisation of the issues.

We would also like to mention that this year we received a comprehensive contribution from a publication group of the Deutsche Gesellschaft für Internationale Zusammenarbeit (GIZ). There are several very interesting examples of good practice as well as interesting analyses concerning the preconditions, challenges and success factors. This analysis makes an important contribution to the further development of our concepts and approaches within the Network. It also shows that there are many commonalities between the countries and regions in the EU and outside, also in the developing and emerging countries. The exchange is extremely rewarding for all parties and should take place systematically at this year's Annual Meeting. Against this background, we would like to thank the GIZ for their involvement in the Network and their readiness to act as hosts and co-organisers of this year's Annual Meeting of the EN RLMM. And last, but not least, we would like to thank Jason Taaffe for his careful and diligent proofreading of this year's contributions.

References

Considine, Marl/Lewis, Jenny M. (2003): Bureaucracy, network, or enterprise? Comparing models of governance in Australia, Britain, the Netherlands, and New Zealand. Public Administration Review, Vol. 63, No. 2: 131-140

Dean, Andrew/Rand, Sigrid (2015): Lessons for Local and Regional Forecasting Arising from the Work of the European Network on Regional Labour Market Monitoring. in: Larsen, Christa/Rand, Sigrid/Schmid, Alfons/Mezzanzanica, Mario/Dusi, Silvia (Eds.): Big Data and the Complexity of Labour Market Policies: New Aapproaches in Regional and Local Labour Market Monitoring for Reducing Skills Mismatches. München: Hampp Verlag: 223-233

Greer, Scott L./Wismar, Matthias/Figueras, Josep (Eds.) (2016a): Strengthening Health System Governance: Better policies, stronger performance. Maidenhead: Open University Press.

Kuhlmann, Ellen/Lauxen, Oliver/Larsen, Christa (2016): Regional health workforce monitoring as governance innovation: a German model to coordinate sectoral demand, skill mix and mobility. Human Resources for Health, 14:71; http://rdcu.be/m4Ul

Lynn, Laurence E. Jr. (2006): Has governance eclipsed government? in: Durant, Robert F. (Ed.): The Oxford Handbook of American Bureaucracy. Oxford: Oxford University Press: 669-690

Martini, Mattia/Andreani, Martino/Trivellato, Benedetta (2016): Addressing Information Needs in Employment Services Provision in Italy: The Role of Codesign Networks. International Journal of Public Administration, http://dx.doi.org/10.1080/01900692.2016.1162802: 1-10

Meuleman, Louis (2008): Public Management and the Metagovernance of Hierarchies, Networks and Markets: The Feasibility of Designing and Managing Governance Style Combinations. Heidelberg: Physica-Verlag

Newman, Janet (2005): Introduction, in: Newman, Janet (Ed.): Remaking Governance: People, Politics and the Public Sphere. Bristol: Policy Press: 1-15

Saltman, Richard B./Dubois, Hans F. W./Durán, Antonio (2011): Mapping new governance models for public hospitals, in: Saltman, Richard B./Durán, Antonio/Dubois, Hans F. W. (Eds.): Governing Public Hospitals. Copenhagen: WHO: 55-74

Tuohy, Carolyn (2012): Reform and the politics of hybridization in mature health care states. Journal of Health Politics, Policy and Law, Vol. 37, No. 4: 611-632

1. HIERARCHY AND MARKET AS DOMINANT GOVERNANCE MODES

The Governance Process in the Swiss Regional Labour Market Observatories

Moreno Baruffini and Luzius Stricker

The objective of this paper is to present an analysis of the level of governance in the different regions of Switzerland and its evolution. We will conclude the paper with an investigation of its impact on the labour market policies.

We follow a conceptual framework which considers three pillars: hierarchy (the government designs and implements policies on the basis of a system of fixed rules and statutes, which are applied by bureaucratic organisations), market (the role of the government is seen as steering on the basis of competition and performance-based rewards) and network (the government negotiates and brokers interests between different actors whilst sharing the leadership internally and externally within collaborative structures of joint action, co-production or co-operation). This framework measures the level of involvement of stakeholders in the development and implementation of policies or programmes. Moreover, these pillars are analysed following the "TAPIC framework" and its five major dimensions.

1. Introduction

This paper provides a brief description regarding the governance of the Swiss economy and of its labour market observatories, which were mainly constituted during the last ten years.

The second section, therefore, gives a brief overview of the economic path that has led the Swiss environment to become the most competitive in the World (WEF 2015).

The current organisation of the Swiss labour market observatories is described in the third section, which discusses their organisation according to "a governance" approach.

The fourth section describes the level of governance in the Swiss labour market, following a conceptual framework developed by Considine and Lewis (2003), which considers three main governance typologies (Table 1). We first explain and analyse the level of governance in the labour market according to this model and we then look at to a more specific level, introducing the five major dimensions constituting the "TAPIC framework" (Greer et al. 2016).

Table 1   The operating logics of different modes of governance

Hierarchy	Market	Network
Authority	Competition	Mutual trust
Legality	Efficiency	Empathy
Accountability	Performance monitor	Acceptance of interdependency
		Consensus

Source: EN RLMM elaboration based on Meuleman (2008).

The last part of this paper sums up the results and presents the new challenges, such as the improvement of the labour market analysis due to the technological advances, to be faced in future.

2. The Swiss economy and labour market[1]

The economic environment

Switzerland has been a federal state since 1848. Authority is shared between the Confederation (central state), the 26 cantons (federal states) and the 2324 communes (in the year 2015). Each of these three levels has legislative powers (to draw up laws and regulations) and executive powers (to implement them). The Confederation, the cantons and regional entities also have judiciary powers (courts), to ensure that the laws are enforced.

---

[1] For a better description refer to Baruffini (2013), on which this and the following chapter are based.

The Confederation's authority is restricted to the powers expressly conferred on it by the Federal Constitution. All other tasks, for example education, healthcare and public safety, are the responsibility of the cantons, which thus enjoy considerable autonomy (Federal Chancellery 2014).

The communes embrace tasks that are explicitly assigned to them by the Confederation or by the canton to which they belong, but they can also legislate when the cantonal law does not specifically refer to issues that affect them directly.

Switzerland has therefore a liberal and competitive labour market, which reflects a long reform period that started in the beginning of the 20th century and followed a slow but steady adjustment in the build-up of the state up since World War II. This has led to the Swiss economic environment becoming the most competitive one in the last few years (WEF 2015).

- In fact, according to Berclaz and Füglister (2003), who studied the Swiss labour market before the great economic downturn in 2008, the main characteristics of the Swiss system are:The *liberal and flexible labour market*, especially involving a high degree of flexibility and low taxes on wages for low-skilled employment.
- A *dual labour market*: the financial sector, insurances and the pharmaceutical industry constitute highly competitive branches, which are oriented towards international markets, while agriculture, construction and artworks are still strictly protected markets.
- A *low unionisation rate*: according to the so-called labour peace, concluded in 1937 between workers' organisation and trade union, strikes and lockouts are prohibited during the period when collective conventions are in force. Moreover, working conditions and wages are negotiated between the social partners without state intervention, except for some basic regulations.

While the employment rate in the service sector rose substantially (from 24% in the sixties to 73% in the twenties), Switzerland still has a high employment rate in different sectors and a high level of employment in manufacturing branches. The Swiss Confederation had a high employment rate of 79.8% among economically active persons aged between 15 and 64 in 2016.

Moreover, for many decades, Switzerland has nearly been in a situation of full employment but since the Euro crisis that affected the European Union in 2011, the economic downturn in Europe has also affected the labour market in Switzerland. In effect, even if the unemployment rate (4.3%, according to ILO unemployment rate) in 2016 is still very low compared to other European countries, the rate is higher, for example, than in the neighbouring regions of Germany.

Nowadays, the key factor of the Swiss labour market is its relationship with the European Union and the European labour market (Segretariato di Stato dell'economia 2013). Switzerland[2], which is not a member of the European Union[3], nevertheless has *"[...] close relations with the European Union on the political, economic and cultural levels. These relations are governed by a whole structure of bilateral agreements concluded over the years between Switzerland and the EC/EU"* (Switzerland European policy – Bilateral agreements). The main recent stages were the so-called *Bilateral Agreements II of 2004,* which cover many economic interests, such as agricultural policy and cooperation in the field of statistics, pensions and professional training and allowed Switzerland to join the Schengen/Dublin Agreement, concerning immigration policy.

Above all, one of the first seven bilateral agreements between Switzerland and the European Union gradually introduced the free movement of persons throughout the EU and Switzerland. Swiss citizens and EU citizens are thus granted the right to freely choose their place of work and residence on the territory of the contracting parties. These agreements have been extended to the EFTA Member States (Liechtenstein, Norway, Iceland).

The Swiss welfare system

"The development of the welfare system took place later in Switzerland" (Berclaz and Füglister 2003) with respect to other European countries, namely in the sixties, with the creation of the national social security institutions. As an example, the concept for an "unemployment insurance" was only included in the constitution in 1975, and not until 1982 did proper legislation come into force. A change, which slightly modified the insurance schema, was introduced in the nineties, when the unemployment rate started to rise.

Switzerland now has an advanced and somewhat polarised system of labour welfare policies, comparable to the type of Nordic welfare of Europe, with strong liberal traits. As a matter of fact, the flexible system with a scheme of compulsory

---

[2] http://www.europa.admin.ch/themen/00500/.
[3] In 1992 Swiss voters narrowly turned down joining the European Economic Area (EEA) or single market.

pension insurance, mandatory health care, and unemployment insurance are comparable to the welfare system in Northern Europe, while the health care system and the pension insurance, which are based on three different "pillars", are characterised by a strong liberal sentiment. The management of these institutions has a stronger market orientation, compared to many public services in the rest of Europe.

The municipal offices of the welfare state, as well as the cantonal labour offices, devise their own measures, in many cases implementing measures of job creation, while all the federal institutions pursue other vocational training methods and the prevention of social exclusion. The federal authorities of the labour market are therefore responsible for the implementation of the "Law on the Placement and Unemployment Insurance", and despite the federal system, there is a tendency in Switzerland for the federal state to be considered an organiser of welfare due to historic reasons.

In any case, the cantons are responsible for the application of federal law on their territory by setting their employment policies and allocating funds for their unemployment benefits (Berclaz and Füglister 2003). With the introduction of regional employment offices and active measures of the labour market in 1995, a more integrated system has progressively come into existence.

Table 2 provides a brief overview of the main actors in the field of employment policy.

Table 2   Switzerland: actors in labour market employment policy

Level	Entity	Office/Commission	Stakeholders
Federal		Swiss Federal Social Insurance Office	Employers' organisations (economiesuisse, Swiss Employers' Union, Swiss Union of Arts and Crafts)
	State Secretariat for Economic Affairs (SECO)	Commission for supervising the compensation funds of unemployment insurance	Trade Unions (Union of Swiss Trade Unions, travail.suisse)
		Parliamentary Committee for Economic Affairs and Taxation	Political parties (Socialist Party, Swiss People's Party, Free Democratic Party, Christian-Democratic Party, Ecology Party)
Inter-Cantonal		Swiss Social Action Institutions Conferences	
		Association of Organisers of Active Labour Market Measures (AOMAS)	
		Association of Swiss Employment Offices (AOST)	
Canton/Local Communes	Cantonal Department of Economic Affairs/Employment Offices	Regional Job Placement Offices	Organisations of the Unemployed
	Cantonal Department of Social Affairs	Active Labour Market Measures' Organisations	
	Tripartite Commissions		
		Public Unemployment Insurance Fund	

Source: Authors' elaboration based on Berclaz and Füglister (2003).

3. The national context: Regional Labour Market Observatories' Organisation

Labour market monitoring does not have a long history in Switzerland. Due to its federalist structure and as previously explained, every canton has set up different types of labour market monitoring, especially in the last twenty years. These range from a simple cantonal office to a more complex system that encompasses public offices, unions, and research institutes. For this reason, at present, there are many regional labour market observatories in Switzerland, of differing degrees of organisation that pursue different activities, according to the needs of the different cantonal authorities.

As an example, one of the first established observatories was the Osservatorio del mercato del lavoro (O-Lav) (Ticino Labour Market Observatory 2012) – recently renamed as Osservatorio delle Dinamiche Economiche (O-De) (Ticino Economic Dynamics Observatory 2017). It was tasked with looking back at the beginning of the bilateral path, on 29 November 2000, when the canton Ticino State Council entrusted the Institute for Economic Research (IRE – University of Lugano) with preparing a draft of the labour market observatory (O-Lav). This was presented on 30 September 2002 and later incorporated into Ti-Lav, the regional labour market control platform, which was defined at the same time. This observatory has no control functions, but the task of analysing the opportunities, risks, and dynamics of the regional labour market.

The observatory technically supports the Tripartite Commission, its working groups and the Office for the Supervision of the Labour Market (USML), while being involved in the implementation of the labour market control and monitoring activity in Ticino. The statistical reference sources are the official statistics by the Federal Statistical Office (FSO). Since 2008, IRE also manages the project PanelCODE, starting from a sample of entrepreneurs belonging to different sectors of Ticino's economy. Every month, it provides valuable information for the investigation of the most important issues, such as the business revenues situation, the level of production, the number of orders, employment and productive capacity and employment barometer. Being survey data, these results complement the official statistics. Finally, the SECO, the State Secretariat for Economic Affairs, has a general coordination role at the federal level.

The current organisation of all the other Swiss observatories that differ in terms of competencies, aims, and duties is characterised by common challenges. Indeed, they are all asked to provide help to cantonal authorities on issues concerning labour market policy implementation, providing an effective and feasible labour market policy evaluation.

Table 3 provides a systematic picture of the Swiss labour market observatories:

Table 3   The Swiss labour market observatories

Observatory	Main theme	Methods	Type
Ticino: Osservatorio delle Dinamiche economiche (O-De)	Trans-border commuter monitoring, wages, skills	Quantitative and qualitative (salary calculator)	Academic institute
L'Observatoire genevois du marché du travail (OGMT)	Wages, benefits and working conditions	Quantitative and qualitative (salary calculator)	Cantonal office
Observatoire fribourgeois du marché du travail (OFMT)	Wages	Quantitative and qualitative (salary calculator)	Cantonal office
Observatoire valaisan de l'emploi (OVE)	Trans-border commuters characteristics, qualifications, skills, age of job seekers	Quantitative and qualitative	Cantonal office

Source: Baruffini (2013).

Considering a first governance definition, as elaborated by the EN RLMM (Table 4), we can state that the general organisation of the Swiss regional market observatories is based on the hierarchy model of governance (cantonal offices implement a set of policies defined by the government) and the market model of governance (the private sector has a strong degree of freedom in choosing the best way to negotiate with the respective social partner).

In the following paragraph, these aspects are analysed following the "TAPIC framework" (Greer et al. 2016) and its five major dimensions, in order to define the Governance of the Swiss labour market monitoring in a conceptual way, following the scheme provided by Table 4.

Table 4   Grid for analysing the functionality of governance in labour market monitoring

Hierarchy	Market	Network
ACCOUNTABILITY	TRANSPARENCY	PARTICPATION
Integrity	Integrity	Integrity
Capacity	Capacity	Capacity

Source: EN RLMM elaboration based on Greer et al. (2016).

4. Dimensions of governance

According to the literature cited by Treib et al. (2005), there are several conceptions of what should be considered "governance". This section will, therefore, present an analysis that will follow the dimensions and concept introduced by that research that will consequently lead to a final classification based on the "TAPIC" framework. The research used for the first-step classification was based, quoting different examples, on what belongs to the European Union framework. However, the dimensions presented in this paragraph are general and will be used to analyse the governance at the Swiss regional level.

As a matter of fact, despite considerable cross-cantonal variations in the mode of policy interventions, as presented before, modern labour markets generally tend to be more regulated and subject to more direct policy intervention than other markets, such as commodity or capital markets.

In particular, the Swiss labour market is based on a specific contracting scheme that implies that both parties, workers and employers operate in an institutional environment, which encompass a set of mutually agreed upon rules. This effectively deters opportunistic behaviour, enabling them to reap the full returns from mutual payoffs and ensures a sufficient degree of flexibility to cope with unknown future events. For several reasons, the establishment of such an environment involves high transaction costs, and free-rider problems can occur when benefits that accrue to third parties from private investments cannot be fully captured by the investors, as in the case with an investment in human capital. Both high transaction costs and the existence of externalities may result in suboptimal outcomes from private market transactions or market failures.

So far, the role of these intermediate and informal kinds of socio-economic coordination has not completely been taken into consideration in policy evaluation research and will constitute one of the most important drivers of change for Swiss regional labour market observatories.

Consequently, a first governance classification (the following quoted definitions and conceptual descriptions are taken from Treib et al. (2005)) could be based on the following points:

- "*Legal vs law*: The first aspect to take onto consideration is the balance of the policy outputs in the form of regulations and decisions are legally binding for the cantonal and for private actors".

As can be noticed in Table 1, the Swiss labour market comprehends both binding and non-binding provisions. The Federal Law on working conditions is strictly binding, but there are many, not binding regulations that the cantonal authorities or the businesses are free to define.

- "*Rigid vs flexible*: Policy outputs may either rely on a rigid mode of implementation, defining detailed standards without much flexibility, or they may leave norm addressees and implementing actors more leeway in adapting them to local circumstances or individual interests".

In the Swiss social policy, the Federal Laws are strictly implemented, and therefore are quite rigid. Cantonal laws, in contrast, are much more flexible, and allow the private sector to negotiate with cantonal authorities.

- "*Presence vs absence of sanction*: Policies also differ with regard to their enforceability. Community law may usually be enforced by an authority".

The SECO has defined a broad range of sanctions for private actors that violate the Federal law.

Concerning individual disputes, the cantons often create special courts for labour disputes and provide for compulsory preliminary conciliation proceedings. A labour dispute involving several employees is instead defined as a collective labour dispute. The cantonal conciliation boards are responsible for handling these disputes. If the dispute extends beyond a canton's border, the Federal Board of Conciliation in Collective Labour Disputes is called upon" (Federal Chancellery 2014).

- *"Material vs procedural regulations*: Policies may either set material standards, or their focus may be a procedural one".

As an example, holiday periods are strictly defined by federal and cantonal laws, but if the relationship between the employer and the employee is not regulated by a fixed-term contract, either party may terminate the contract at any time. However, when terminating a contract, a certain period of notice must be given.

- *"Fixed vs malleable norms*: This dimension refers to the more or less fixed and context-dependent character of the norms included in a particular policy instrument".

As already stated, there are few rules in the Swiss environment are but they are quite fixed.

- *"Only public actors involved versus only private actors involved*: Concerning the governance, two extreme poles can be distinguished: either only public actors or only private actors are involved in policy-making. On the one hand, a hierarchical state leaves the policy process to public actors. On the other hand, only private actors are involved in self-regulation by firms without state intervention or in self-organisation of communities. Between these two poles, there are several modes of governance which involve both public and private actors, like different forms of "policy networks" or bureaucracies that have been restructured according to the New Public Management approach which entrusts formerly public tasks to private businesses".

The general setup of the Swiss labour market is more oriented towards self-regulated governance, with a general framework defined by the Federal government.

- *"Hierarchy versus market*: Irrespective of whether public or private actors are involved in decision-making, the institutional structure of their interactions can either be hierarchical, which gives one or a few actors the possibility to reach collectively binding decisions without the consent of the others, or it can resemble a market structure, where every actor remains free to choose their desired courses of action. In between these opposing extremes, there may be several other types of institutional structures".

The Swiss labour market is organised in between, with a precise hierarchical structure, but without strict control of the decision-making process.

- *"Central versus dispersed locus of authority*: A related institutional dimension is whether the locus of authority is centralised or dispersed".

Switzerland is one of the prominent European examples of federalism, with a solid and well-established authority scheme.

- *"Institutionalised versus non-institutionalised interactions*: Modes of governance may be distinguished according to the degree of formal institutionalisation of decision-making and implementation processes".

In the Swiss context, many governance processes that belong to the labour market monitoring activity are not based on the federal law and are therefore characterised by less institutionalised procedures. In contrast, cantonal legislation usually implies clear rules and is typically based on a legislative approach, which defines the roles of defining, implementing and controlling all the labour market monitoring activity.

Table 5   Grid for analysing the functionality of governance in labour market monitoring

Mode	Quality Criteria				
	Transparency	Accountability	Participation	Integrity	Capacity
Hierarchy (H)					
Market (M)					
Network (N)					
H+N+M					
H+M					
H+N					
M+N					

Source: EN RLMM elaboration based on Meuleman (2008) and Greer et al. (2016).

Following all the description provided above, we can consequently state (Table 5) that in Switzerland the functional modes of governance and combinations of modes in regional labour market monitoring for evidence-based policy-making are based on a mix of hierarchy (the government designs and implements policies on the basis of a system of fixed rules and statutes, which are applied by bureaucratic organisations) and market (the role of the government is seen as steering on the basis of competition and performance-based rewards). There is a strong prominence of authority, efficiency, and competition.

Applying the TAPIC framework, in particular:

- Transparency: the decision-making follow both a bottom-up approach (cantonal) and a top-down approach (federal);
- Accountability: both federal and cantonal authorities have a binding power on controlling and sanctioning;
- Participation: the "labour peace" ensures participation to both organisations and trade unions;
- Integrity: according to (WEF 2015) processes are organised in a non-corrupt and institutionalised manner;
- Capacity: expertise on policy formulation, implementation and evaluation exists but is spread across many actors.

"Quality criteria" are generally set by a central authority (the SECO) and sometimes, due to the strong federalist structure, cannot be efficient in an effective but fragmented labour market monitoring, since all the national, regional and local framework and institutional conditions strongly affect the functionality of the modes of governance and their configuration.

5. Conclusions

This paper has presented some of the main features of the regional Swiss labour markets, characterised by the presence of a flexible system with strong liberal tendencies.

Despite considerable cross-cantonal variations in the mode of policy interventions, the Swiss labour markets generally tend to be more regulated and subject to more direct policy intervention than other markets, and moreover, due to the Swiss federal structure, every canton set up a different structure, and every regional labour market is on a different path.

We have analysed the level of governance in those different regions and its evolution and we have tried to catch its effect on the labour market policies, following a conceptual framework that takes into consideration three pillars: hierarchy, market, and network. We consequently argued that the functional modes of governance and combinations of modes in regional labour market monitoring for evidence-based policy-making are based on a mix of hierarchy and market.

Moreover, we extended the analysis with a two-stage process, at first considering different conditions of the labour market monitoring and then defining it according to the "TAPIC framework" and its five major dimensions.

Many Swiss regions are still in the process of installing such a system for the observation of their labour market and the Swiss labour market is far from having established a common monitoring system; many actual mega-trends, such as digitalisation, will also affect the development of this monitoring system.

References

Berclaz, Michel/Füglister, Katharina (2003): The Contentious Politics of Unemployment in Europe: Political Claim-making, Policy Deliberation and Exclusion from the Labor Market – National Template for Switzerland. UNEMPL

Considine, Mark/Lewis, Jenny M. (2003). Bureaucracy, network, or enterprise? Comparing models of governance in Australia, Britain, the Netherlands, and New Zealand. Public Administration Review, Vol. 63, No 2, pp. 131-140

Greer, Scott L./Wismar, Matthias/Figueras, Josep (Eds.) (2016): Strengthening Health System Governance: Better policies, stronger performance. Maidenhead: Open University Press.

Meuleman, Louis (2008): Public Management and the Metagovernance of Hierarchies, Networks, and Markets: The Feasibility of Designing and Managing Governance Style Combinations. Heidelberg: Physica-Verlag.

Osservatorio delle dinamiche economiche O-DE (2017): Competitività Economica 2017 Rapporto sulla struttura economica ticinese. Istituto di ricerche Economiche, Università della Svizzera italiana Lugano

Osservatorio del mercato del lavoro O-LAV (2012): Le politiche regionali del mercato del lavoro: margine di manovra, sviluppo e competitività. Istituto Ricerche Economiche, Università della Svizzera italiana Lugano

Per il Consiglio federale: Segretariato di Stato dell'economia (2013): Rapporto sulla politica economica esterna 2012 e Messaggi concernenti accordi economici internazionali e Rapporto concernente le misure tariffali adottate nel 2012

Treib, Oliver/Bähr, Holger/Falkner, Gerda (2005): Modes of Governance: A Note Towards Conceptual Clarification. European Governance Papers

World Economic Forum (WEF) (2015): The Global Competitiveness Report 2015-2016

Websites

Federal Chancellery, Parliamentary Services and the Federal Office of Statistics, 2014: https://www.ch.ch/

Switzerland European policy – Bilateral agreements: https://www.eda.admin.ch/dea/en/home/bilaterale-abkommen.html

Labour Market, Economic Policy and Economic Growth Perspectives in Russia

Nina Oding

1. Introduction

Today, Russia faces a challenging task of modernising its economy and raising its competitiveness. Crucial aspects of this process are human resources and innovation fostering. By turning to the innovation mode of development, Russia recognises it is the only way to diminish its reliance on natural resources and diversify the economy.

The type of governance and the similar economic policies and strategies could play a special role by contributing to or by hindering the processes of accumulation of human capital and its realisation in the labour market.

This paper describes how the Russian labour market adjusts to economic circumstances and contributes to building up the country's capacity to become part of the world economy. The paper examines the following questions: what are the institutional factors of labour market functions? Do the institutional factors contribute to the process of economic and social development? How should the government take advantage of bridging the gap between labour market data and political process? We hope to find the answers to these questions by studying the regional labour markets, their management and strategy.

In Russia, both in periods of high growth and crisis, the labour market does not show significant changes under the influence of traditional factors. The peculiarities of the Russian labour market model include specific mechanisms of adaptation to shocks. Variations in the labour market influenced by the economic dynamics are manifested in the reduction of wages while preserving jobs. It creates difficulties for the observation and analysis of labour market data.

There is a system of institutional and structural factors ensuring stability in the labour market. The combination of these factors creates major problems that accumulated in the field of employment, where for an extended period of time, the job structure is maintained without a significant formation of new jobs. This peculiarity becomes an obstacle for the evidence-based political decision-making as well as for economic development.

It is necessary to consider the characteristics of the labour market, which determine the provision and use of labour market information to identify the kind of mode of governance presented in the Russian economy. Also, regional differences and the existence of good practices should be taken into account to identify future development prospects for management and policy-making.

The article describes the peculiarities of the institutional conditions of the labour market as factors that determine the low level of unemployment and the type of employment in an economy that does not facilitate the realisation of human potential and economic development. These features are typical for the entire Russian labour market, but at the level of specific regions may or may not be taken into account when forming the mode of governance. The most vivid example here is the experience of Republic Tatarstan, one of the advanced regions in Russia regarding the real practice of development.

2. New factors of the economic growth

While Russia's economy is experiencing negative conditions for economic growth, it faces numerous international challenges, as well as significant trends in the global environment that affect not only its competitiveness but also its labour market development. Among the most important aspects of the change are the consequences of globalisation, the increasing importance of knowledge as the main driver of growth, the creation of industries and jobs where human capital can be requested.

Economists have different opinions about the key growth factor. For some (Barro 1998, Krueger and Lindahl 2001) human capital plays the crucial role, for others, for example Acemoglu et al. (2001) the quality of the institutions are the main determinants of economic growth. As in many theoretical discussions, empirical evidence, measurement methods and the solution of endogeneity problems in econometric strategy acquire particular importance (Acemoglu et al. 2014).

Some authors (Hausmann et al. 2005, Lyubimov 2016) treat human capital and institutions as complementary factors of economic growth. Even with "bad" institutions, improving the quality of education can accelerate economic growth and poor education can limit it, even more than bad) institutions.

Thus, by considering the institutional framework and human capital levels, this creates some preconditions regarding relevant and targeted information for labour market development as well as evidence-based policy decisions in the country and its regions.

The basic trends of world development are as follows:

- Globalisation, the international division of labour and international production cooperation;
- Global competition in the markets for resources, goods, and services;
- Global competition in the labour market, professional mobility;
- Rapid change in the composition of professions, updating necessary knowledge and skills.

Based on the results of the Human Development Index (HDI), taking into account the income, education, and longevity of the population, Russia as a whole belongs to a group of countries with a high level of development. The main factors that positively influence the country's place in the global rating are related to the high degree of education, the enormous capacity of the domestic market, the spread of information technologies in society and education, and finally the stimulation of innovation in the sciences by the state.

Collecting and analysing data from different sources determines the current and the future development of labour market and economic policy measures. These data are official aggregated data from the Federal State Statistics Service (Rosstat) of Russia and its regional offices, as well as data from the OECD database and European job movement map. Two surveys are also crucial for collecting data, namely the survey of the population on employment issues (ONPZ), as well as the survey of wages by profession (OZPP), which are regularly conducted by Rosstat. However, in the presence of such significant sources of information, the analysis of labour market processes is no easy undertaking.

Phenomena such as the large scale of informal employment over an extended period of time, combined with significant human capital in Russia attracts researchers because of the disparity compared to the situation in other developing countries.

In the developing economies, informal employment reflects the structure of supply in the labour market that is not relevant regarding education and qualifications. In Russia, the problem lies in the sphere of demand for labour: companies require employees of technical specialties, but universities produce lawyers and economists as researchers Gimpelson and Kapelyushnikov (2013) point out, the expansion of informality in the presence of significant human capital is a clear symptom of the institutional failure of the state, which does not provide the right conditions for business development. In addition, Russian labour legislation is one of the most stringent in Europe, supplemented by excessive administrative pressure on the business through additional controls and inspections.

The dual tasks of improving the quality of institutions and the use of human capital for the modernisation of the economy and society is a significant challenge for the Russian governance system. If in the previous period, economic growth relied on natural resources and substantial domestic demand, then after the crisis, the activation of the use of human capital for innovations should be placed at the centre of economic policy. Focus on quality workplaces, consistent improvement in the quality of the education system, and the development of the health system are top priorities for public policy.

3. Low unemployment

Over the period of 2000-2016, macroeconomic indicators have implied a stable state of the labour market. According Rosstat statistics the employment rate remains quite high (more than 65% on average), and unemployment is low (less than 7% on average). Unemployment in the major cities remains low, but in the single-industry towns and the North Caucasus, the problem of employment is acute.

The situation does not change even during crises; the Russian labour market demonstrates an automatic reaction to economic recessions by maintaining a relatively high employment rate, while experiencing growth in the rate of unemployment, and lower labour costs. The companies respond by slight decrease in the employment and sharply reduce wages of the employees or transfer employees to part-time employment especially in the event of crises, which have already hit the Russian economy twice since the beginning of the 2000s.

This feature manifested itself during the last crisis of 2014-2016 when the low unemployment was due to the traditional way of adapting to crises by reducing wages and underemployment of workers (Gimpelson and Kapelyushnikov 2014).

Typical ways to cut costs are actions (including violations of labour laws) such as: delaying payment of wages and sending employees on unpaid leave. In sectors with the greatest decline and the greatest informal employment (wholesale and retail trade, construction, services to the population), it is possible to reduce employment at the expense of individual entrepreneurs and their employees. This model reflects a certain consensus between the businesses, the state, and the population. It thus facilitates a lower risk of social protests against the state, higher costs for businesses and provides some employment for the population (RANKHIGS 2016).

Perhaps, it is worth agreeing with the researchers of employment problems that in the Russian model the social consequences of the decrease in the real wage are more significant than the risk of growth of unemployment. Therefore, this feature of adaptation to negative economic trends has a positive socio-political effect, since it avoids an increase of poverty due to the growth of the number of the unemployed (RANKHIGS 2016). However, the reverse side of this process is the so-called ""working poverty"; almost five million people employed receive a salary at the level of the minimum wage, which is even lower than the established subsistence level of 7,500 roubles or about 120 euros per month.

Some researchers note that the stabilisation of employment is largely due to extremely flexible wages, which allows labour costs within enterprises to be restrained and the mass release of workers to be avoided (Gimpelson and Kapelyushnikov 2013). However, on the other hand, stable employment with reduced earnings represents a shift in focus to another area of social policy— the provision of benefits for public sector services and public utilities for the working population. According to Liliya Ovcharova, the director of the Institute of Social Policy, in the last crisis, the drop in the standard of living affected 70% of Russian families, and the poorest sections of the population are getting poorer (Petryaev 2017).

Also, the consequence of the functioning of the Russian labour market is the fact that the crises of 2008-2009 and 2013-2016 showed that the opportunities for the development of the Russian economy on the old basis do not allow Russia to overcome the backlog in the technological development of production and living standards of the population. The predominance of output and export of natural resources and active state participation in the economy are the biggest obstacles to developing new small and medium size business in the sphere of high-quality technologies.

It is very likely that domestic economic policy and structural weaknesses of the economy played a significant role in the prolonged recession in recent years. An important part of the problem of the economy lies outside of the labour market.

4. Informal employment

During the period of economic growth (2000-2007) the Russian economy did not react to economic growth by creating new jobs, instead it partly shifted and went into the shadow sphere disappeared as an object of observation and taxation. By 2011, the informal sector employed about 20% to 30% of all employed by different estimations, which is much higher than in developed countries, although less than in Latin America. However, the range of estimates not only indicates the complexity of this phenomenon

Informal employment is a product of the 1990s and played a significant role in the adaption of the population to the radical changes in the economy and society. According to various estimates, there are between 15 million to 30 million citizens in Russia who are officially unemployed, but who have incomes from which taxes are not collected. According to the Federal State Statistics Service in 2016, employment in the informal sector of the economy reached 15.4 million people (21.2% of all employed), an increase of more than half a million people. People who avoid paying taxes affect the stability of the public services sector, including pensions.

According to the researchers of the RANKHiGS Laboratory of Research on Corporate Strategies and Behavior of the firms (2016), informal employment deprives the state budget of between one trillion to three trillion roubles per year. The total revenue of the consolidated budget of 2016 was about 27 trillion roubles.[4] The reintegration of these workers into proper and legal employment would increase the income of the state and, especially the savings of the pension fund (RBC 2017).

---

4 Or 415 billion Euro, 1 Euro=65 Rubl.

As noted in the same study, informal employment plays a major role in stabilising the labour market and mitigating crises, its volumes occupy a stable niche adequate to the structure of the economy and the labour market. It is in many ways a substitute for unemployment and is unlikely to play a significant role in creating new jobs and increasing labour productivity. One can assume that the volumes of informal employment are in a certain equilibrium state, adequate to the existing structure of the economy and the labour market. By itself, a significant proportion of the informal sector signals a hostile institutional environment. However, in 2017, legislators and the government decided to step up their efforts to drive informal workers "out of the shadows" in various ways, such as depriving them of the opportunity to receive free medical services.

A proper response to these attempts was described in the report of 2014 "The Russian Labour Market: Trends, Institutions, Structural Changes" (2014) in the Higher School of Economics, commissioned by the CSR. Among the important points in the report is the hypothesis that overestimating the estimates of informal employment in the Russian Federation without more complex and detailed criteria of "informality", would lead to a decrease in estimates of the share of employed in the informal sector by about half – from 20-25% to 10-15%.

5. Structure of employment

Information on the professional structure of the workforce is crucial for understanding the results and orientations of the educational system. The fair presentation of reliable information regarding the professional structure of the workforce, the dynamics of the distribution of workers by major professional groups makes it possible to determine the prospects for a professional employment structure, as well as restrictions on the possibilities for economic growth and parameters of economic development forecasts.

At the same time, the employment structure remains extremely unsatisfactory — the low rate of new job creation leads to the conservation of a large segment of employees with low labour productivity. During the economic growth of the 2000s, the total number of employees in the economy grew, but job numbers in the non-government sector were declining. At the same time, the number of employed in the informal sector of the economy, primarily in the service industry, has grown. Observations by the Higher School of Economics show that it took until 2015-2016 for the share of employment in the service sector of the economy to peak - that is, the "de-industrialisation" of the economy is complete, and we can state that the development of the service sector of the Russian Federation is no longer in a transition period.

People employed in the budgetary sector (education, healthcare, public administration, culture) gradually replaced those employed in the commercial sector. The ratio of employees working in the public sector exceeded 30% (and in the area of large and medium-sized enterprises and organisations exceeds 40%). The structure of employment is not shifting in the direction of a diversified, high-tech and innovative economy.

It should be pointed out that the situation differs significantly in regions where services and small business are only concentrated in cities.

6. Education and labour market demand

Another significant feature of employment in Russia is that the coordination between labour and education markets is disrupted — about one in three employed does not use the knowledge and skills that are available to him.

Russia is characterised by the ubiquitous spread of the "over-education" of the workforce; there are more students than school graduates. Even secretaries, lower-level workers and drivers have diplomas from higher education institutions. Thus, the availability of a degree is not a signal for the Russian regarding the level of education and knowledge of the employee.

Job seekers with the same diploma and the same specialty, can get jobs, receiving extremely different income, even in similar positions. The salary depends not so much on education, skills, and abilities as on the place of work, the company. For example, engineers, managers and secretaries working at Gazprom will receive salaries five to seven times higher than their counterparts in other businesses. At the same time, entrepreneurs complain about the shortage of employees with the necessary qualifications. To attract specialists, they are forced to increase their remuneration. In turn, specialists change jobs like gloves, since they consider their current work as a place of temporary respite before moving to a new, even higher-paid one. Hence, it becomes unprofitable for the employer to invest in personnel.

Moreover, the shortage of high-quality workers applies not only to managers but also to skilled employees and specialists. Companies are forced to carry out "pre-training" of new employees on small professional issues and skills. They need to adapt to a specific workplace in a particular company, but also fill gaps of a general professional nature and even in basic education. In fact, one can state that the state system of education, particularly at the level of professional educational institutions, does not cope with the training of personnel and the formation of the necessary qualifications of human capital. At the same time, the practice of training employees is rather widespread in business, especially when it concerns engineering personnel and skilled workers (Oshchepkov 2011).

The actual separation of the university system from the needs of the real economy becomes a threat in the medium term. If there is no deeper alignment of higher education institutions with professional communities in the next decade, the remaining gap in the training of personnel for the new economy will intensify, undermining the country's potential in the global competition for ideas and resources.

To a certain extent the main improvements of the educational system are developing even nowadays. In the next five to ten years, peer-to-peer evaluation systems for course and diploma papers, as well as online ratings of teachers of higher education, will be formed in Russia. Adult education will undergo radical changes. In particular, additional education will be transformed into a lifelong learning environment.

7. Regions and their potential

The report (2014) mentioned above only contains general information and a recommendation – the decentralisation of labour market regulation from the federal level to the regional level. As the authors reasonably believe, "the federal rigidity in establishing minimum levels of payment reduces the efficiency of the labour market of the Russian Federation, due to its flexibility remains a unique mechanism for mitigating economic crises." This is crucial for the regions with advanced socio-economic positions, for example, St. Petersburg, Moscow, Krasnodarskiy kray.

The diversity and differentiation of the levels of development of the territories in Russia make it possible to identify areas with significant potential for modernising the economy. Regions also differ in their labour markets, functioning quite autonomously, with a certain degree of success regarding employment, job creation and the size of wages. Strong heterogeneity and weak cohesion must inevitably be taken into account when making decisions that affect the whole country. Accordingly, economic policy measures should also consider these circumstances, and in addition, provide an opportunity for an independent policy in the labour market.

These regions occupy the top lines of the rating of the Human Development Index for the regions of Russia (Table 1). As pointed out in (UNDP 2006-2007) *"over a quarter of Russia's population lives in regions where the HDI is above the national average, and 15% of the population live in the most affluent subjects of the Russian Federation (Moscow, Tyumen region with its autonomous districts, St. Petersburg and Tatarstan), whose human development indices are comparable to those of developed countries. Such regions have sufficient means and resources to develop their human potential alone"*.

Calculations of the Human Development Index (HDI) of the Russian regions for 2004, 2009 and 2010 show that the index has increased for the vast majority of subjects of the Russian Federation, although the dynamics vary. The fastest growing HDI resource-export regions are those which have experienced a growth in per capita GRP, especially in those regions where oil is produced. What the index in several depopulating regions of the central district of Russia slightly decreases because of a reduction in the proportion of students, due to the small number of generations entering the school age.

Table 1 The Human Development Index (HDI) of the regions of Russia in 2010[5]

Region	GRP/PPP, $	Income index	Life expectancy, years	Longevity Index	Literacy, %	Education index	HDI	Rank
Russia	19,674	0.882	68.83	0.731	99.7	0.916	0.843	
Moscow	39,226	1.000	73.56	0.809	99.99	0.984	0.931	1
St. Petersburg	24,551	0.919	71.49	0.775	99.9	0.969	0.887	2
Tumenskaya oblast'	60,363	1.000	69.72	0.745	99.7	0.916	0.887	3
Sakhalinskaya oblast'	51,900	1.043	65.01	0.667	99.7	0.903	0.871	4
Belgorodskaya oblast' As	23,190	0.909	71.29	0.772	99.7	0.917	0.866	5
Respublika Tatarstan	23,747	0.913	70.43	0.757	99.7	0.922	0.864	6
Krasnoyarskiy kray	27,100	0.935	67.76	0.713	99.6	0.915	0.854	7
Respublika Komi	24,836	0.920	67.20	0.703	99.7	0.936	0.853	8

Source: UNDP (2013), pp. 150-151.

Among them, apart from Moscow and St. Petersburg, is the Republic of Tatarstan —the region located in the centre of European Russia. Tatarstan is the most prosperous among the national republics of Russia, and it has been among the five best regions regarding all indicators of human development for many years.

In 2012-2014, a large-scale study of the state of human capital and the opportunities for its development and use in modernising the region's economy was conducted in Tatarstan[6].

The Republic of Tatarstan ranks eighth in Russia regarding population (3,780,600 people) and its capital, Kazan, is part of a group of 13 Russian cities with more

---
5 These are just regions at the top of ranking.
6 In the framework of the project "Strategy for Tatarstan 2030" commissioned by the regional administration.

than a million inhabitants. In general, the economy of the Republic of Tatarstan is developing by Russian standards. Nowadays the Republic of Tatarstan faces several complex tasks: it needs to stimulate the development of an innovative economy, provide demand for human capital and, at the same time, provide a sufficient supply of valuable human capital. Since 2016, Tatarstan has experienced positive growth in the majority of macroeconomic indicators, including the gross regional product, the volume of industrial production, the retail trade turnover and some investments. Based on the results of a survey of Tatarstan's population (statistic agency) regarding employment issues, the labour force since the second half of 2010 exceeded 2 million people. In 2012, the economically active population was made up of 2.0928 million people, or 55.4% of the total population of the republic, of which 2.0116 million people were employed in the economy. In early 2017, the total level of unemployment was at 3.8%. It is much lower than the average for the Volga Federal District (4.5%) (which includes Tatarstan) and Russia as a whole (5.3%). There are 14,581 people registered as unemployed in the Republic (Tatarstat 2012).

The overwhelming majority of the unemployed for the period from 2003 to 2010 were looking for work with the help of friends, relatives, and acquaintances (over 70%). Over 25% appealed directly to the administration, to the employer or applied to the Employment Service. Over 20% used print and responded to ads. During the crisis period from 2008 to 2010, over 30% applied to the Employment Service. The Employment Service actively addresses people over 50, with primary and secondary education.

The population census data (1998, 2010) shows the growth of persons with higher and secondary training in Tatarstan and the drop in the number of individuals with incomplete secondary and primary school.

One of the problems in the regional labour market is the imbalance between the professional and qualification structure of graduates in schools of all levels and the needs of the labour market. The labour market is experiencing a professional deficit of the working professions, whose prestige has been significantly lowered; also, the continuity of the staff is lost because of their aging. Regarding sectors, there is a shortage of workers in construction, engineering and metalworking, transport, housing and communal services.

The constant monitoring of the labour market by the State Statistics Committee and the Ministry of Labour and Social Protection provides the basis for the development of employment policies and decision-making on overcoming the crisis phenomena in the labour market. In particular, the authorities identified the most important aspects of this market: a shortage of working specialties, inadequate training of personnel in the education system and brain drain. Accordingly, they developed programs for each of these areas.

A number of the enterprises surveyed in the framework of the mentioned project indicated that they recruit specialists with higher education degrees for working professions. Employing graduates with a speciality degree for working professions is an example of the inefficient use of labour. However, the model elaborated at OAO TATNEFT in cooperation with the Almetyevsk State Petroleum Institute looks more optimal from this point of view, where students train in the system of acquiring the working profession at the stage of training at the University.

According to experts, there is a shortage of specialists not because they are out of the market, but because graduates do not want to go to work in the industrial enterprises. It is because of the relatively low level of wages at most companies and specific labour conditions, the steady rhythm of work, dangerous production environments, and so on. So graduates of higher education institutions with a professional profile tend to search for jobs in the service sector with a comparable level of payment. However, these offer substantially easier conditions to work in.

Looking at the number of students per 10,000 people of the population, Tatarstan is one of the leading regions in the Russian Federation. It is inferior in this indicator to Moscow, St. Petersburg, Tomsk and the Novosibirsk regions (Rosstat 2011). The problem of "brain drain" from the Republic is already a recognised fact. If we consider the structure of educational migration flows, then we will see that substitution is taking place. The most talented from the regions rush to the regional centre, the most talented from the centre of the region rush to the capital of the country.

Since in the coming years there will not be a significant redistribution of workers regarding the level of vocational education, one can believe that in the future we can predict further tensions in the labour market. Some specialties that are not in demand and make these tensions obvious include specialties in the humanities, social sciences, managerial and legal profiles. These specialists will replenish the unemployed group and are forced to undergo retraining and change their profession.

The Employment Committee conducted monitoring surveys of employers in 2007 on training needs for 2008-2012 for the purpose of forecasting the personnel requirements of the economy of the Republic and the formation of volumes and profiles of training qualified workers and specialists in the system of professional education of the Republic of Tatarstan. Analysis of the results shows that the need for training for the next five years is 144,000 people for 1,327 professions and specialties. The greatest need for the training of workers – 113,000 people, or 78% of the total demand for personnel.

Now all sectors of the economy need workers; the government of the Republic of Tatarstan decided to radically change their approach to the issue of vocational training for young workers. A new concept for the development of professional education was developed and approved. The concept is based on the creation of sectoral educational clusters, consolidating the efforts of schools from a vocational school to a higher educational institution and the business community (Bondarenko 2006).

However, considering the presence of a rather large shortage of skilled workers and specialists with specific knowledge and skills, there is no significant demand for highly qualified specialists for an innovative economy.

This circumstance can be explained like this: innovation in a market economy is a consequence of free competition in the markets. In the absence of free competition and property rights protection, the incentives for generating innovations are rather weak. The current stage of economic development of the national economy and economy of Tatarstan is based on the production of natural resources for export. In these conditions, incentives to invest in industries that are not related to the extraction, processing, and transportation of resources are weakened. Therefore, only economic freedom, competitive markets, the rule of law and rights to private property are the factors that automatically generate innovations, demand for them, investments in an innovative product and can bridge the gap between an idea and an innovative product. On the other hand, educated people, aiming for innovation, can make demands for the development of market relations, which is crucial for the Republic of Tatarstan, where conditions for innovation have already been created and development institutions (funds, technology parks, free economic zones) are functioning. However, the potential for innovations and high technologies is still unduly considered the basis of the regional economy. However, in the medium to long-term perspective, it is critical to concentrate efforts and develop economic policy measures in this direction. The core of this policy should be the reorientation of the labour market towards new jobs and production, and for this, it is necessary to change the system of management and regulation of the labour market as well as the ways of the training specialists.

8. New aspects of economic policy and the labour market

The study of the problems of accumulation and retention of human capital in the Republic of Tatarstan is based on multidimensional processes of collecting information from open sources, expert assessments and interviews with the principal players in the course of developing an innovative economy.

The participants of the Tatarstan project elaborated on the scheme and sources of information gathering and the method of forming the research database. They collected the information from statistical bodies and authorities, data from the Ministry of Education and the Ministry of Labour of the Republic of Tatarstan, as well as information from mass media, independent studies and other analytical sources in order to identify the effects of the accumulation of human capital (Figure 1).

Figure 1   Basic model for labour market policy development

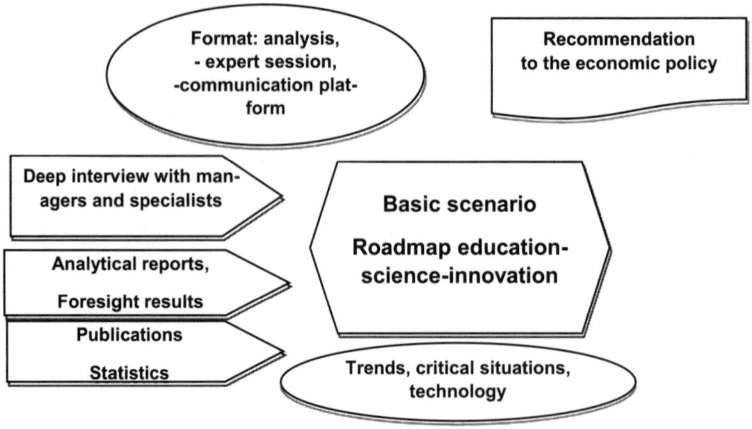

```
        ┌─────────────────────┐       ┌──────────────────────┐
        │  Format: analysis,  │       │   Recommendation     │
        │  - expert session,  │       │ to the economic policy│
        │  -communication plat-│      └──────────────────────┘
        │         form         │
        └─────────────────────┘

┌─────────────────────────┐
│ Deep interview with man-│
│  agers and specialists  │        Basic scenario
└─────────────────────────┘
┌─────────────────────────┐      Roadmap education-
│   Analytical reports,   │      science-innovation
│    Foresight results    │
└─────────────────────────┘
┌─────────────────────────┐
│      Publications       │
│       Statistics        │     Trends, critical situations,
└─────────────────────────┘            technology
```

Source: own elaboration.

Observing and analysing phenomena in the labour market is subject to the task of shaping the demand for highly qualified specialists for an innovative economy, which in turn depends on the structure of the economy and the quality of institutions. The focus the management system put on improving the business climate, ensured the freedom of entrepreneurship and competition for the development of new firms and industries that will increase the demand for human capital.

Due to changing priorities, from supporting full employment to innovative production, local problems of the labour market and the sphere of education were identified: the discrepancy between the needs of the economy and the parameters of the training system, as well as the lack of involvement in international cooperation. Also, a new specific problem was discovered — the leakage of highly qualified specialists to the federal capital. Observers noted the high mobility of talented young people and experienced specialists, who leave in larger numbers than those arriving to Tatarstan.

The so-called trap of an average premium for higher education is significantly lower than in Moscow and other large cities, also abroad (Koritzkiy 2012). The Republic of Tatarstan, on the one hand, lags behind regions that can give substantial premiums from higher education at a similar level of economic development, on the other, from regions that, with a lower premium from higher education, give better living conditions.

The solution for this problem could be the creation of beneficial conditions for the lives of families of young professionals, for example by providing short-term courses and internships, which will offset the wage gap in comparison to Moscow, where the additional premium is absorbed by high prices for rental housing, healthcare and childcare, and recreation. As a pilot project, it was proposed to implement the program "Creating an Enabling Environment for Employees of Innovative Companies", which includes three areas: the creation of a system to stimulate self-realisation of specialists, the socialisation and establishment of specialists on the territory of the Republic, and the support of their working and recreational conditions.

The tasks of the developed strategy for Tatarstan 2030 also include the participation of innovative companies in the international division of labour and international production and technological cooperation. For this purpose, tax incentives are planned for innovative companies, state support for exports, the creation and development of technology parks and Innopolis, encouragement for inter-firm cooperation and collaboration, and the creation of private venture funds and business angels.

Measures to enhance interaction between the education system and innovative companies in the region include the involvement of the companies in the discussion and improvement of curricula, programs, an organisation of fellowships and implementation of joint projects. In the long term, it is necessary to increase the autonomy of higher education institutions, decentralise decision-making in them while tightening the control of the boards of trustees. Minimise all bureaucratic costs for those universities that already now want to develop independently. Stimulate the arrival of business in universities and investment on the part of education that is already paid. At the same time, seek permission for higher education institutions to issue diplomas for graduation.

9. The governance types

Governance models in Russia definitely can be attributed to a hierarchical type in which central and regional governments develop and implement policies and regulations based on legislation and rules (Yakovlev 2014). However, it is hardly possible to speak about the existence of a certain mode, because with the development of society and communications, the growing problems associated with legality and accountability. One of the most important aspects of the change are the effects of globalisation, the increasing importance of knowledge as the main driver of growth and the creation of new industries and jobs.

The challenges present both opportunities and threats that are likely to affect labour market but also the very mission and purposes of governance mode. Also, the various forms are shaped by social and cultural as well as institutional practices, which also constitute essential elements of governing (Newman 2005).

New actors appear in the arena; they become subjects, and not objects of the management process. In Russia, this is manifested in the active role of business, associations and non-governmental organisations involved in the development of programs and strategies. A management system whose purpose is to increase the potential and use it for the benefit of people, including strategic planning and economic policy, must inevitably take into account the state and prospects of the labour market in the regions.

The solution of the task of increasing the growth rates of the economy demands a change in the basic principles of management and the transition to more modern methods in management technology. In the last decade, the traditional hierarchy model has been blurred to some extent, and this process has begun at the regional level. A vivid example of this practice is the experience of Tatarstan described above. There, various groups of stakeholders took an active part in the process of creating strategic documents, the formation of thematic commissions, developing proposals and monitoring decisions made.

Government bodies become the arbiter and negotiator for cooperation and joint actions based on trust and consensus.

In the process of joint work on strategic documents and roadmaps, there was an awareness of the boundaries of information, in particular about the labour market, which eluded observation and inhibited discovering new phenomena in the sphere of employment, such as precariat, remote work, flexible schedules, ubereconomy. The use of information on these new phenomena while in the process of developing strategic documents and making informed decisions will overcome the gap between precise information on the labour market and economic policy.

In addition to this, the blurring of the traditional linear hierarchical management structure is also taking place in the state management system, the ideas of implementing the "project office" developed as the corporate form of governance applying business-type managerial models. It significantly changes the nature of the relationship with different actors.

It allows us to speak about the availability of mode Network elements and to a lesser extent Market (performance monitoring) with the strengthening of the communication process. From the TAPIC framework, elements of successful management, such as accountability and participation, arise to achieve success in the provision and use of labour market information.

However, for the firm dominance of the network-oriented governance with participation model in the region, there is no essential dimension - integrity (the existence of non-corrupt institutions). As for capacity and transparency, which are also considered crucial for all actors.

Using the example of Tatarstan, one can see that the utilisation of a mode of governance, combining hierarchy and Network, makes it possible to provision and use of labour market information is especially functional for evidence-based employment politics.

References

Acemoglu, Daron/Gallego, Francisco A./Robinson, James A. (2014): Institutions, Human Capital, and Development, in: Annual Review of Economics, Vol. 6, No. 1, pp. 875-912

Acemoglu, Daron/Johnson, Simon/Robinson, James A. (2001): The Colonial Origins of Comparative Development: An Empirical Investigation, in: American Economic Review, Vol. 91, No. 5, pp. 1369-1401

Barro, Robert J. (1998): Determinants of Economic Growth: A Cross-Country Empirical Study. Cambridge, MA: MIT Press

Bondarenko, Nataliia (2006): Defitsit kvalifikatsii personala: trebovaniia rabotodatelei i vozmozhnosti i ogranicheniia sistemy profobrazovaniia (Deficit of skilled personnel: the demand of employers or possibilities and limitations of the system of professional education), in: Vesnik obshchestvennogo mneniia, No. 6, pp. 37-45

Gimpel'son, Vladimir/Kapeliushnikov, Rostislav/Roshchin, Sergeĭ (Eds.) (2017): Rossiĭskiĭ rynok truda: tendentzii, instituty, strukturnye izmeneniia (Russian labor market: tendencies, institutions, structural changes), Moskva: TSeTI (TceTi, Centre of Labour Research), LIRT I NIU VSHÉ, pp. 1-148

Gimpelson, Vladimir/ Kapeliushnikov, Rostislav (2014): Between Light and Shadow: Informality in the Russian Labour Market, IZA Discussion Paper No. 8279, pp. 1-31

Gimpel'son, Vladimir/Kapeliushnikov, Rostislav (2013): Zhit' v teni ili umeret' na svetu: neformalnost' na rossiĭskom rynke truda (To live in shadow or to die under in the light: Informality in the Russian labour market), in: Voprosy ekonomiki, No. 11, pp. 65-88

Hausmann, Ricardo/Rodrik, Dani/Velasco, Andrés (2005): Growth Diagnostics, Inter-American Development Bank

Koritskiĭ, Alekseĭ (2012): Otsenka vliianiia chelovecheskogo kapitala na ekonomicheskiĭ rost: teoriia, metodologiia, empiricheskaia proverka, Novosibirsk: Krasnoiarskiĭ Gosudarstvennyĭ Universitet, p.19

Krueger, Alan B./Lindahl, Mikael (2001): Education for Growth: Why and for Whom?, in: Journal of Economic Literature, American Economic Association .Vol. 39 No. 94, pp. 1101-1136

Lan'shina, Tat'iana/Zemtsov, Stepan/Barinova, Vera (2017): Beznadsorniĭ trud: chto mozhet predlozhit' gosudarstvo samozan iatym, podrobnee na RBK: http://www.rbc.ru/opinions/economics/15/02/2017/58a440ec9a79473c4c9a2a09

Lyubimov, Ivan (2016): Corrupt Bureaucrats, Bad Managers, and the Slow Race between Education and Technology Helsinki, No. 12, pp. 1-14

Newman, Janet (2005): Introduction, in: Newman, Janet (Eds.): Remaking Governance: People, Politics and the Public Sphere, Bristol: Policy Press, pp. 1-15

Oshchepkov, Alekseĭ (2011): Otdacha ot vysshego obrazovaniia v rojssiĭskikh regionakh (The return from higher education in the Russian regions), in: Ekonomicheskiĭ zhurnal VSHE, No. 4, pp. 468-485

Petriaev,Yuriĭ (2017): Dolia semeĭ, imeiushchikh sredstva dlia razvitiia snizilas' na chetvert' do 30%, in: Vedomosti, No. 4303

RANKHiGS (2016): 2014-2015 gody: Ekonomicheskiĭ krizis — sotsial'noe izmerenie (Economic crisis—social dimenstion), in: Izdatel'skiĭ Dom "Delo", No. 3, pp. 1-112

Rosstat (2011): Regions of Russia. Socio-economic indicators, pp. 990, online: http://www.gks.ru/free_doc/doc_2015/region/reg-pok15.pdf

Tatarstat (2012): Obrazovanie v Respublike Tatarstan: Kazan', pp. 176

United Nations Development Programme UNDP (2006): Human Development Index in the Regions of Russia, online: http://www.undp.ru/nhdr2006_07eng/Chapter9.pdf

United Nations Development Programme (UNDP) (2013): Doklad o chelovecheskom razvitii v RF: ustoĭchivoe razvitie: vyzovy Rio, pp. 150-151, online: http://www.undp.ru/documents/NHDR-2013.pdf

Yakovlev, Andrei (2014): Russian Modernization: Between the Need for New Players and the Fear of Losing Control of Rent Sources, in: Journal of Eurasian Studies, Vol. 5, No. 1, pp. 10-20

Websites

NEWSru (2017): http://www.newsru.com/finance/14apr2017/survivers.html

State Statistical Service Tatarstat (2010, 2011, 2012): http://tatstat.gks.ru/

http://tatstat.gks.ru/wps/wcm/connect/rosstat_ts/tatstat/ru/statistics/

Precarious Employment Governance in Russia: Challenges, Practice, Scientific Validity

Vyacheslav Bobkov, Vadim Kvachev and Irina Novikova

1. Introduction

There are several forms of employment regulation in the Russian Federation:

- Hierarchy – governance in accordance with the rigid system of statuses and rules on the ground of a centralised decision-making pattern;
- Market – governance in the form of providing rules and conditions by the state for workable competition;
- Network – governance in the form of actors' interest alignment and decision-making consensus.

Government regulation of employment, including not only labour activity but also entrepreneurship, is performed by means of key legal instruments among which are: the Law on the Civil Service of the Russian Federation[1], the Labour Code[2], the Civil Code[3] and the Code of Administrative Violations[4] etc. All the other regulations are based on above mentioned enactments.

2. Current system of employment regulation in Russia

Hierarchical form of governance in Russia includes the establishment of prescriptive norms and rules concerning all forms of labour activity and entrepreneurship by the state. Among them are:

- Government regulation of employment in the public service sector, managed by the Law on the Civil Service of the Russian Federation[5];
- Government regulation of employment in other sectors.

---

[1] Federal Law No. 1032-1(19 April 1991).
[2] Federal Law No. 197 (30 December 2001).
[3] Federal Law No. 521 (30 November 1994).
[4] Federal Law No. 195 (30 December 2001).
[5] Federal Law No. 58 (27 May 2003).

In Russia, only under these criteria, are employees considered to be state civil service workers, who work directly in areas of the government. This includes employees who work in organisations, which are financed by federal, regional and municipal budgets, educational and healthcare organisations, cultural organisations and others. As a matter of fact, these two groups of employees differ in the conditions of employment, salary and pension coverage. It is very distinct from state civil servants as the employment of people isn't regulated by any particular law to be paid from the state budget. Standards regulating this type of employment can be found in the articles of the Russian Labour Code. Article 144 of the Russian Labour Code deals with the system of payment to employees in government-financed organisations, Article 25 guarantees the compensation of employees in government-financed organisations and so on. The Labour Code also regulates employment of the State's non-budgetary funds, such as the Pension Fund of the Russian Federation, the Social Insurance Fund of the Russian Federation, the Federal Compulsory Medical Insurance Fund and other foundations established by the state.

Market regulation of employment in the market sector is settled by the Labour Code, in particular by defining the establishment of labour relations, the duration of working hours, the schedule of work and rest, the minimum wage, social guarantees at the workplace, temporary incapacity for work terms, unemployment, healthcare, pension insurance, etc.

Employment regulation in the market sector includes an instrument, which is established by the Law Concerning Employment in the RF, Labour Code and Civil Code as well as by variety of local normative acts.

According to the Labour Code, an employer can define the work status and the duration of working time within the limits of legislation, the proper forming of wages (art. 135, 143 of the Labour Code), set wages (art. 135 of the Labour Code), workplace discipline (Chapter 30 of the Labour Code), corporate business travel guarantee (Chapter 24 of the Labour Code), etc. Work for natural persons acting as their own employers as well as work for small businesses qualified as micro-enterprises are regulated separately (Chapter 48 of the Labour Code).

The Law on Employment in the Russian Federation states the rights of employers (art. 26). The Civil Code defines entrepreneurial activity of a Russian citizen in two ways – if the citizen acts as a legal entity (art. 4) or if the citizen acts without forming a legal entity (Chapter 3). Local normative acts regulating employment in the private sector affect the interests of employees and the self-employed. At the present time, are 61.9% of all employed in Russia work in the private sector and 7.1% are self-employed.[6]

Network forms of employment regulation in Russia were established by the Federal law on the Fundamentals of Social Control in the Russian Federation[7]. The most effective form of network governance in employment is the Employment Promotion Coordinating Committee, which was created to build a consensus in employment policy implementing at all levels of governing. Social partnership in labour relations is one of the most important network institutes as it helps to reconcile the interests of the employer, the employee and the state (art. 23-55 of the Labour Code).

Specialised areas of social control are defined by regulatory acts by the Social Councils of federal ministries, agencies and services[8]. Social Councils are formed by representatives of civil society. Social Councils have advisory powers to discuss all the initiatives of government structures. The main coordinating body of the Social Control system is the Civic Chamber of the Russian Federation and its regional departments[9].

A relatively new form of civil society influence on the employment of public authorities is social media. There is a law which permits citizens to announce an initiative on a special government-run Internet platform. If the initiative collects hundreds of thousands of signatures federally or 5% of the standard residential population regionally or municipally, the public authorities are obliged to review it and to either initiate a bill or take other measures to implement it[10]. More detailed analysis in accordance with EN RLMM criteria is presented in Table 1 in the Annex.

---

6 Trud i zanyatost' v Rossii. Rosstat (2015), Table 3.7. s. 107, Tabl. 1.37. P. 15 URL: http://www.gks.ru/free_doc/doc_2015/trud15.pdf.
7 Federal Law No. 212 (21 July 2014).
8 Decree of the President of 4 August 2006 No. 842; Government Decree of 2 August 2005 No. 481.
9 Federal Law No. 32 (4 April 2005).
10 Decree of the President of 4 March 2013 No. 183.

3. Premises of applicable legislation enforcement for regulation of new forms of employment for the purpose of precarity minimisation

Evolution of the market capitalist system in Russia is attended by the development of new forms of precarious employment. According to the ILO approach, precarious employment is spilt into two categories of contractual agreement: labour contracts for a limited period of time (terminal contracts, short-term contracts, temporary contracts, seasonal contracts, daily work contracts, contingent contracts); type of labour relations (multilateral and disguised labour relations, fictional self-employment, subcontracting and agency contracts). These categories are instantiated by four precarious conditions of labour: low wages, low level of protection from employment termination, lack of access to social security and minimal guarantees, associated with standard employment, and barriers to access employees' labour rights (ILO 2012). Currently, precarious employment is a common practice. It is used quite a lot, not only in subjective intentions of some employers but in the substance of the Post-Fordist market capitalism work flexibility. By various estimates, between 30% to 50% of Russian employees are affected by different forms of precarious employment. Above, as mentioned, the instruments of governance very rarely regulate precarious employment Bobkov et al. 2017, Bobkob et al. 2014). Stand-alone initiatives do decide some important issues but they are not systematic. According to official data, there were 20 million employed in the informal sector alone in the beginning of 2010[11]. In 2014, the Russian government launched an initiative to legalise informal employment but the state focused on the task of tax collection. This is, of course, an important problem but as long as government priorities differ from employee and employer interests, the problem of precarity will not be solved. Decision-makers should focus on protecting social and labour rights of employees as well as the creation of a friendly work environment. Only under these conditions, will employers and employees start to come out of the informal sector voluntarily.

For example, in the period of 2014 to 2016, the Russian government changed legislation, in order to prohibit agency work[12]. These changes included strengthening administrative sanctions for the finishing of contracted service instead of labour contracting and regulating teleworking[13]. However, the informal sector

---

[11] Press-Conference of Deputy PM Olga Golodets on G20 Ministerial Meeting, July 2013. Official web-site of Russian Government. URL: http://government.ru/news/3189/ dDate of access – 20 May 2017)
[12] Federal Law No. 116 (5 May 2014) Федеральный закон РФ от 5 May 2014 No. 116-ФЗ
[13] Federal Law No. 60 (5 April 2013)

wasn't reduced after the legislation development and there is a good reason for this. Amendments were focused on compulsory measures, which didn't have clear fundamental terms for enforcement.

According to official statistics, 0.09% of workers were remote workers in 2016[14]. It is a well-known fact that telework in Russia has a wide distribution in the labour market. That said, the vast majority of such workplaces only exist in the informal sector, especially taking into account secondary employment.

In 2017, several new laws aimed at the legalisation of informal employment will come into action. They are devoted to labour conditions at micro-enterprises[15] and to tax holidays for some categories of the self-employed[16]. These normative acts raise questions in their legitimacy and could damage public perception, which would fail to decrease the scale of precarious employment.

From our point of view, new flexible forms of employment should be developed on the basis of systematic classification and with due regard to existing regulation in current laws. Some new flexible forms of employment, in fact exist, but aren't regulated by any legislation. In the following classification, we looked at the modelling the system used by Eurofound (Mandl 2015). This method could be used to develop Russian legislation, taking into account unused normative capacity of some existing norms. More detailed information on legal instruments which can be used to regulate these forms is presented in Table 2 in the annex to illustrate these points.

For example, on-call work is usually regulated by informal verbal agreement. However, the employer and the employee discuss deadlines. For decreasing a level of precarisation of such employment, regulation of these labour relations is needed. In particular, the subscriber contract could be used in this context in the process of legislation development. Working time could be recorded in articles 92, 93, 94, 101, 102, 104, 105. This type of employment could also be disclosed in Chapters 48 and 48.1 of the Labour Code.

Successful outcomes of these proposed regulation changes depend on the effective application of all three forms of governance: hierarchical, market and network. It is indisputable that the primary mechanism is net governance because

---

[14] Obsledovanie rabochej sily. Federal State Statistics Service. 2016. URL: http://www.gks.ru/wps/wcm/connect/rosstat_main/rosstat/ru/statistics/publications/catalog/doc_1140097038766 (date of access 20 May 2017).
[15] Federal Law No. 348 (3 July 2016).
[16] Government Decree of 27 August 2005 No. 858.

it can expose and evaluate new forms of employment. The second most important method is, of course, market governance because it allows formulating and coordinating employer and employee interests. After these two forms have been applied, hierarchical mechanisms of enforcement can be adopted.

4. Conclusion

An employment regulation system exists in the Russian Federation which uses hierarchical, market and net governance forms and enables reacting to changes on the labour market.

Employment regulations in the Russian Federation have the following limitations:

Hierarchical governance:

- More wide-spread explanatory work concerning the enforcement is required;
- Decision-making process expertise should be formalised to consider opinion different subjects;
- Governance in this form is mainly aimed at budgetary recharge, not at creating facilities for employees and employers;
- Adoption and enforcement of laws are not free from corrupt conduct.

Market governance:

- There is a lack of trade-unions at the primary level;
- A considerable part of labour relations is regulated informally (envelope salary; verbal agreements; fiscal evasion).
- There is a lack of employee participation in management under the conditions of precarious employment.
- Decision making of market actors is aimed exclusively at their own cost minimisation and upholding of interests.

Network governance:

- Expert community do not always represent all the professional and social groups.

Russian legislation is used insufficiently for regulating precarious forms of employment. Some particular decisions are very important but they are not systematic.

Current Russian legislation contains necessary premises for governing new forms of employment. Systematic classifications of this forms should lead to following adaptation and development of current legislation for purposes of precarious employment regulation.

References

Bobkov, Vyacheslav/Veredyuk, Olesya/Aliyev, Ulvi (2017): Risks of Society Stability and Precarity of Employment: A Look at Russia, in: International Journal of Social Quality, Vol. 7 pp. 21-43

Herrmann, Peter/Bobkov, Vyacheslav/Csoba Judit (Eds.) (2014): Labour market and Precarity of Employment: Theoretical reflections and Empirical Data from Hungary and Russia. Bremen: Wiener Verlag für Sozialforschung

ILO 2012: From precarious work to decent work: outcome document to the workers' symposium on policies and regulations to combat precarious employment/International Labour Office, Bureau for Workers' Activities. Geneva: ILO, 2012. URL: http://www.ilo.org/wcmsp5/groups/public/---ed_dialogue/---actrav/documents/meeting-document/wcms_179787.pdf (date of access 20 May 2017)

Mandl, Irene/Curtarelli, Maurizio/Riso, Sara/Vargas, Oscar/Gerogiannis, Elias (2015): New forms of employment, Publications Office of the European Union, Luxembourg

Websites

Federal web portal of regulation drafts. URL:
http://regulation.gov.ru/# (date of access – 20 May 2017)

Обследование рабочей силы. Федеральная служба государственной статистики. 2016. [Obsledovanie rabochej sily. Federal State Statistics Service. 2016]. URL:
http://www.gks.ru/wps/wcm/connect/rosstat_main/rosstat/ru/statistics/publications/catalog/doc_1140097038766 (date of access – 20 May 2017)

Press-Conference of Deputy PM Olga Golodets on G20 Ministerial Meeting, July 2013. Official web-site of Russian Government. URL:
http://government.ru/news/3189/ (date of access – 20 May 2017)

Trud i zanyatost' v Rossii. Federal State Statistics Service. 2015. URL:
http://www.gks.ru/free_doc/doc_2015/trud15.pdf

Legal acts

Decree of the President of 04 August 2006 No. 842

Decree of the President of 04 March 2013 No. 183

Federal Law No. 273 (25 December 2008)

Federal Law No. 1032-1 (19 April 1991)

Federal Law No. 521 (30 November 1994)

Federal Law No. No. 197 (30 December 2001)

Federal Law No. 195 (30 December 2001)

Federal Law No. 58 (27 May 2003)

Federal Law No. 32 (4 April 2005)

Federal Law No. 60 (5 April 2013)

Federal Law No. 116 (5 May 2014)

Federal Law No. 212 (21 July 2014)

Federal Law No. 348 (3 July 2016)

Government Decree of 2 July 2005 No. 481

Government Decree of 27 August 2005 No. 858

ANNEX

Table 1 Classification of different types of employment regulation in Russia

	Transparency	Accountability	Participation	Integrity	Capacity
Hierarchy (I)	Basic Russian legislation (Law Concerning Employment in the Russian Federation, Labour Code, Civil Code, Law Concerning State civil service in RF etc.) available for everyone involved in labour relations; explanatory work concerning labour legislation application is insufficient.	Employee, employer, representatives of employees and employers, employment promotion coordinating committee, monitoring institutions.	Strict law enforcement; possibility to discuss draft bills using network instruments of communication; possibility to announce an initiative; instruments of public opinion consideration though ill-conceived in terms of formal procedure.	Federal Law on Countering Corruption[17]; Federal Labour Inspectorate; pre-court institutions of employment disputes; courts; integrity of employment regulation sufficiently institutionalised; adoption and enforcement of the law are not free from corruption.	Federal web portal of regulation drafts[18]; employment regulations decision making procedure requires to be more formalised in terms of contributor's roles.

---

17 Federal Law No. 273 (25 December 2008).
18 Federal web portal of regulation drafts. URL: http://regulation.gov.ru/# (Date of access – 20 May 2017)

Market (M)	In terms of the law application market governance is faced with the same problems similar to hierarchical governance issues; company internal agreements, Local normative acts, accessible to potential labour relations participants as well as to their representatives, generally these regulations' clarification is sufficient.	Employee, employer, representatives of employees and employers, employment promotion coordinating committee, monitoring institutions; market actors.	Tariff industrial agreements and collective labour agreements; labour contracts and supplementary labour contracts based on negotiations between employee and employer; lack of employee participation in management under the conditions of precarious employment.	Employer and employee representatives often do not participate in activity of trade-unions. A considerable part of labour relations is regulated informally (envelope salary; verbal agreements; fiscal evasion).	Social partnership institutions; trade-unions; employers' association; governance generally aimed on budgetary recharge instead of creation market facilities for employer and employee. Decision making of market actors is aimed exclusively at their own cost minimisation and upholding of interests.
Network (N)	Social partnership agreements in the social labour sphere; Social Council's and Civic Chamber's public hearings; public initiatives are transparent and generally accessible for everyone involved in labour relations.	Employee, employer, representatives of employees and employers, employment promotion coordinating committee, monitoring institutions; Federal Labour Inspectorate; market actors. All-Russian and trans-regional trade-unions and their territorial bodies; Federal Ministries', Federal Agency's and	Social Partnership institutions entirely participate in employment regulation decision-making process; internet voting is lacking; Labour Code provides too rigid conditions for strike holding. Consequently, this instrument of employment governance is	Network governance processes institutionalised; these forms of employment governances are less corruptible.	Network governance is implemented by an expert community; nevertheless, an expert community doesn't always represent all professional and social groups.

| | | Federal Services' Social Councils. | used insufficiently. | | |

Table 2 New flexible forms of employment and Russian legal acts, which could form the basis for their governing

Eurofond classification of new flexible forms of employment	Characteristic of form	Capabilities of current legislation application for regulation of new flexible forms of employment
Strategic employee sharing	A group of employers forms a network which hires one or more employees for individual task work in the participating network organisations.	Labour Code: Article 72.1 Transition of an employee to a different permanent job Labour Code. Article 72.1 Temporary transition of an employee to a different permanent job Article 104. Added up calculation of working hours Article 105. Dividing the working day into parts Article 150. Remuneration of labour when performing work requiring different qualifications Article 151. Remuneration of labour when combining jobs and performing the duties of a temporarily absent employee Article 48. Force of the agreement Chapter 48. Special procedures for employees working for individual employers
Job sharing	An employer hires two or more employees for mutual work.	Labour Code: Chapter 44. Special procedures for off-hour employees Article 150. Remuneration of labour when performing work requiring different qualifications Article 151. Remuneration of labour when combining jobs and performing the duties of a temporarily absent employee Article 48. Force of the agreement

		Chapter 48. Special procedures for employees working for individual employers
Interim management	An organisation leases an employee from another company for temporary work or a single task.	Law Concerning Employment in the Russian Federation.
		Article 18.1. Activity in the field of agency work
		Labour Code:
		Chapter 53.1. Special procedures for the employees sent to work temporary to private individual or entity in an agency work contractual relationships
		Chapter 48.1 special procedures for employees working for individual employers – microenterprises
		Chapter 48. Special procedures for employees working for individual employers
Casual work	Employment isn't stable and continuous. An employer is under no obligation to provide work on a regular basis but can call an employee to work on demand at any moment.	Civil Code:
		Article 429.4. Subscriber contract.
		Labour Code:
		Chapter 45. Special procedures for the employees who concluded a labour contract for two months
		Article 92. Reduced length of working time
		Article 93. Incomplete working time (part-time working)
		Article 94. Length of daily working time (shift)
		Article 101. Irregular working hours
		Article 102. Work on flexible-time scheme
		Article 104. Added up calculation of working hours
		Article 105. Dividing the working day into parts
		Chapter 48.1 special procedures for employees working for individual employers – microenterprises
		Chapter 48. Special procedures for employees working for individual employers
Intermittent work	An employer recruits employees on a regular or irregular basis for particular work within a specific project or for seasonal work. This	Labour Code:
		Article 59. The term labour contract
		Article 92. Reduced length of working time

		employment is characterised by a fixed term based on a particular task implementation or on the number of working days.	Article 93. Incomplete working time (part-time working)
			Article 94. Length of daily working time (shift)
			Article 101. Irregular working hours
			Article 102. Work on flexible-time scheme
			Article 104. Added up calculation of working hours
			Article 105. Dividing the working day into parts
			Chapter 46. Special procedures for seasonal employees
			Chapter 47. Special procedures for shift workers
			Chapter 48.1 special procedures for employees working for individual employers – microenterprises.
			Chapter 48. Special procedures for employees working for individual employers
	On-call work (zero-hours contracts)	Continuous employment relation between employer and employee in which work is provided on an irregular basis.	Civil Code:
			Article 429.4. Subscriber contract.
			Labour Code:
			Article 92. Reduced length of working time
			Article 93. Incomplete working time (part-time working)
			Article 94. Length of daily working time (shift)
			Article 101. Irregular working hours
			Article 102. Work on flexible-time scheme
			Article 104. Added up calculation of working hours
			Article 105. Dividing the working day into parts
			Chapter 48.1 Special procedures for employees working for individual employers – microenterprises
			Chapter 48. Special procedures for employees working for individual employers
	Full mobility	Frequent changes in location and variety of locations within the workplace with a combination of different working time regimes as	Labour Code:
			Article 49.1. Special procedures for teleworking
			Article 101. Irregular working hours
			Article 102. Work on flexible-time scheme

	well as the composition of individual and collective workplaces.	Article 104. Added up calculation of working hours
		Article 105. Dividing the working day into parts
		Article 150. Remuneration of labour when performing work requiring different qualifications
		Article 151. Remuneration of labour when combining jobs and performing the duties of a temporarily absent employee
		Chapter 48.1 Special procedures for employees working for individual employers – microenterprises
		Chapter 48. Special procedures for employees working for individual employers
Site mobility	Mobility with frequent changes of workplaces in a geographically constrained area.	Labour Code:
		Article 72.1. Transition of an employee to a different permanent job. Transferring an employee to a different working place
		Article 72.1. Transition of an employee to a different temporary job
		Article 101. Irregular working hours
		Article 102. Work on flexible-time scheme
		Article 104. Added up calculation of working hours
		Article 105. Dividing the working day into parts
		Article 150. Remuneration of labour when performing work requiring different qualifications
		Article 151. Remuneration of labour when combining jobs and performing the duties of a temporarily absent employee
		Chapter 48.1 Special procedures for employees working for individual employers – microenterprises
		Chapter 48. Special procedures for employees working for individual employers
Multi-location workplaces	A number of fixed workplaces which change infrequently though with special mobility.	Labour Code:
		Article 282. General articles for off-hour work
		Article 101. Irregular working hours
		Article 102. Work on flexible-time scheme

		Article 104. Added up calculation of working hours
		Article 105. Dividing the working day into parts
		Article 150. Remuneration of labour when performing work requiring different qualifications
		Article 151. Remuneration of labour when combining jobs and performing the duties of a temporarily absent employee
		Chapter 48.1 Special procedures for employees working for individual employers – microenterprises.
		Chapter 48. Special procedures for employees working for individual employers
Networked workplaces	Limited physical mobility with work in different places; work types in this position include 24-hours software development and complicated engineering and technical tasks.	Labour Code:
		Article 282. General articles for off-hour work
		Article 101. Irregular working hours
		Article 102. Work on flexible-time scheme
		Article 104. Added up calculation of working hours
		Article 105. Dividing the working day into parts
		Article 150. Remuneration of labour when performing work requiring different qualifications
		Article 151. Remuneration of labour when combining jobs and performing the duties of a temporarily absent employee
Voucher-based work	An employer acquires vouchers from a third person (as a rule from the government) which will be used as a payment for services from an employee.	Law Concerning Employment in the Russian Federation. Article 18.1. Activity in the field of agency work
		Labour Code:
		Chapter 53.1. Special procedures for the employees sent to work temporary to private individual or entity in an agency work contractual relationships
Portfolio workers	Employees have several workplaces or contracts in different fields of work intra-company.	Labour Code:
		Article 282. General articles for off-hour work
		Article 101. Irregular working hours
		Article 102. Work on flexible-time scheme

		Article 104. Added up calculation of working hours
		Article 105. Dividing the working day into parts
		Article 150. Remuneration of labour when performing work requiring different qualifications
		Article 151. Remuneration of labour when combining jobs and performing the duties of a temporarily absent employee
		Chapter 48.1 Special procedures for employees working for individual employers – microenterprises.
		Chapter 48. Special procedures for employees working for individual employers
		Civil Code:
		Article 23. Entrepreneurial Activity of a Citizen
Ad-hoc employee sharing	An employer who cannot provide work for employees sends them to work for another company (labour contract between primary employer and employee is preserved).	Law Concerning Employment in the Russian Federation. Article 18.1. Activity in the field of agency work
		Labour Code:
		Chapter 53.1. Special procedures for the employees sent to work temporary to private individual or entity in an agency work contractual relationships
		Article 104. Added up calculation of working hours
		Article 105. Dividing the working day into parts
		Chapter 48.1 Special procedures for employees working for individual employers – microenterprises
		Chapter 48. Special procedures for employees working for individual employers
Crowd employment	Employment organised via online platform which allows potential employers to hire employees for particular works and services.	Civil Code:
		Chapter 39. Compensated Providing of Services.
		Article 23. Entrepreneurial Activity of a Citizen
		Labour Code:
		Article 92. Reduced length of working time
		Article 93. Incomplete working time (part-time working)
		Article 94. Length of daily working time (shift)

			Article 101. Irregular working hours
			Article 102. Work on flexible-time scheme
			Chapter 48.1 Special procedures for employees working for individual employers – microenterprises
			Chapter 48. Special procedures for employees working for individual employers
			Chapter 49. Special procedures for outworkers
Collaborative employment	Cooperation between non-regular workers, self-employed entrepreneurs and micro-enterprises for collaborative delivery of services.	Civil Code:	
		Chapter 39. Compensated Providing of Services.	
		Labour Code:	
		Article 101. Irregular working hours	
		Article 102. Work on flexible-time scheme	
		Chapter 48.1 Special procedures for employees working for individual employers – microenterprises	
		Chapter 49. Special procedures for outworkers	
Umbrella organisations	Delivery of particular administrative services such as billing or fiscal management service	Civil Code:	
		Chapter 39. Compensated Providing of Services.	
		Labour Code:	
		Article 101. Irregular working hours	
		Article 102. Work on flexible-time scheme	
		Chapter 49. Special procedures for outworkers	

A Conceptual Model of Collaborative Support System for Labour Market Governance

Ciprian Pânzaru and Claudiu Brândaș

1. Abstract

The labour market is a very dynamic and complex system involving a series of actors, decision-making processes, policy-making processes and legislation. Within this system, there may often appear issues related to the lack of transparency and accountability leading to informational asymmetry, arbitrary and non-participatory decision-making.

In this context, the transparency of information and standardised communication is necessary to ensure a good labour market governance. Our approach is focused on the analysis of the labour market governance architecture in order to develop a conceptual model for a hybrid and collaborative support system for labour market governance. This system will provide support for transparency, monitoring, and participation in a collaborative framework, in order to increase the efficiency of labour market governance. Beyond its theoretical implications, the model could also be used in providing a coherent framework for the construction of a better labour market governance structure.

2. Introduction

Economic and demographic factors associated with the specific pattern of socio-economic and political developments have contributed to shaping the current landscape of the Romanian labour market. Currently, the Romanian labour market is characterised by deep labour shortages, higher labour regulations volatility, and a weak relationship between the education curriculum and the labour market needs (Manpower 2016; World Economic Forum 2014; Panzaru and Brandas 2015; Panzaru 2012, 2015).

In this context, a good labour market governance shall be a solution for improvements in the functioning of the labour market. Labour Market Governance (LMG) includes the totality of institutions (e.g. policies, norms, laws, regulations, structures, mechanisms and processes) that affect the functioning of a labour market

(ILO 2011). LMG can be conceptualised as the effects of interactions among government, social, political and economic actors, where all actors are providers of information and expertise. These interactions involve information flows, conflicts, interests, ideas, etc.

Our study is focused on the analysis of the labour market governance architecture in order to develop a conceptual model for a collaborative support system for LMG. The paper is organised in two main parts. In the first part, we presented the characteristics of the Romanian labour market governance. In the second part of the study, we developed a conceptual model for a hybrid and collaborative support system for the LMG.

3. Labour market architecture

The Romanian labour market is dominated by a large number of actors organised on multiple levels. Among these, there is the Ministry of Labour, and its agencies with regional and local subsidiaries (e.g. National Employment Agency), public organisations (e.g. Social and Economic Council) and private organisations (e.g. trade unions, employers' associations).

The representation of relations between actors who form the architecture of the Romanian LMG is presented in Figure 1.

Figure 1   The architecture of Romanian labour market governance

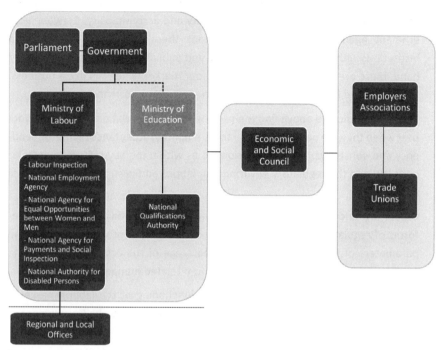

Source: own elaboration.

At the macro-level, the LMG architecture is a mixed one which combines self-governing private organisations on the market, hierarchical relationships between government agencies or public institutions involved directly or indirectly in labour market management and the network-based relationship between all these actors.

LMG is not an alternative to government, in terms of policy-making, besides LMG involves "large quantities" of government. From our point of view, LMG is an agreement among actors based on networks of relations, but organised at the same time on markets and hierarchies. In the case of the Romanian labour market, it is possible to talk about three groups of actors: government agencies, hybrid institutions and private institutions.

Government agencies and public institutions involved in labour market management are primarily organised according to hierarchical principles. Their organisational mode is based on authority, legality and accountability. Between government agencies and private institutions there are the so-called hybrid institutions with elements of both private and public organisations. On the other hand, there are private players on the labour market which run like a business, being oriented towards competition, efficiency and performance.

The actors indicated above find themselves in complex relationships which work best when they are based on mutual trust, empathy, acceptance of interdependency and consensus. They play various roles within the key LMG elements: labour law and the regulatory environment, labour administration and industrial relations.

Labour law and the regulatory environment include all policies, laws and other forms of regulation in the field of labour and employment which establish the parameters of the LMG. It covers a broad range of subjects concerning work, employment, social security, social policy and related human rights (ILO 2011).

The legal framework which regulates the functioning of the labour market is comprised of legislative provisions issued by the Parliament, the Government or the Ministry of Labour. Apart from these, there is also the legislation of the European Union as well as the international treaties signed by Romania.

The Government represents the main actor of the LMG. It is "the general management of public administration", it elaborates strategies in order to implement the government platform and formulates legislative initiatives. Alongside the Government, in the regulatory environment of the LMG there is also the Parliament, as this is the national legislature of Romania.

The Ministry of Labour is also a main actor in the regulatory environment of LMG. The Ministry of Labour is the institution which elaborates strategies and policies of job vacancy filling, professional formation and social protection for the unemployed. The activity of Ministry of Labour is supported by public institutions such as: the National Agency of Employment (NEA), the National Qualifications Authority (NQA) and Labour Inspection (LI).

These institutions represent the main actors of labour administration. Labour administration refers to all public administration activities in the field of national labour policy – including policy setting and implementing. The quality of the labour market governance is partly determined by the efficiency and effectiveness with which labour administration services are delivered to the clients of the labour administration system (ILO 2011).

One of the most important functions of the LMG is to ensure the efficient allocation of human resources to cope with the changing demand for jobs and skills. This task is managed by employment services provided by public or private agencies.

NEA is the Public Employment Service of Romania. It represents the main actor of labour administration. NEA's territorial offices are the County Agencies of Employment and Local Units of Employment. The NEA coordinates the Agency of Bucharest, 41 county agencies (with 70 local agencies and 141 offices), eight county centres of vocational training for the unemployed, eight regional centres of adult vocational training, as well as a National Centre for the Vocational Training of the Personnel. The NEA has the following responsibilities (National Employment Agency n.d.):

- Organises, provides and finances, services of vocational training for unemployed persons;
- Advises unemployed persons and intermediate contacts between them and employers;
- Makes proposals regarding the elaboration of the budget project for unemployment insurances;
- Manages the budget of unemployment insurances and presents the situation to the Ministry of Labour;
- Proposes legislative projects in the matter of employment, vocational training and social protection of the unemployed to the Ministry of Labour;
- Manages services of establishing, paying and keeping track of financial aids and allowances financed by the budget of unemployment insurances;
- Implements programs financed by EU funds.

In addition to Public Employment Services (PES), there are many private employment agencies. In contrast to PES, the private employment agencies have a market-based business model.

Labour inspection is another important actor of labour administration. It provides control in the field of labour, employee safety and health and market supervision. At the same time, labour inspection also ensures the management of the Employee Account Registry. The general Employee Account Registry comprises information about all contracts of employment. Labour inspection is also responsible for controlling informal labour. Labour inspection coordinates territorial labour inspectorates – in every county and in Bucharest.

A good LMG needs to respond to industrial accidents, occupational diseases, maternity and involuntary unemployment. Thus, within LMG regarding the labour administration component there are other three institutions: the National Agency for Equal Opportunities between Women and Men, the National Agency for Payments and Social Inspection and the National Disability Authority (Ministry of Labour, n.d.).

The mission of the National Agency for Equal Opportunities between Women and Men is that of promoting the principle of equality of opportunity between women and men, in order to eliminate any form of gender discrimination in all policies and national programs, including the labour market. The National Agency for Payments and Social Inspection manages funds being allocated from the state budget for the payment of social care benefits and funds for social service programs. The National Authority for Disabled Persons protects and promotes the rights of disabled persons and supports them in the employment process. All these agencies have regional and local offices.

Alongside agencies coordinated by the Ministry of Labour, the LMG architecture also contains agencies belonging to other ministries. For example, The National Qualifications Authority (NQA) is coordinated by the Ministry of Education (Ministry of Education n.d.). This authority (NQA) regulates and coordinates the general framework of education and continuous professional formation of adults. NQA elaborates the national framework of qualifications and manages the National Registry of Qualifications, the National Registry of Authorised Training Providers, and the National Registry of the Graduates from Authorised Training Programs for Adults. Also, NQA coordinates and controls the authorisation process of training providers and evaluation centres for professional competencies, as well as the certification of professional competencies evaluators.

The third key element in the LMG is represented by the industrial relations (ILO 2011). This element refers to the relation between employers and workers (Lewis et al. 2003). LMG is improved if the tripartite constituents participate in the process. In the Romanian structure of LMG, the main role in the industrial relations component is owned by The Economic and Social Council (ESC). This is a public tripartite, autonomous institution, whose aim is that of facilitating the tripartite dialogue between employers' associations, trade unions and representatives of associations and nongovernmental foundations of the civil society. From this point of view, we consider ESC a quasi-autonomous non-governmental organisation (Skelcher 1998, Wettenhall 1981). It has a role in the processes of national government, but it is not a government department or part of one. The Economic and Social Council is an advisory forum of the Romanian Parliament and Government (Economic and Social Council n.d.). In our approach, ESC represents the link between governmental agencies and private institutions involved in the management of the labour market.

ESC consists of 45 members representing employers' associations, trade unions and associative structures of the civil society. They are appointed following a recommendation from the Ministry of Labour. The specific areas of activity of the ESC are:

- Economic policies;
- Fiscal and financial policies;
- Labour relations, social care, wage policies and equality of opportunity;
- Agriculture, rural development, environment protection and sustainable development;
- Consumer protection and fair competition;
- Cooperation, liberal professions, and independent activities;
- Citizens' rights and freedoms;
- Health policies;
- Policies for education, youth, research, culture and sports;

ESC approves legislative projects for domains mentioned above.

The architecture of LMG is also composed of private organisations. In this category, there are employers' associations and trade unions.

Employers' associations are divided into branches. Their role is to represents the interests of employers in relation to authorities and trade unions. A number of at least 15 employers can form an employer association. As a matter of fact, employers' associations can be formed with even a minimum of five members in branches where they possess more than 70% of the overall volume of production. Employers' associations can be organised in cross-sectoral confederations. A confederation is representative if it is comprised of companies from at least

25% of the branches of activity and gathers 7% of the number of employees. Representativeness is obtained every four years, through judicial decision.

Trade unions represent a form of voluntary organisation of the employees for defending their rights and promoting their professional, economic and social interests in the relation with the employer. A trade union can be established by at least 15 persons of the same branch or profession. Trade unions participate in the negotiation and signing of the collective labour agreement. In order to be a negotiating partner for an employer, a trade union shall be representative (e.g. at least one-third of the number of employees from the company must be members)

The most critical concerns among the LMG actors are the lack of transparency, accountability, participation, integrity and capacity.

In this context, the Government, Parliament and Ministry of Labour have to ensure a good and stable regulatory environment for an appropriate functioning of the labour market.

However, the most extensive criticism of employers concerns the legislative instability in the field of the labour market. The legislative and fiscal instability is one of the "obstacles" which companies and business people in Romania encounter. The lack of medium and long-term predictability is hampering the appropriate management of business. In a recent study (TMF Group 2015) foreign companies based in Romania indicated the following major challenges: the frequent shift in legislation (54%), obtaining appropriate support from the state (51%) and implementing the legislative demands (49%).

There are also problems concerning transparency in information flow about labour demand and supply and about labour regulatory information. This situation often generates informational asymmetry. For example, employers have to report to the NEA all job vacancies within five working days since they became vacant. Also, they are obliged to announce the filling of the vacant positions within a day since the positions were filled. In reality, not all employers comply with these rules. On the other hand, regulations concerning the labour market are not spread in an appropriate manner and information can't reach all beneficiaries.

Another critical aspect of the labour market is the relation between trade unions and state. Trade unions depended on state funding and frequently, trade union leaders are at the same time political figures with public functions.

Sometimes, both trade unions and employers' associations work as distributional coalitions (Olson 2008). Their purpose is that of creating collective benefits for their executive members.

The representativeness of employers' associations is also a problem. Although the law states the conditions in which such an organisation can be established, there are situations in which the number of members is overstated, precisely with the purpose of forcing representativeness. Many important companies decide to remain outside of these organisations. For example, multinational companies, generally, are not members of employers' associations.

In order to deal with these governance deficiencies, we proposed a conceptual model for a hybrid and collaborative support system for labour market governance (LMG-CSS). In the next section, we present this model.

4. Model design and description

Based on our analysis presented in the previous section, in the design of the LMG-CSS conceptual model, we start from the fact that LMG is a complex system of rules, procedures, monitoring and assessment methods, processes and relationships between the actors of the system. The collaborative decision-making process can be viewed as a global network of brains based on cloud, mobile and social networks (Brandas and Didraga 2014). In developing the model, we considered the TAPIC framework and how IT&C can offer support for a good LMG. In the CSS model, actors, processes, information flows, roles and responsibilities were integrated with the support of IT&C.

The main objectives of LMG-CSS conceptual model are:
- Providing support for transparency;
- Monitoring;
- Participation in a collaborative manner.

The goal of LMG-CSS is to increase the efficiency and efficacy of LMG processes.

The architecture of LMG-CSS is structured on three levels:

- Processes, in order to ensure transparency, collaboration, and monitoring;
- Users and beneficiaries;
- Technologies which ensure the support for execution of the processes.

Figure 2   Structure of the LMG – CSS process

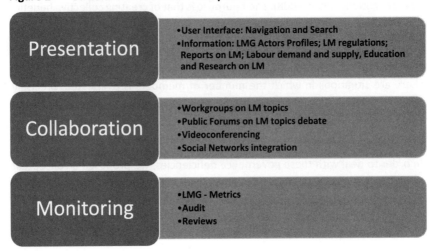

Source: own elaboration.

At the first level – processes – there are the following components (Figure 2):

- Presentation, provide integration and information concerning to:
  - Status, role and characteristics of the labour market actors;
  - Labour market regulation;
  - Labour demand and supply;
  - Education and vocational training;
  - Research.

- Collaboration, provide support for online and off-line collaboration and communication between labour market actors. Collaboration allows:
  - Developing the workgroups on labour market issues;
  - Developing public debates forums;
  - Developing newsletters about labour market regulations and laws;
  - Videoconferences.

- Monitoring allows visualisation of the quantitative and qualitative indicators concerning labour market processes (different access level depends on the role of each labour market actor). The monitoring process contains:
  - Labour market metrics and indicators;
  - Audits;
  - Reviews.

The second level – users and beneficiaries – are different groups of LMG actors depending on the role of each actors in LMG Architecture (Figure 1) as follows:

- Agencies of Ministry of Labour: provide and extract information in the presentation process, participate in the collaboration process (workgroups and public debates) and provide reports (metrics and reviews) for the monitoring process;
- Ministry of Education: provides and extracts information in the presentation process, participates in the collaboration process (workgroups and public debates);
- Economic and Social Council: provides and extracts information in the presentation process, participates in the collaboration process (workgroups and public debates) and provides reports for the monitoring process;
- Employers' Associations and Trade Unions: provide and extract information in the presentation process, participate in the collaboration process (workgroups and public debates) and provide reports (metrics and reviews) for the monitoring process.

The third level – technology – refers to IT&C technology used for execution of the processes. The main technologies are the Internet, Cloud Computing, Mobile Computing, Social Networks, Data Mining, Machine Learning and Cognitive Computing.

In Table 1 we present the way in which the LMG-CSS conceptual model provides support for a good LMG.

Table 1   LMG-CSS and the dimensions of successful governance

Model's Process	Transparency	Accountability	Participation	Integrity	Capacity
Presentation	X	X		X	X
Collaboration	X		X		
Monitoring		X		X	X

Source: own elaboration.

We consider that our model can ensure a good functionality for LMG regarding transparency, accountability, participation, integrity, and capacity.

Beyond its theoretical implications, the model could also be used in providing a coherent framework for a construction of a better labour market governance structure.

5. Conclusions

LMG has received attention only recently. The impacts of factors and institutions affecting the labour market outcome are being intensified, making the role of LMG more important than ever. In the current complex environment, LMG can provide the mechanisms for consultation, interaction and exchanges of information between all labour market actors.

This paper brings an interdisciplinary insight to a possible approach of a LMG based on IT&C. We consider that a collaborative support system for labour market governance (LMG-CSS) can provide support for transparency, monitoring, and participation in a collaborative framework, in order to increase the efficiency of labour market governance.

Our research suggests that the use of technology in LMG can improve efficiency, bring transparency in the decision-making processes and diminish the information asymmetry. These measures would lead to an increase of trust and accountability between all actors involved in labour market management.

References

Brândaș, Claudiu /Didraga, Otniel (2014): Collaborative Decision Support Systems: Cloud, Mobile and Social Approaches, in: Proceedings of the IE 2014 International Conference, Bucharest: ASE Printing House, pp. 15-8

Brândaș, Claudiu/Pânzaru, Ciprian (2015): Analysing of the Labour Demand and Supply Using Web Mining and Data Mining, in: Larsen, Christa/Rand, Sigrid/Schmid, Alfons/Mezzanzanica, Mario/Dusi, Silvia (Eds): Big Data and the Complexity of Labour Market Policies: New Approaches in Regional and Local Labour Market Monitoring for Reducing Skills Mismatches, München: Hampp Verlag, pp. 71-87

International Labour Organization (2011): Asian Decent Work Decade resource kit: labour market governance, Regional Office for Asia and the Pacific, Bangkok, online: http://www.ilo.org/wcmsp5/groups/public/---asia/---ro-bangkok/documents/publication/wcms_098156.pdf

Lewis, Philip/Thornhill, Adrian/Saunders, Mark (2003): Employee Relations: Understanding the Employment Relationship, Harlow: Pearson Education

Manpower (2016): Talent Shortage Survey, online: http://manpowergroup.com/talent-shortage-2016

Olson, Mancur (2008): The rise and decline of nations: Economic growth, stagflation, and social rigidities, Yale: University Press

Pânzaru, Ciprian (2015): On the Sustainability of the Romanian Pension System in the Light of Population Declining, in: Procedia-Social and Behavioral Sciences, No. 183, pp. 77-84

Pânzaru, Ciprian (2012): The role of skills development in the local labour market, in: Larsen, Christa/Hasberg, Ruth/Schmid, Alfons/Atin, Eugenia/Brzozowski, Jan (Eds): Skills Monitoring in European Regions and Localities. State of the Art and Perspectives, München: Hampp Verlag, pp. 105-140

Skelcher, Chris (1998): The appointed state: Quasi-governmental organizations and democracy, London: Open University Press

TMF Group (2015): The Business Environment in Romania, online: http://www.businesscover.ro/mediul-de-afaceri-din-romania-si-problemele-investitorilor-straini

Wettenhall, Roger (1981): The quango phenomenon. Current Affairs Bulletin, Vol. 57, No. 3, pp. 14–22

World Economic Forum (2014): Matching Skills and Labour Market Needs: Building Social Partnerships for Better Skills and Better Jobs, online: http://www3.weforum.org/docs/GAC/2014/WEF_GAC_Employment_MatchingSkillsLabourMarket_Report_2014.pdf

Websites

Agenţia Naţională pentru Ocuparea Forţei de Muncă [National Employment Agency]: http://www.anofm.ro/

Agentia Nationala pentru Egalitatea de Sanse intre Femei si Barbati [National Agency for Equal Opportunities between Women and Men]: http://anes.gov.ro

Agenţia Naţionala pentru Plati si Inspectie Sociala [National Agency for Payments and Social Inspection]: http://www.mmanpis.ro/

Autoritatea Nationala pentru Calificari [National Qualifications Authority]: http://www.anc.edu.ro/

Autoritatea Nationala pentru Persoanele cu Dizabilitati [National Authority for Disabled Persons]: http://anpd.gov.ro

Consiliul Economic si Social [Economic and Social Council]: http://www.ces.ro/

Inspectia Muncii [Labour Inspection]: https://www.inspectiamuncii.ro/

Ministerul Muncii si Justitiei Sociale [Ministry of Labour]: http://www.mmuncii.ro

Labour Market Governance in England: Devolution and Localism

Andrew Dean

1. Abstract

This short paper summarises the current trend in England towards the devolution of skills governance to sub-regions and city regions. It describes the devolution of powers during the 2010-2015 Coalition Government and its continuation in a modified form by the current Conservative Government. It discusses the emerging issues, opportunities and uncertainties that have arisen and comments on the political priorities and strategies that have led to the reorganisation in labour market and economic governance. Finally, it concludes that there are some fundamental issues that are not being addressed and that the approach to devolution has more to do with central government and ideological pre-occupations than with any conscious plan to enhance or reform labour market policies and governance.

2. Background

Devolution of Powers to the Scottish Parliament, and Welsh and Northern Ireland Assemblies has been part of the UK political landscape for many years. However, following the decision by the Scottish voters to remain part of the United Kingdom in September 2014 the UK Government announced:

It is also important we have wider civic engagement about how to improve governance in our United Kingdom, including how to empower our great cities and we will say more about this in the coming days. (David Cameron, cited in Sandford 2016a) reported on BBC Website (2014).

This announcement followed the production of several reports during 2014 making proposals for the transfer of additional powers to local authorities, or to local areas. Themselves building upon the 2012 report No Stone Unturned: in Pursuit of Growth ("The Heseltine report"), which recommended the merging of various national funding streams to provide much greater local responsibility for economic development. Efficiency in public service provision, triggered by continuing reductions in local government funding, was also prioritised within these more recent reports (Sandford 2016a). Changes proposed include:

- Giving new powers in specific policy areas to local authorities
- The transfer of additional budgets alongside those powers
- Enhanced power over local taxes (council tax and business rates), additional local taxation powers, and more flexibility around borrowing and financial management
- The creation of combined authorities and/or directly-elected mayors (Sandford 2016b, 2016c)

Some of these developments remain very new, notably the role of elected mayors and although England provides the longest-standing case of local democracy in Europe, the outcome of such changes has been mixed in terms of both success and acceptance by national political parties within municipalities (Kukovic et al. 2015).

Governance is (by definition) not simply a matter of the state's role or configuration; it also involves those of commercial interests, together with an institutional dimension, encompassing networks, habits of cooperation/antagonism and issues of legitimacy. O'Brien and Pike (2015) looked at both London and Manchester as examples of devolution in action. They concluded that in neither has the recreation of metropolitan governance capacity resulted in strong, institutional capacity that is capable, independently, of generating impacts that rival those that flow from central government's "implicit spatial policy". Drawing on a list, proposed by Le Gales (2002) and reporting work by Gordon et al. (2013), the authors summarised the current condition of each city and overall concluded that neither city was yet near to meeting the specification of what a metropolitan collective actor would/should embody. We are still some way from recognised autonomy or true devolution in a form which would be recognised in other countries.

3. Recent developments

During 2014 and 2015 a number of government reports made proposals for devolution of powers to local authorities or local areas in England. Most were published by think-tanks, with some coming from political parties. The proposals government viewed for local devolution covered functions in the following areas:

- Housing: capital funding from the Homes and Communities Agency, plus housing benefit;
- Further education and skills: funding from the Skills Funding Agency and Education Funding Agency, and associated programmes;
- Employment, principally the Work Programme;
- Transport: including local capital investment plans, trunk roads, and bus regulation;
- The probation service.

Further proposals were also made for extension of local control over school education, various social/welfare programmes and the commissioning of health and social care services. Ahead of the May 2015 General Election, all three major UK political parties had pledged greater devolution through various means. The Conservative Party's 2015 manifesto stated:

We will devolve far-reaching powers over economic development, transport and social care to large cities which choose to have elected mayors. We will devolve further powers over skills spending and planning to the Mayor of London. And we will deliver more bespoke Growth Deals with local councils, where locally supported, and back Local Enterprise Partnerships to promote jobs and growth (Conservative Party 2015).

4. Devolution deals in England

As of November 2016, devolution deals with eleven areas have been agreed. Discussions have also taken place on further devolution to Greater London. Below are the devolution deals agreed as of November 2016:

- Greater Manchester;
- Sheffield City Region;
- West Yorkshire;
- Cornwall;
- North-East;
- Tees Valley;
- West Midlands;
- Liverpool City Region;
- Cambridgeshire;

- Norfolk/Suffolk;
- West of England;
- Greater Lincolnshire.

Devolution deals have been negotiated in private between government teams and local authority leaders. Once the deal document has been agreed and published, each council involved must then itself approve its participation in the deal. This has been referred to by the government as "ratification". Commonly the majority of local councillors are not provided with information on a devolution deal until the final document is published. This "deal making" is also important in understanding why central government is a keen advocate of elected mayors and is in itself, the author would argue, a by-product of the prevalent neoliberal market-oriented approach to governance.

5. Implementation of devolution deals

Many aspects of the deals are to be implemented under the Cities and Local Government Devolution Act 2016 whilst other elements of the devolution deals do not concern statutory functions, and as such are easier to implement.

Limited information is available about the impact of exiting the European Union on devolution deals. The main impact is likely to be on EU structural funding, which was to be passed to local areas under many of the deals. The government has stated that it will guarantee any spending of these funds that is agreed before the UK leaves the EU. Local areas have also sought involvement in the "Brexit negotiations", arguing that powers returning to the UK on leaving the EU should be considered for devolution to local or devolved areas. Greg Clark, the previous Secretary of State for communities and local government, claimed that he had "argued successfully … for English local government to be part of the negotiations on the terms of our exit" (Sandford 2016a).

6. Deals "under negotiation"

To have their proposals taken into account in the autumn 2015 Spending Review, any further proposals for devolution from local areas were required to be submitted to the Treasury by 4 September 2015. Any later bids would implicitly receive lower priority. In the event the government received 38 bids for devolved powers by 4 September 2015. Deals have been reported as under negotiation in a number of areas:

- West Midlands;
- Hampshire/Isle of Wight;
- Lancashire;
- Dorset.

Whilst bids from Gloucestershire, Cheshire and Warrington and Cumbria have been reported as foundering on the areas' opposition to a directly-elected mayor. In other cases, adjacent areas have sought to join other "regions" for example, Warrington Council has had unofficial discussions with regard to joining the Liverpool City Region. Devolution bids, or expressions of interest/prospectuses, have also been published in Leicestershire; North and East Yorkshire; Surrey and Sussex; Greater Essex; and Devon/Somerset.

7. Deals "experiencing difficulties"

A number of devolution deals have run into obstacles since their initial agreement with the government. In most cases, though not all, difficulties have normally centred around local reactions to the creation of directly-elected mayors:

- The North-East deal collapsed on 7 September 2016 when four of the seven participants voted against it in full council;
- Derbyshire and Nottinghamshire agreed a draft "North Midlands" deal in January 2016, but subsequently a number of district councils pulled out
- Lincolnshire County Council and North Kesteven District Council rejected the Greater Lincolnshire deal in November;
- Five district councils pulled out of the Norfolk/Suffolk deal;

8. Content of devolution deals

The devolution deals agreed to date can be characterised as consisting of "a menu with specials". A number of items have been made available to most areas, but each deal also contains a few unique elements (typically consisting of commitments to explore future policy options). The following sections outline the nature of the "menu" powers that have been made available to most of these areas. The devolution deals agreed so far have many similarities in terms of powers to be devolved. In terms of restructuring the further education system, requested deals typically consist of moves towards local commissioning of the Adult Skills Budget from 2016-17, followed by full devolution of the budget from 2018-19. Some areas are also taking on the Apprenticeship Grant for Employers. In support of skills, most areas, local and central business support services will be united in a "growth hub" and UK Trade and Investment will be required to partner with local business support services. Other key elements of devolution are:

- The Work Programme;
- EU structural funds;
- Fiscal powers;
- Integrated transport systems;
- Planning and land use.

Very little information has been made available so far on the funding arrangements for any of these responsibilities. In terms of labour market governance, the key areas proposed for reform are economic development, employment and skills and aspects of welfare (the Work Programme). The proposed changes for these are dealt with in term in the following sections.

9. Devolution of economic development

Proposals for further devolution of economic development powers are rare in the recent literature, since much public spending on economic growth, business support and regeneration is already devolved to the 39 Local Enterprise Partnerships (LEPs) in England. Economic development is often interwoven with many of the other policy areas and much of the case for proposed devolution of powers to local areas rests on their ability to stimulate economic growth more effectively after those powers have been devolved. This driver of economic growth and productivity linked to devolution is critical in understanding both the approach taken and the intended result and how the latter has driven the former.

The government brought together a number of pre-existing funds into the Single Local Growth Fund in 2013, in response to the recommendations of the 2012 Heseltine Review (No Stone Unturned). This proposed the creation of a "single pot" of funding totalling some £49 billion over five years. To fund local growth the government established a Local Growth Fund as the main source of funding for local areas' growth schemes, alongside the 2014-20 round of the European Structural Funds, which will be distributed by LEPs in their areas. There have now been three calls for Local Growth Fund "deals" and many millions of pounds have been allocated, predominantly to infrastructure projects. A proposal was also made for funding from UK Trade & Investment, and "a role in shaping the industrial policy for creative industries", to be provided to combined authorities (IPPR/PwC 2014).

10. Devolution of employment and skills

Currently, further education funding is provided by the Education Funding Agency (EFA) who look after 16-19yrs programmes and the Skills Funding Agency (SFA) who look after apprenticeships and further education funding and provision. Proposals for devolution in this policy area have included:

- Further education funding for 16-19-year-olds to be transferred to councils and local partners;
- Statutory responsibilities of the Department for Work and Pensions, Skills Funding Agency, Education Funding Agency and local authorities regarding further education funding should be merged, and managed locally;
- Devolution of funding for adult skills, further education and apprenticeships to combined authorities, together with Education Funding Agency funding and careers advice;
- Commissioning of further education for 16-24-year-olds should be devolved to combined authorities where they exist;
- "Metro Investment Funds", to provide additional funding for higher education research and teaching, to be established;
- Creation of a "youth transitions service", directed at younger people, run by local authorities or combined authorities.

The language accompanying these requests frequently cites knowledge of the local economy and "meeting employer demand" as the core drivers and as such this latter driver has not changed for many decades and can be found liberally within all employment and skills literature in England. The recent report looking at non-metropolitan areas (Non-Metropolitan Commission 2015) echoed the above asking for government to give local partners the responsibility for managing and commissioning local skill services in the interests of local learners and businesses, including:

- Devolving the skills funding still managed nationally to local level (including 16-19 provision);
- Managing college mergers or closures, and facilitating market entry by new providers such as University Technical Colleges;
- Developing much better local evidence on the value of courses to help learners decide on the option that gives them the best chance of a job.

11. Devolution of the work programme

The Work Programme is a marketised Department for Work and Pensions initiative, administered by JobCentre Plus but contracted out to providers covering local areas, to provide personalised support to unemployed people. Current contracts under the scheme were extended in late 2014, and now run until 2017. Proposals for greater local control over it include:

- The Work Programme to be devolved to combined authorities, with funding continuing to be provided to them on the basis of success in finding sustained employment for people;
- Retention of control of the Work Programme by central government, but letting provider contracts on the basis of local geographical boundaries, and allowing local areas to feed into the design of the contracts;
- A separate programme for people out of work with long-term health conditions, to be run by combined authorities or upper-tier local authorities.

Once again, linking the provision to both employer need and the local economy are core parts of the argument for devolution.

The government has stated on a number of occasions that it has had no preconceived ideas about which powers should be devolved, or to which areas. However, there are a number of evident similarities between the devolution deals agreed to date. Powers over business support services, adult skills funding, transport budgets and bus franchising, and land management feature in almost all of the deals. By contrast, involvement in health services and policing, for instance, have been offered in only a small number of areas. The negotiations have been conducted in secret, leading to speculation about the intentions underlying central government's approach.

12. Directly-elected mayors and combined authorities

Directly-elected mayors were first introduced to the UK by the Local Government Act of 2000. A directly elected mayor and a cabinet is one of three different "governance arrangements" or "political management arrangements" available to local authorities: the others are a leader and cabinet, and the traditional "committee system", where decisions are made by policy committees and approved by full council. Elected mayors may be introduced in England and Wales, but not in Scotland or Northern Ireland.

Initially, an elected mayor could only be created following a referendum in favour in the relevant local authority. The majority of referendums on creating elected mayors have resulted in "no" votes. Consequently, since 2007, local authorities have also been able to create an elected mayor by resolving to do so and currently 16 local authorities have elected mayors. This figure does not include the Mayor of London and the Greater London Authority, which are covered by separate legislation and have quite different powers to local authority mayors. The 2010 Coalition agreement committed to holding mayoral referendums in the twelve largest cities (by population) in England. Leicester and Liverpool subsequently established mayors following resolutions by their respective city councils. A third city, Bristol, voted "yes" in a referendum held in May 2012 and elected its first mayor in November 2012. The remaining nine cities rejected the mayoral system in May 2012. Mayors do not have powers over and above those available to non-mayoral local authorities (Sandford 2016c).

The persistence of the mayoral experiment resides in a consistent interest, across the main UK-wide parties, to "do something" about the perceived inadequacies of leadership at local level (Fenwick and Elcock 2014). Authors have cited three main reasons why the mayoral model of local governance is gaining adherents across the world (Hambleton 2013):

- It is clear to the public, as well as other stakeholders, who is leading the locality – this reduces confusion and clarifies accountability;
- The process of direct election gives the mayor enormous legitimacy to lead – it enhances his or her ability to influence other actors (sometimes referred to as the "soft power" of the mayor);
- A directly elected mayor can use the position to address the strategic leadership challenges facing the locality, including international challenges, as well as to take tough decisions.

The newly elected Mayors are intended to provide visible and accountable leadership; but roles for locally elected councillors, and prospects for community and citizen engagement, remain unclear. A number of authors report that the public has yet to be adequately engaged in what is in danger of becoming a technocratic transfer of power. It is also not clear if mayoral elections will attract sufficient public interest to ensure turnouts (and attendant legitimacy) significantly higher than the (average) 15% achieved for the directly elected Police and Crime Commissioners introduced in 2012 (Berman et al. 2012).

In practice due to differing Devolution Deals England's new elected mayors will have differing degrees of power over different matters. In most areas, they will have an effective veto over decisions. Under most deals, mayoral spending plans are to be subject to rejection by cabinet members on a two-thirds majority. Despite the differing levels of formal power, the mayor's profile will be such that they are likely to become associated, in the public eye, with any new initiatives or policy changes in all of the "devolved" areas.

A number of criticisms have been made of the lack of public consultation in most devolution negotiations. The 2009 and 2016 Acts require a statutory consultation process when a new combined authority is created or when new powers are devolved to it. These have taken place in the areas that have been offered devolution deals. However, the negotiations leading to devolution deals are non-statutory and informal, and have been conducted confidentially.

Combined authorities are a legal structure that may be set up by local authorities in England. They can be set up with or without a directly-elected mayor. Combined authorities may be set up by two or more local authorities. The first combined authority to be established was the Greater Manchester Combined Authority, in 2011. In the previous section, we saw that the government has negotiated "devolution deals" with several areas. Each of the existing combined authorities has negotiated a deal, and new mayoral combined authorities have been proposed in other participating areas.

Some new combined authorities have adopted shortened "brand names", instead of their lengthy formal ones, for everyday communication, such as the "North-East Combined Authority" which is formally the "Durham, Gateshead, Newcastle-upon-Tyne, North Tyneside, Northumberland, South Tyneside and

Sunderland Combined Authority". At the time of writing the combined authorities are: Greater Manchester; Liverpool City Region; Sheffield City Region; West Yorkshire; North East; Tees Valley; and West Midlands.

Most of the Devolution Deals agreed so far have featured a new directly elected mayor covering a combined authority area. The IPPR report (Cox and Hunter 2015) suggests that in practice any substantial devolution of power required a mayoralty:

"...despite the rhetoric around locally tailored deals, it has become increasingly clear that the government does have some unwritten rules, particularly around scale and governance. County proposals that have been considered too small have been challenged, while, more significantly, in almost all cases where there is anything other than modest ambition, the government would appear to be insisting on the introduction of a directly elected mayor."

The report stated that elected mayors were inappropriate for areas which did not have a single urban centre and urged the government to clarify what alternative governance arrangements would find favour in devolution deal negotiations. Shortly after taking office as Prime Minister, Theresa May asserted that the government's position on mayoralties had not changed. The Centre for Public Scrutiny, which is pursuing research into the governance and accountability surrounding combined authorities, has stated:

"... the asymmetry involved [between the deals] also provides an additional impetus for transparency. Local people – anyone, indeed, not involved in the negotiations – need to understand what devolution priorities are being arrived at and agreed on. ... At the very least, the broad shape and principles of a bid for more devolved powers should be opened up to the public eye. "

The Centre for Cities report Firm Views (Clarke and Jeffries 2015) indicated that businesses supported enhanced powers for local government, and found substantial support for additional taxation powers for local government. The report also found substantial regional variation in business concerns:

"For example, in Bristol businesses felt that housing and planning must be the priority for the economy and therefore more local control over where and what sort of housing and developments could be built were seen as essential. In Birmingham, the focus was on alleviating transport pressures and using public assets more efficiently. In Manchester businesses were very positive about more

powers being devolved, but there were concerns over the ground-breaking devolution of health budgets given their magnitude, and possible limited local capacity and institutional inexperience."

There are also issues of accountability (Wood et al. 2015). Combined authorities represent sub-regional rather than local government. Proposals for combined authorities have typically mapped on to Local Enterprise Partnership boundaries, which are business not community led and reflect "functional" economic areas over other understandings of local identity and interests. It is argued by some that the evidence base is weak for devolution's ability to actually stimulate economic growth – at least against the certainty of short-term spending cuts.

Combined authority boundaries may not cross those of district or unitary council authorities. However, they can cross county council boundaries. This allows combined authority boundaries to reflect "functional economic areas", meaning that they are not bound by traditional local government geographies. Some combined authorities took on "associate members" alongside their "full members". Five district councils from Derbyshire and Nottinghamshire are currently "associate members" of the Sheffield City Region, and York City Council (an exclave) is an associate member of the West Yorkshire combined authority. The West Midlands has several district councils as associate members. Local authorities may not be members of more than one combined authority; but there would appear to be nothing preventing a local authority being a member of one and an "associate member" of another.

13. Beyond the city regions

Non-metropolitan areas account for roughly half of England's economy and population. However, their mix of businesses and the challenges faced by areas of less dense population; diffuse transport networks; smaller market towns; green belts; and small cities, are different, as is the pattern of governance. The future of the economy and public services in these areas have received less attention and this is largely down to an unwillingness locally to merge into combined authorities and to choose a democratic model embracing an elected mayor.

The continued survival of local government has been put down to being a result of the centralised structure to political management in English local government which has generated a high level of organisational capacity and a pragmatic sensibility that ensures the institution remains in place even in challenging circumstances. Other local organisations, such as voluntary sector bodies and quangos, have less capacity are less likely to survive political upheaval. Such resilience has come to the fore in the period of fiscal austerity since 2009 when local authorities have had to manage severe declines in their budgets whilst taking on additional functions. The organisational capacity and pragmatism of English local government creates path dependence. Its very efficiency at managing services may have shut off options for new ways of working (John 2014).

14. Devolution, localism and neo-liberalism

Since 2010, local government has seen its budget reduced by 40% under the government's austerity drive, more than any other part of the public sector. A number of authors, notably Meegan et al. (2014) and Peck (2012) have examined the changing role of governance in relation to neo-liberalism. Capital and second-tier cities have been heralded as potential centres of international competitiveness, key to regional and national growth and sites for the "neo-liberalisation of spatial and scalar relations" (Peck and Tickell 2002). They link this to the state asserting market rules in more and more spheres of social life and promoting deregulation of state activity in the interests of markets and profit-making, privatisation of public assets and cutbacks in public expenditure on public services – termed by some as "roll-back neo-liberalisation" (Peck and Ticknell 2002).

By contrast, Oosterlynck and Gonzalez (2013) argue cities have also been "at the heart of the global financial crisis", which has challenged this narrative and revealed the unstable nature of the neoliberal economic growth model on which it is based. Unstable or not, it appears certainly in England that despite the global financial crisis, neo-liberalism and financialisation remain deeply embedded in the economic and political order (Callinicos 2012). This can be seen in England and the UK where, after a brief flirtation with Keynesian macro-economic policy by the Labour Government when the impacts of the crisis were first felt, the "geographies, modalities and pathways..." (*Brenner* et al. 2010) of post-crisis austerity under the succeeding Coalition Government gave rise to a more extensive and intensive commodification of space, the public sphere and even of citizens themselves.

A need for a re-balancing of the economy, most clearly apparent in the local and national drive for economic and productivity growth, is part of a new narrative alongside a "localism" agenda in which core second-tier city regions are being encouraged to negotiate devolved powers through novel forms of private sector urban governance to promote economic growth, representing the rolling-out of new institutions and policies, but in the context of an already neo-liberalised landscape and the most severe cuts in local government expenditure in recent history.

Austerity has one of its aims to reduce public sector spending as a proportion of gross domestic product. In terms of fiscal policy, it has increased value added tax and personal allowances for income tax, reduced Corporation Tax and the top rate for income tax. Yet, it is reductions in public spending that mark out its austerity programme and reinvigorated "shrink the state" neo-liberalism. Drawing on the US experience Peck (2012) sees the turn to austerity policies and politics as a more proactive and prescribed form of fiscally mediated retrenchment, charting the emergence of "austerity urbanism", a phenomenon that he argues is a feature of neo-liberalisation and the failure of successive waves of neoliberal reforms to generate sustainable economic development.

Certainly, in England (and the UK) cities have received the greatest fiscal retrenchment because they remain disproportionately reliant on public services and public employment with large municipal bureaucracies and organised workforces with pay and pensions that are targets for reform. It is also true that it is cities that have been at the forefront of the "Devolution Agenda" and associated "City Deals".

Chapain and Renney (2011) argue that the relatively lower level of financial autonomy of English local authorities in relation to their counterparts in other Organisation for Economic Co-operation and Development (OECD) countries to some extent protected them when the recession first struck. However, more deprived areas have tended to be more disproportionately affected by cuts by central government (Hastings et al. *2012*) with cities in the North of England impacted particularly hard since 2010. The localisation of business rates, while increasing local autonomy, is also likely to prove regressive, reinforcing benefits to localities with stronger economies and penalising localities with higher levels of deprivation.

In the context of austerity, city authorities are being forced to look at reforming their public service delivery variously through charging for some services, outsourcing others and collaborating with other authorities (Meegan et al. 2014). The (previous) Coalition Government's removal of grants targeted at disadvantaged areas inevitably had an immediate impact on cities like Liverpool, which lost some £101 million from area-based grant, 17% of its total funding, in a single year. Indeed, the previous Coalition Government abolished all urban policy initiatives targeted at disadvantaged areas. It also abolished the English regional development agencies (RDAs) and the Integrated Regional Offices of central government. The regional approach to economic development of the previous government was been replaced by a localism approach built around the promotion of 39 local enterprise partnerships (LEPs) at sub-regional level.

LEPs have to be business-led, which means a business Chair alongside other business people on the LEP Board, the leaders of the local authorities in the LEP area and other representatives from the public sector and civic society usually including local universities. There are no requirements, for example, to have representatives from local trades union or voluntary and community sectors, although these could be invited to join.

15. Concluding thoughts

Clearly there is a major tension in policy between austerity urbanism in the shape of reductions in local government spending and, on the other hand, the desire to promote local economic development, especially in the large cities (Meegan et al. 2014). However, there are concerns that without generating new sources of income, local government will be unable to fund its "discretionary" services. It is these discretionary services that include many employment and skills programmes and other local economic development activity.

Although the Coalition Government of 2010-2015 piloted devolution, its signature policies of "localism" and the "Big Society" focused on non-state actors, providing rights and opportunities for communities to challenge local government and establish their own services. The current Conservative Government is promoting devolution as a strategy to stimulate economic growth based on greater sub-regional autonomy and increased competitiveness across and between English localities. The "localism" of the previous Coalition administration has developed into a strategy for stimulating economic growth based on greater sub-regional autonomy and increased competitiveness across and between the regions. Local authorities have been invited to come forward with joint proposals to form combined authorities, which can "bid" to take over powers currently held by Whitehall.

We have seen that combined authorities have the opportunity to champion local identities and acquire new economic development powers from Whitehall. However, devolution could be a strategy to decentralise austerity, shifting responsibility to the local level for deeper cuts (56% by 2020) and inevitable service reductions (Lowndes and Gardner 2015). The emerging patchwork of "devolution deals" challenges the redistributive assumptions of the grant regime and could leave disadvantaged areas at particular risk of failure.

There has been some international criticism of the UK's plans. Among economists, Joseph Stieglitz, Paul Krugman and Thomas Piketty have all been vocal opponents of austerity as a response to the international sovereign debt crisis. The Organisation for Economic Co-operation and Development warned that the previous Chancellor of the Exchequer's planned deficit reduction measures have the potential to impact negatively on the UK's growth (Giles 2015) and the IMF suggested that advanced economies could be better served by living with high levels of debt, rather than aggressive debt-reduction programmes (cited in Ostry et al. 2015).

In terms of skills and employment, as with all other aspects, decentralisation has both political and operational dimensions and clarity is needed as to what sort of power is being devolved in the case of the new Devolution Deals. It looks very much like central government is holding onto *political* power, whilst decentralising operational responsibilities (and responsibility for contracting budgets). Just what the real benefits to Mayors and others from gaining these operational powers is yet to be made clear other than the promise of future powers - linked to performance against centrally agreed targets.

Devolution is having different effects for different service areas as the focus of the Devolution Deals has been overwhelmingly upon economic development (investment, planning, transport and other infrastructure, jobs and skills). A risk is that economic development develops a privileged status (in terms of access to funds and policy influence) to the disadvantage of other local services including social care, housing, education, culture and leisure.

To conclude, skills and employment policy finds itself caught up in a devolution of power in which we find a new process of deal-making founded upon territorial competition and negotiation between central national and local actors unequally endowed with information and resources, leading to highly imbalanced and potentially inequitable outcomes and where major geographies remain excluded through a desire not to elect mayors or opt for combined authority status. In those currently included in this process to secure the "best deal", local actors are expected to present attractive and viable local propositions to government in return for the prospect of securing new resources, policy freedoms and flexibilities. The parameters of the deal are uncertain, rendering the principal-agent relationship somewhat fluid and opaque (O'Brien and Pike 2015). This extension of deal-making as a model for public policy is not only a very obvious expression of marketised neoliberal thinking, but it is likely to have a profound impact on the governance and economics of decentralisation and devolution.

References

Berman, Gavin/Coleman, Charley/Taylor, Mark (2012): Police and Crime Commissioner Elections 2012, London: House of Commons Library

Brenner, Neil/Peck, Jamie/Theodore, Nik (2010): Variegated neoliberalization: geographies, modalities, pathways, in: Global Networks, Vol. 10, No.2, pp. 182-222

Callinicos, Alex (2012): Contradictions of austerity, Cambridge Journal of Economics, Vol. 36, pp. 64-77

Chapain, Caroline/Renney, Craig (2011): Impacts of the recession on local authorities, in: Bailey, David/Chapain, Caroline (Eds): The Recession and Beyond: Local and Regional Responses to the Downturn, London: Routledge, pp. 82-97

Clarke, Edward/Jeffrey, Simon (2015): Firm views: What do businesses really think of devolution to city-regions? Centre for Cities Report

Conservative Party (2015): Strong Leadership; A Clear Economic Plan; A Brighter, More Secure Future

Cox, Ed/Hunter, Jack (2015): Empowering counties: Unlocking county devolution deals, IPPR Report 2015

Department for Business, Innovation and Skills (2012): No stone unturned: in pursuit of growth – The Lord Heseltine review

Fenwick, John/Elcock Howard J. (2014): Elected mayors: Leading locally?, in: Local Government Studies, Vol. 40, No. 4, pp. 581-599

Giles, Chris (2015): OECD Warns Britain to Spread Spending Cuts More Evenly, in: Financial Times, June 3

Gordon, Ian/Harloe, Michael/Harding, Alan (2013): The Uncertain Development of Metropolitan Governance: comparing England's First and Second City-Regions, in: Keil, Rodger et al. (Eds.): Governing Cities through Regions: Canadian and European Perspectives: Wilfred Laurier University Press

Hambleton, Robin (2013): Elected mayors: An international rising tide?, in: Policy & Politics, Vol. 41, No. 1, pp. 125-128

Hastings, Anette/Bramley, Glen/Bailey, Nick/Watkins, David (2012): Serving Deprived Communities in a Recession. York: Joseph Rowntree Foundation

IPPR/PwC (2014): Decentralisation Decade, Core Cities Group, Competitive Cities, Prosperous People

John, Peter (2014): The great survivor: The persistence and resilience of English local government, in: Local Government Studies, Vol. 40, No. 5, pp. 687-704

Kukovic, Simona/Copus, Colin/Hacek, Miro/Blair, Alasdair (2015): Direct mayoral elections in Slovenia and England: traditions and trends compared, in: Lex Localis, Journal of Local Self-Government, Vol. 13, No. 3, pp. 697-718

Le Gales, Patrick (2002): European Cities. Social Conflict and Governance, Oxford: Oxford University Press

Lowndes, Vivien/Gardner, Alison (2015): Local governance under the Conservatives: super-austerity, devolution and the "smarter state, in: Local Government Studies, Vol. 42, No. 3

Meegan, Richard/Kennett, Patricia/Jones, Gerwyn (2014): Global economic crisis, austerity and neoliberal urban governance in England, in: Cambridge Journal of Regions, Economy and Society, Vol. 7 No. 1, pp. 357-375

Non-Metropolitan Commission (2015): Devolution to Non-Metropolitan England: Seven steps to growth and prosperity

O'Brien, Peter/Pike, Andy (2015): City deals, decentralisation and the governance of local infrastructure funding and financing in the UK, in: National Institute Economic Review, Vol. 233, August, pp. R14-R26

Oosterlynck, Stijn/González, Sara (2013): "Don't Waste a Crisis": Opening up the City Yet Again for Neoliberal Experimentation, in: International Journal of Urban and Regional Research, Vol. 37, pp. 1075-1082

Ostry, Jonathan. D./Ghosh, Atish R./Espinoza. Raphael (2015): When Should Public Debt Be Reduced? https://www.imf.org/external/pubs/ft/sdn/2015/sdn1510.pdf

Paine, David/Calkin, Sarah (2016): New devo deals expected in Autumn Statement, in: Local Government Chronicle, 16 November 2016

Peck, Jamie (2012): Austerity urbanism, in: City: analysis of urban trends, culture, theory, policy, action, Vol. 16, No. 6, pp. 626-655

Peck, Jamie/Tickell, Adam (2002): Neoliberalizing space, in: Antipode, Vol. 34, No. 3, pp. 380-404

Sandford, Mark (2015): Combined Authorities. House of Commons Library BRIEFING PAPER 07065, 5 May 2015

Sandford, Mark (2016a): Devolution to local government in England. House of Commons Library BRIEFING PAPER. Number 07029, 23 November 2016

Sandford, Mark (2016b): Combined Authorities. House of Commons Library BRIEFING PAPER 06649, 23 November 2016

Sandford, Mark (2016c): Combined Authorities. House of Commons Library BRIEFING PAPER 05000, 17 October 2016

Websites

BBC Website (2014): http://www.bbc.co.uk/news/uk-politics-29271765

The Reaction of Social Partners to the Application of the "Jobs Act": A Comparison Between Digital Communication Strategies

Renato Fontana, Vera D'Antonio, Martina Ferrucci, Carmine Piscopo

1. Introduction

On the 4th of September 2015, the Cabinet definitively approved the last four implementing decrees of the enabling act n. 183 of the 10th of December 2014. This legislative measure is known as the "Jobs Act", which reforms the Labour market and abolishes article 18 of the 1970 Labour Code prepared by Gino Giugni and approved by then Minister of Labour Giacomo Brodolini.

The aim of this paper is not to take a stand on the efficaciousness of the above mentioned Italian measures. Considering the extremely difficult historical situation from the employment point of view, especially for young people and women, the aim is instead to stress the communication strategies adopted by the social partners when referring to the Jobs Act. By social partners we are referring to the labour unions (Cgil) and the employers' organisations (*Confindustria* and *Confcommercio*) in particular. We have also dedicated special attention to the position of the press, summarised in the articles published by the *Corriere della Sera* in three precise periods of time.

The Italian labour market, after its darkest years, has registered an inversion in this trend. In 2015 the unemployment rate went down for the first time since 2008, passing from 12.7% to 11.9%[1]. If Europe's recovery has been defined as "slight", Italy's one should be labelled as "very slight". Despite the positive result, we must signal that the recovery has not been sufficient to bring the number of unemployed Italian workers below the level of 2008. The situation is no different if we look at the other side of the coin, namely the employment rate. It is increasing, but at a more contained pace than in the rest of Europe: + 0,6% in comparison with 2014[2].

---

[1] Cfr. Eurostat, Unemployment rate - annual data; http://ec.europa.eu/eurostat/web/products-datasets/-/tipsun20
[2] Cfr. Eurostat, Employment, domestic concept - annual data; http://ec.europa.eu/eurostat/web/products-datasets/-/tipsna60

Table 1   Unemployment rate – annual data

	2007	2008	2009	2010	2011	2012	2013	2014	2015	2016
DE	8.5	7.4	7.6	7.0	5.8	5.4	5.2	5.0	4.6	4.1
ES	8.2	11.3	17.9	19.9	21.4	24.8	26.1	24.5	22.1	19.6
FR	8.0	7.4	9.1	9.3	9.2	9.8	10.3	10.3	10.4	10.1
IT	6.1	6.7	7.7	8.4	8.4	10.7	12.1	12.7	11.9	11.7

Source: Eurostat, Unemployment rate - annual data; http://ec.europa.eu/eurostat/web/products-datasets/-/tipsun20.

Table 2   Employment rate – annual data

	2007	2008	2009	2010	2011	2012	2013	2014	2015	2016
DE	1.7	1.3	0.1	0.3	1.4	1.2	0.6	0.8	0.9	1.2
ES	3.3	0.2	-6.3	-1.7	-2.7	-4.0	-2.6	0.9 p	2.5 p	2.7 p
FR	1.4	0.5	-1.1	0.1	0.8	0.3	0.2	0.4	0.2 p	0.6 p
IT	1.2	0.2	-1.7	-0.6	0.3	-0.3	-1.8	0.1	0.7	1.3

Source: Eurostat, Employment, domestic concept - annual data; http://ec.europa.eu/eurostat/web/products-datasets/-/tipsna60.

As it is imaginable, the economic recovery is slower and requires greater effort in the countries which were more strongly hit by the crisis, such as Italy. However, if we look at the employment rates divided according to age brackets, we notice that, in the considered context, young people are always the most penalised. Between 2008 and 2015 young people (aged between 15-34) saw their work opportunities drop by 11.1% (variation of the employment rate), while over the same period there was an increase of 9.2% in the employment rate of the over 50 years old (Fontana et al. 2016).

The labour reform wanted by Matteo Renzi's government is inserted, therefore, in a general picture which aims at providing the conditions to tackle the problem of unemployment in Italy, and in particular the unemployment of young people and women. This problem does not seem to have been solved, even partially, by the measures adopted. Here is some data in brief. At the end of 2016, the unemployment rate in the age bracket 15-24 was above 40%. Out of over 60 million residents in Italy, and over 25.5 million of people eligible to work, Istat (Istituto Nazionale di Statistica 2016) registered that only 22.5 million had a job. That is slightly more than one third of the residents, exactly 37%.

Despite its dialogue with the various institutional players, the government was not always able to adopt all the requests of integration and improvement presented, sometimes because the political will was not there or due to budget issues. The deregulation systems and the incentives for the creation of new job posts strained the public debate on the topic, which is inserted in a wider context where the model of a permanent job position is replaced by a much more flexible model, with a regulatory substrate respectful of the European protection standards It may not be the Danish model, but in Italy flexibility without protection is also called "job insecurity". The government responsible for the laws mentioned above seems to be aware of this.

In this specific case, the Jobs Act, passed by the Italian Parliament with various legislative measures between 2014 and 2015, was introduced in the midst of ferocious protests, especially coming from the unions. This tension did not create an atmosphere of constructive participation, but on the contrary a harsh debate on the topic, often characterised by irreconcilable positions. In this purely legislative scenario, **digital platforms** played a role of primary importance. Without considering the legislative meaning of the measures, and paying attention to the informational and communicative aspects connected to them, we have observed *de facto* a *strong editorial and multimedia production of contents* of the social partners to underline the many aspects – both positive and negative – of the act. The impact that the communication of the social partners has had on the territory reveals very well the partial "sharing" and later on "acceptance" of the new law. The great and daily work of connection between politics and population, in this specific case, was performed mainly by the social partners involved in our research.

The hypothesis at the basis of the present paper is based on the fact that *"the polemical polarization between the supporters of the latest labor reform and its detractors made the debate become stagnant with mutual accusations of untruthful and false behaviors"* (Seghezzi and Nespoli 2017: 2). In this sense, the political communication did not help public opinion and even those who should have guaranteed the application of the measures understand the main aspects of the labour market reform. It is as if the "war of figures" had provoked sort of a class struggle revival without any historical, political and cultural elements to justify its presence. In other words, a class struggle *after* the class struggle, paraphrasing a famous book by Luciano Gallino (2012).

In any case the inversion of the trend towards fixed-term contracts instead of open-ended ones did not take place (see Table 3); even if many people would have benefited from this opportunity, the model of increasing protection contracts has been relevant and it has not changed the public opinion's widespread *sentiment* about the uncertainty connected to the ungovernability of the ongoing changes. There was significant growth in 2015: according to the INPS observatory on job insecurity, indeed, the increase of open-ended contracts numbered 934,000 (Seghezzi and Nespoli 2017).

Table 3   Employees with a contract of limited duration (annual average) % of total number of employees from 15 to 64 years

	2005	2010	2014	2015	2016
DE	12.6 b	13.0 b	11.8	11.8	11.9
ES	27.5 b	20.7	19.9	20.9	21.8
EU28	11.7	11.7	11.7	11.9	12.0
FR	:	:	13.6	14.2	14.3
IT	9.1	9.6	10.4	10.8	10.9

Source: Eurostat, Employees with a contract of limited duration (annual average); https://data.europa.eu/euodp/it/data/dataset/rKXDQCrvVjmOz4CgEbnSbw.

Companies were certainly encouraged to hire staff by the generous reduction of labour contributions rather than by the desire to make investments in human capital, using innovation as the main requisite of change to bring back the economy to the condition of competing in terms of resources and ideas for the future. The most recent data provided by Istat (2016) reveals that the increase of employment mostly affects the age bracket of over 50-years old and hardly affects young people between 15 and 34. From this point of view nothing has changed.

The communicative flows concerning the law take place in this heated context. Thus, we have tried to understand the sense and the weight of some forms of communication which seem to be very conditioned by the socio-political position adopted and without the correctness and completeness useful to untie the knots which continue to pester the labour market in Italy.

The aim of the screening we present here is therefore the study of the media representation of the Jobs Act, moving from the documents and the initiatives of the social partners produced between the end of 2014 and December 2016. In particular, we will analyse the texts published on the digital platforms of the organisations using content analysis techniques which more than others participated to the reflection and the debate on the relevance of the Jobs Act, including those representing respectively employees and employers. What emerged in particular from this analysis are the communicative policies of the CGIL on one side and of the Confindustria on the other, leaving a marginal role to other similar institutional subjects.

In this scenario, considering the strategic importance of the press, we have analysed the texts published on the digital platforms both from a quantitative (with a questionnaire adjusted to the particular subject of the research) and a qualitative point of view.

Finally, since the press exercises so much influence on public opinion and on the collective imagery of a significant part of the population, we have examined the writings in the digital edition of Italy's most important newspaper, both for its numbers and its authority: the *Corriere della Sera*.

2. The Communication Strategies of the CGIL

Founded in 1906, the *Confederazione Generale Italiana del Lavoro* (CGIL) is the oldest Italian union. With over 5 million members, it is the most representative labour union in Italy. It is organised in two directions: a vertical one with a division per work category (metalworkers, civil servants, farmers, old-age pensioners, etc.) and a horizontal one characterised by a territorial or local aggregation of the various work categories.

Together with the CISL, which can count on over 4 million members, and the UIL[3], which has over 2 million members[4], CGIL is among the most important unions in the country.

As a consequence of its historical relevance, we have decided to focus on the communication strategy of the CGIL with reference to the measures considered. The authors of this work studied the communication strategy of Italy's first union towards the labour market measure, called the "Jobs Act". In particular, we have analysed the contents and the protagonists of the communications in order to understand how the workers' representatives, and therefore the real "protagonists" of the Jobs Act, reacted to the introduction of this new law. As already anticipated in the introduction, the unions' position against the law provoked a campaign against the abrogation of article 18, but it also initiated a debate on the employment policies politicians, industrialists and workers expect for the future.

In detail, we have considered all the articles published on the official website – www.cgil.it – related to the Jobs Act. We considered all the posts of 2014 and then the posts present in the first four months[5] of every year from 2015 to 2017, for a total of 95 pieces of news.

The objective of this research is to identify the main communication dynamics of the union, but especially to study in depth the language and the formats used in the mediation of the message connected to the topic "Jobs Act" between politicians and workers. To reach these objectives, we have used a data sheet (Table 4) with the main information: testimonies, presence of data, etc.

---

3 See CISL, presentation page of the official website https://www.cisl.it/la-cisl/cose-la-cisl.html consulted on 07/05/2017
4 See UIL, page dedicated to membership application on the official website http://www.uil.it/tesseramento_cat.asp consulted on 07/05/2017
5 The Jobs Act was approved in December 2014. We chose to analyze the first four months for every year to study the progress of the debate in time.

Table 4   Data sheet

Publication Date	Title and Subtitle
Testimonial	References to data and sources
Two Keywords	References to generational categories
Gender References	References to social partners

Source: own elaboration.

In addition, every piece of news has been classified with two thematic keywords, combined to the following macro-categories (Table 5):

Table 5   Keywords

Social Safety Nets	• Focus on layoffs, allowances, maternity allowances, etc.
Employment	• Focus on employment growth, hiring, etc.
Unemployment	• Focus on unemployment increase, dismissals, etc.
Economic policies	• Focus on stability law, crises and structural investments
Development policies	• Focus on employment incentives, projects, European policies, visions of the future
Rights	• Focus on the reduction of labour rights, on the reduction of rights for women and on the reduction of protection measures
Contracts	• Focus on contract typologies or on the renewal of collective contracts
Job insecurity	• Focus on the forms and on the difficulties of job insecurity
Political disputes	• Meetings and agreements with the political world
Demonstrations	• Protests and strikes

Source: own elaboration.

The official site www.cgil.it is only one of the numerous portals belonging to the union. Its organisation also has branches locally that have their own institutional website and communication strategy. Not being able, however, to take into consideration every single territorial unit, we have focused on the national strategy. The CGIL has its own publishing house which manages scientific journals of academic and cultural prestige, but these publications do not belong to the *corpus* of the research. We have not considered attachments, links or documents outside the official website.

The only exception is represented by the initiative http://www.adessolosai.it/, a thematic portal strongly used by the CGIL to inform citizens on the "real" (from the point of view of the CGIL) impact of the Jobs Act. This portal will be considered an integral part of the national strategy and will therefore be analysed.

2.1 The Jobs Act and the reduction of the union's bargaining power

"The Cgil has the important role to protect work from the unlimited and unconditioned action of the market. It does this through the never-ending activity of building and rebuilding solidarity at work and among workers, thanks to its daily engagement in representation and contract bargaining. [...] By means of the category organisations, it stipulates employment contracts and it simultaneously offers protection, aimed at defending, declaring and conquering individual and collective rights, from welfare systems to rights in the working place"[6].

With the abrogation of art. 18, the union has lost a great part of their bargaining power. Indeed, following a dismissal, even if recognised as illegitimate, the employer is no longer forced to re-hire the dismissed employee. This small change hits one of the main tasks of a union, that is to protect work, denying the worker the possibility to participate in the discussion or, in technical terms, the "bargaining" process.

Moving forward from this circumstance, it is clear that the political position of the CGIL, and also of the other unions, has been and is strongly against the Jobs Act.

Over the last three years, the most debated issues brought forward by the union have been those regarding the weakening of workers' rights, layoffs and public

---

6 See CGIL presentation page of the official website http://www.cgil.it/chi-siamo/ consulted on 07/05/2017.

works contracts. In particular, the latter can be considered highly representative both of the effects and the doubts created by the introduction of the Jobs Act and of the "increasing protection" work contract. The CGIL has at various times defended the rights of employees working in sectors and activities subject to public works contracts: every time a company changes, despite keeping one's job, the employee may see his/her length of service unrecognised. In other words, they could be always seen as newly hired. This is an issue which was later solved thanks to the intervention of the union.

The measure, which is the subject of our research, is in fact rich of applicative shortcomings, partially tackled and solved by the workers' unions. Furthermore, the complex legal and technical aspects linked to working issues make union mediation a cultural point of reference and a place of information and clarification, often free or low-cost, for all citizens.

2.2 The Communication Dynamics of the Official CGIL Website

The 95 articles analysed stress the role of two great personalities through their declarations: Susanna Camusso, general secretary of the CGIL since 2010, and Serena Sorrentino, general secretary of "Funzione Pubblica" (the sector that unites public employees) since 2016. Most of the campaign against the Jobs Act has been assigned to them. The two voices have different specificities and communicative functions: Susanna Camusso is the leader of a union and faces topics in a wider sense. Her language is more direct and can prey on people's emotions. Serena Sorrentino is nearly always present when there is data to explain. Her contribution is more technical and objective. Susanna Camusso is present in 25 out of 95 posts, while Sorrentino is present in 21 out of 95 posts. The last step of the podium is left to Fabrizio Solari, the confederal secretary of the CGIL, all concentrated in March 2015. In 33 cases out of 95, instead, no reference is made to a specific personality.

In terms of time, the largest share of messages is concentrated in 2014 (44 out of 95 cases) and the share decreases as the years continue: 34 out of 95 in 2015, ten out of 95 in 2016 and seven out of 95 in 2017. In this regard, Camusso's interventions are mainly of a political nature and are concentrated in 2014 (20 cases out of 25), that is immediately before or close to the approval of the law.

Later on, once the measure has been approved, the issue is discussed by Sorrentino (with ten out of 21 cases in 2015), who tries to tackle the topic from a quantitative point of view, discussing the figures on unemployment and employment.

Data is used in 22 cases out of 95 and ISTAT[7] is the most quoted institute (twelve out of 22), followed by INPS[8] (eight out of 22). In the texts, generational issues are mentioned only in 16 cases, while gender and equal opportunity issues are debated less frequently (only mentioned in nine cases). This last aspect is connected with the protests of the self-employed over their rights, in particular for what concerns maternity leave and illness. In addition to the so-called "VAT number possessors" (with six cases out of 95), the other "collective actors" are entrepreneurs and factory workers, both with five cases out of 95.

Considering the classification of keywords, the majority of the articles published on the CGIL website (25 cases out of 95) refer to workers' rights, with important references to development policies (36 cases out of 95) and criticism to the economic policies carried out by the Government (33 cases out of 95). The last heated topic for the union is the focus on contracts, which develops into a discussion about the numerous contract typologies and the renewal of the national collective contracts.

---

7 Istat - Istituto nazionale di statistica, a public research body. It is the main producer of official statistics for Italy. See http://www.istat.it/it/istituto-nazionale-di-statistica; last visit 12/05/2017
8 INPS – "Istituto Nazionale della Previdenza Sociale (INPS) is one of Europe's biggest and most complex social security offices, with a budget which is second only to that of the State. INPS manages the near totality of Italian social security funds, insuring the majority of self-employed workers and employess of the public and private sectors." See https://www.inps.it/nuovoportaleinps/default.aspx?iMenu=11; Last visit 12/05/2017

Table 6   Top 30 high frequency words

Italian	English		Italian	English	
Lavoro	Work	604	Imprese	Enterprises	79
Cgil	Cgil	387	Appalti	Public contracts	79
Lavoratori	Workers	354	Politica	Politics	77
Governo	Government	215	Cassa	Allowance	76
Contratto	Contract	168	Crisi	Crisis	75
Jobs Act	Jobs Act	161	Politiche	Policies	74
Anno	Year	144	Paese	Country	74
Diritti	Rights	136	Serena Sorrentino	Serena Sorrentino	72
Ore	Hours	135	Segretario generale	General Secretary	72
Tutele	Protection	130	Parte	Party	71
Legge	Law	114	Sindacato	Union	69
occupazione	Employment	110	Dati	Data	68
Italia	Italy	105	Giovani	Young people	62
Tempo	Time	93	Fatto	Fact	62
Susanna Camusso	Susanna Camusso	91	Renzi	Renzi	60

Source: own elaboration on CGIL datasets.

What also clearly emerges from the analysis of the high frequency words is how the contents proposed by the CGIL are strongly oriented towards grounds which are typical ones of union bargaining, such as "rights", "contract" and "hours". We notice that the concept of "employment" is used more than "unemployment". Widely present are the two main female figures of the union, as are the two words "crisis" and "data". Renzi's presence is marginal, especially considering the overexposure of the word "Government". The topic "young people" appears in the classification, but subdued in comparison to other more used words such as "protection", "public contracts" and "politics".

2.3 "Adesso lo sai": The CGIL informs the citizens

From the study of the contents extracted from the national portal of the CGIL emerges a communication modality which is not addressed to the common citizen. The articles published online are a collection of the official declarations of the big union. Many of these are detailed and they often contain an interview or a statement (for example of Camusso or Sorrentino) to comment on data or the political situation. We have not found infographics or extra material capable of simplifying the reading or of synthetically providing at least some of the most important information. In addition, the continuous references to economic policies or to the slight statistical differences between the data on employment and the data on unemployment cannot be considered topics easily accessible by the greater public. For instance, the articles with declarations of Sorrentino contain only and exclusively comments to Istat and Inps data.

On the contrary, the web portal "Adesso lo sai" ("Now you know") - www.adessolosai.it – is a useful instrument of information for the citizens. Created with a modern and attractive interface, thanks also to a clever use of graphic and short texts, the website points out only the six main critical aspects of the Jobs Act. The excellent job done is complemented by the availability of a more complete volume[9] for those who wish to study the act in depth and by the possibility to do a "job quiz", which measures your knowledge of the act.

The presence and the distribution of the CGIL on Italy's national territory is articulated in such a way that the monitoring of its overall communication strategy is a hard task. However, being Italy's most important union, the CGIL has played a decisive role in all the developing phases of the measures. In our opinion, the most representative message of the information and protest campaign organised by the CGIL against the Jobs Act can be summed up in this short title: *"from the protection (of rights) we pass on to the increasing monetization of rights"*[10].

---

9 CGIL, (2015) "Guida al Jobs Act" in I quaderni di WikiLabour; See http://www.wikilabour.it/GetFile.aspx?File=%2fJobs-Act%2fGuida%2fGuida-Jobs-Act_DEF.pdf. Accessed on 12 May 2017.
10 CGIL, (2014), Jobs act: Cgil, dalle tutele si passa alla monetizzazione crescente dei diritti published on 26 December 2014. See Dalle tutele si passa alla monetizzazione crescente dei diritti; Accessed on 12 May 2017.

3. Event communication at the service of employers' organisations

After examining and understanding the communication strategies adopted by the unions to protect the workers, we now move on, briefly, to the main organisations representing the interests of the employers, *Confindustria* and *Confcommercio*.

For reasons of space and prominence we are not able to retrace the long history that has made it possible for these and other employer organisations to control in one way or another the Italian labour market for more than a century. It is sufficient to provide a short identikit of the above mentioned social players, to then continue on to the analysis of the communication strategies adopted following the final implementation of the enabling act 183/2014.

Confindustria is the *Confederazione Generale dell'Industria Italiana* which associates the big size industrial enterprises; *Confcommercio* is the *Confederazione Generale Italiana delle Imprese, delle Attività Professionali e del Lavoro Autonomo*, and it associates trade and tourism businesses. The former, founded in 1910, can count on around 222 member organisations. The latter groups together over 700,000 enterprises. It is superfluous to reconfirm that these and other union organisations are going through a period of loss of credibility and a crisis of identity, (Cella 1999, Carrieri 2012, Ballistreri 2015) because they are not able to propose concrete strategies and satisfactory actions regarding the needs of a labour market that is more and more under stress. However, it is true that the membership numbers they continue to have, are enough to renew the credit and the public consideration they can still count on.

The analysis which has been carried out in order to understand the communication strategies used to talk about the Jobs Act in the aftermath of the parliamentary approval, is based on information from the databases of the official websites of Italy's two most important employer organisations. In both cases, the keyword "Jobs Act" search on the internal portal search engines encompassed a period of time which covers the years 2015 and 2016.

What immediately stands out is the massive use of events as a *tool of internal communication, and at the same time, as an educational measure*, to spread knowledge and manage informational flows addressed to employees and members, with the explicit objective to provide practical indications to update their professional competences.

This is even truer in the case of *Confindustria*: considering the one hundred statements published on the official portal between 2015 and 2016, more than half (50.49%) are invitations to training and refresher events, for a total of 51 events organised in the country. *Confindustria* organised, with extremely high peaks of frequency in the first months of 2015, 21 seminars, 17 "in-depth" or "study" meetings, eleven conferences, a workshop and a fee entry course. *Confcommercio*, on the other hand, was less receptive to using a strategic communication tool for the training and the motivating of its internal resources, organising barely 15 events in the period considered. In the near totality, they were "information sessions" (ten out of 15). The two employer organisations have one fact in common: after an initially enthusiastic and widely spread use of events, organisational activity started decreasing as time went by and after the gradual "assimilation" of the legislative decrees, until it completely stopped in June 2016 (Graph 1).

Graph 1   Frequency distribution for number of events (2015-2016)

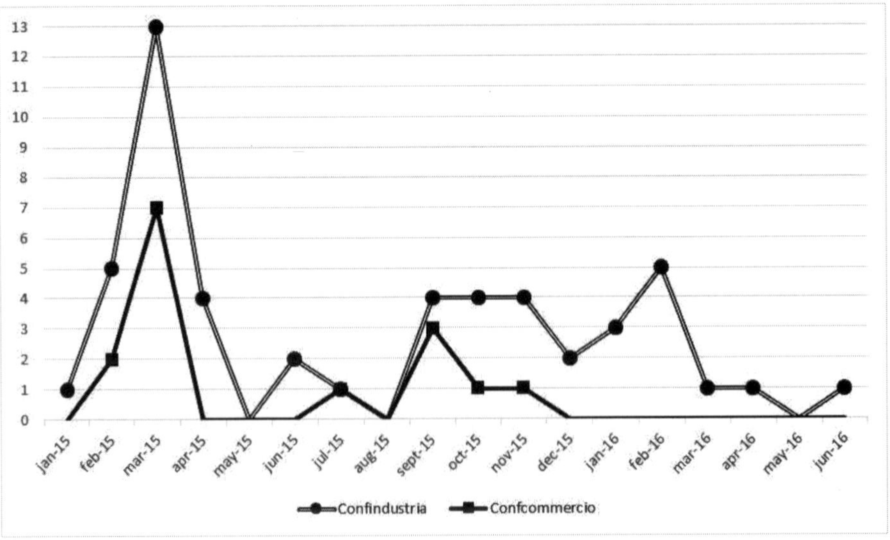

Source: own elaboration on Confindastria and Confcommercio datasets.

The first seminars or conferences organised, mainly in Northern Italy – an interesting fact to which we will return – stress the *element of novelty*. Most of the titles of the events organised in the first months after the presentation of the enabling act are made up of words like *change, new, evolution*. The widely shared and accepted idea is to take stock of the main novelties introduced by the Jobs Act and to provide the first practical indications, engaging experts, technicians and bodies called to interpret and apply it.

The statements and the invitations which promote participation in these events contain words of praise for the law, speaking about a legislative *corpus* "desired by the entrepreneurial system" which moves in the direction "of enterprise organisation flexibility, for such a long time wanted by business organisations". They also talk about "an epochal regulatory intervention" which aims at "stabilising work relationships", bringing "advantages" both to the enterprises and the workers.

For what concerns the timing of the events, it is possible to identify two particularly proliferous moments which proceed in parallel, as it was proper to expect, with the steps made by the Reform in its *iter*. The first "round" of events concerning the Jobs Act is concentrated during the month of March 2015, reaching 20 events over a period of 30 days – an average of one seminar for every working day of the month. These follow the entry into force of the legislative decrees n. 22[11] and 23[12]. As is inherent to the *educational* purpose of the seminars, the topics in this first phase concentrate on the introduction of the *increasing protection labour contract* and on the new guarantee measures in case of work relationship termination (Table 7).

---

11 Legislative Decree 4 March 2015, No. 22 (Provisions for the re-ordering of the social safety net regulations in case of unvoluntary unemployment and for the recollocation of unemployed workers, in accordance with the law 183/2014).
12 Legislative Decree 4 March 2015, No. 23 (Provisions for the increasing protection labour contract, in accordance with the law 183/2014).

Table 7 Tag clouds of event titles in year 2015 (1) and 2016 (2)

2015	2016
Tag Cloud 1	Tag Cloud 2

Lemmas 1*	# occurrences 1	Lemmas 2*	# occurrences 2
Lavoro/*Job*	24	Novità/*Newness*	5
Contratto/*Contract*	9	Lavoro/*Job*	4
Tutele Crescenti/ *Increasing-protection Entitlement*	9	Cassa Integrazione/ *Unemployment Insurance*	3
Cambia/*Change*	9	Riforma/*Reform*	3
Nuovo/*New*	9	Ammortizzatori Sociali/ *Social Safety Net*	3

Source: 66 statements in Confindustria and Confcommercio datasets.

* In this case, we have omitted the "Jobs Act" lemma because of its presence in the vast majority of the titles under consideration.

Attention rises again, although with less relevant numbers, starting from the month of September 2015, when the publication of the last four legislative decrees in the Gazzetta Ufficiale (23 September 2015) finally completes the mosaic of the Jobs Act. In this second "round", the debate moves from the increasing protection contracts to the social safety net.

The events organised in this phase move from the analysis and the comment of the latest measures entered into force and which concern especially the social safety net in the case of a stable work relationship, and they appear as real"second appointments' connected to the Spring edition: they were often reorganised in the same locations and the same speakers were often recalled in order to, we imagine, not only give continuity to the training project, but also argumentative coherence to the opinions proposed.

Once concluded the drawing up of the "new framework of labour market rules", following the enacting decrees approved during the year, 2016 opens with less engagement in terms of creation of occasions to meet and discuss. In the first semester of the year Confindustria, for instance, organised eleven events, all concentrated in the northern part of the country, in which the proposal is once again to take stock on the "novelties" of 2016 for what concerns work and social security, with a specific focus on the "reform" of the "social safety net", on the regulations about distance control and safety at work and, especially on the "unemployment allowance" as a measure against job insecurity in times of crisis. A crisis which is not only occupational.

On the contrary, Confcommercio, does not seem to continue its organisational activities begun in 2015, and from November of the same year it does not set up or in any case it does not promote any study or informative event on its official portal.

Among the personalities called to intervene as experts and professionals with the task of interpreting and applying the regulation, Riccardo Del Punta, a lawyer and Professor of Labour Law at the University of Florence, and Arturo Maresca, a lawyer and Professor of Labour Law at the Sapienza, University of Rome stand out. The latter was present at more than eleven events.

The colleagues Maria Magri and Fabio Pontrandolfi, managers of Confindustria in the area of work and welfare, are less pervasive, but equally active, having intervened on four occasions, both in the north and in the south of the peninsula in various panels.

Overall, the presence of lawyers and legal professionals is preponderant and they are clearly called to intervene as legal analysts more than as simple speakers, because they can provide a complete juridical picture of the reform and allow the member companies to benefit from their experience and know-how.

The geographic distribution of the events organised in the period considered also deserves to be mentioned. A quick glance at the map created for this purpose (Graph 2) is enough to convince oneself of the clear supremacy, if not of the total concentration, of the events in the regions of Northern Italy. Ferrara is the most engaged city, having been selected as preferred location for seminars and meetings on four different occasions. It is closely followed by Gorizia, La Spezia, Milano, Novara, Pesaro, Pistoia, Ravenna, Roma and Rovigo. It is notable that Rome, the capital, is located more to the south than many other cities with at least three events organised by both organisations over the period of two years.

Among the twenty Italian regions Veneto is ranked first concerning the organisations' presence and representation. This is true in particular for Confcommercio that set up ten out of the 15 events in the region, in particular in the smallest towns of the provinces of Vicenza and Belluno (Feltre, Lonigo and Marostica among the others).

Graph 2 Geographic distribution of the events in the peninsula (2015-2016)

Source: our elaboration on Confindastria and Confcommercio datasets.

The South of Italy is once again absent, with the exception of Apulia, where Brindisi is the only city south of Rome to hold at least three events in the period considered. Even Naples cannot compete with the neuralgic centres of the industrial North. In other words, Southern Italy was not able to attract the attention of the organisers, remaining marginal in the coordination of the experts to be sent to the member enterprises.

4. Beyond the reform: Protagonists and storytelling surfing the online pages of the *Corriere della Sera*

In a country afflicted by an employment crisis which in particular hit the most disadvantaged sectors of the population, the introduction of the Jobs Act has been the metaphor of the will to invert negative trends moving from an institutional intervention. Notwithstanding the contents and the directives of the reform, it is undeniable that this initiative has provoked an intense and controversial debate, amplified by media and in particular by the main information channels in Italy. The strategic role played by the press in this case has been decisive on one hand in the forming of the conscience of influencers and opinion leaders (traditionally a privileged audience of journalism), and on the other hand, in addressing the portion of public opinion most affected by the reorganisation of the labour market, such as entrepreneurs/managers – 54% of them collect their information from newspapers (Audipress 2016) – and young people. In the *panorama* of Italian journalism, a leading role is held by the *Corriere della Sera*, a historical Milanese newspaper founded in 1876, and which is still the most widespread newspaper with its 240,119 readers (ADS January 2017), and which immediately after the sport newspapers, is the most read newspaper among the young people aged between 18 and 24 (Audipress 2016 III).

However, the widespread development of the new technologies has obliged scholars to rethink the power of online information sources, which are more and more capable of arousing public opinion and of cultivating citizens' imagery, particularly when they wish to spread awareness on governance policies and actions. This is not only the consequence of the fact that web audiences are generally more active and aware than traditional media ones (see, among others, Jacobelli 2001), but also due to the fact that online papers have a practically unlimited power of penetration thanks to the presence and the chain sharing of news on the main social network sites. For instance, in contrast to the correspondent paper editions, whose purchase is clearly intentional and planned (in other words, it implies the will to be informed), the digital editions are able to strengthen ideas and opinions without depending on the user's planned intention to read, amplifying the effects of a message's diffusion. Furthermore, *corriere.it*, as well as its paper edition, stands out in the *panorama* of online press for its number of users (979,576 Audiweb 2017)[13].

Moving from these presuppositions, we will try to understand not only the position taken by the *Corriere della Sera* online when writing about the Jobs Act, but also try and reflect on the direction public opinion could take in its convictions thanks to the representations deployed.

The last part of our research therefore makes reference to all the articles present on *corriere.it* which match the selection criteria (inserting the keyword "Jobs Act" in the search engine inside the website). Specifically, we analyzed all the contents published in the month in which the law was passed, December 2014 and with the aim of verifying the presence of changes in the storytelling, also those spread in the months of December 2015 and 2016 (we decided to analyse that month because the law entered into force in the same month). The choice of a relatively wide time range represents the wish to intercept not only the changes in media exposure, but also the direction in which these changes are moving.

The resulting *corpus* is made up of 177 articles: 82 in 2014, 27 in 2015 and 68 in 2016. We then studied the texts selected on two levels: a *quantitative* analysis one, aimed at identifying the topic's development over the entire period of reference, the lemma/headline keyword occurrences, the people and the personalities most engaged, the significant stakeholders/bodies/organisations and the narrative frame adopted by *corriere.it*; and a *qualitative* one, aimed at understanding if the rendering of this topic is inserted in a context of for/against, positivity/negativity, effectiveness/ineffectiveness of the Act.

The first reference to the Jobs Act present in the online edition of the paper dates back to 2013, when only two articles regarding the topic were published. A topic which would become extremely relevant a year later. In fact, in 2014 we witnessed an impressive jump in publications: from two to 460. However, news cy-

---

13 In reality, *corriere.it* is not the first ranked online newspaper considering number of users, but the second after *repubblica.it* (1,600,296, Audiweb 2017). However, if we consider that the digital edition of the Corriere della Sera, in contrast to its direct competitor, is a subscription service and that its internet traffic (the flow of data across the internet) is 98% (versus 96% in the case of repubblica.it, Audiweb 2015 in Guastella 2015), we can with a certain margin of certainty consider corriere.it the most representative newspaper in the panorama of information spread via the internet in Italy.

cles make news' life relatively short and as was predictable, in the two-year period 2015-2016 the number of short articles started decreasing slowly, but inexorably, passing from 447 to 407 (on 10 May 2017 the number of documents with the keyword amounted to 108).

The peculiarities in the annual distribution of the articles, even if they do not predictably allow us to establish well defined trends, permit us to talk about a certain linearity in the "physiologic" rhythm of the news: the issue which appears extremely desirable in the two months preceding the approval of the law on 10 December 2014 (October and November), seems to die out in the spring of the following year. We will have to wait until December 2016, that is the passing of a sufficiently long period of time before starting to make the first evaluations of the effects created when *corriere.it* will show again a peak of interest for the Jobs Act (Graph 2).

The under-representation of this topic in July (at least compared to the other months) is a unique, ironic constant, so as to underline the idea that even if employment provokes a heated debate, it cannot be considered a topic for the summer.

Graph 2   Monthly presence of the Jobs Act 2014-2016

Jobs Act Corriere.it - 2014	Jobs Act Corriere.it - 2015	Jobs Act Corriere.it - 2016
109 105 82 46 30 25 17 16 11 8 7 4	70 61 43 40 35 35 34 32 27 26 24 20	68 52 43 42 36 32 32 28 25 20 15 14
October, November, December, September, March, January, February, May, April, August, June, July	March, February, April, May, January, June, September, August, December, October, November, July	December, May, June, March, February, April, September, October, January, August, November, July

Source: *corriere.it* – articles responding to the key words "Jobs Act" 2014-2016.

Greater differences as to the editorial choices for the headlines are noticeable (Table 8).

In this case, what emerges is the weight that current affairs have in determining the narrative frame used for the storytelling of the reform. In 2014, in fact, the stories related to the general strike against the reform, which took place on 12

December of the same year, are the predominant stories. It is no coincidence that the most frequent lemmas are "Strike", "Marches", "Camusso", "CGIL", "Square" and so on, placing Matteo Renzi, the Prime Minister at the time, in the background. The study of the headlines gives the reader the idea of a population that is reacting to the decree with decisively little enthusiasm (Table 8 – Tag Cloud 1 and Lemma/Occurrence 1).

In 2015 space was given in the headlines to the various nuances of the Jobs Act: in this case we can find lemmas such as "Growth", "Work", "Banks", "Unions", but also "Graduate", "Pay", "Reforms" and "Hired" (Table 8 – Tag Cloud 2 and Lemma/Occurrence 2). It almost seems that after the law entered into force the storytelling of the Jobs Act moved towards a certain maturity and narrative balance. A balance that was to be short lived. In 2016 news reports once again show their appeal in the construction of facts and this time what prevails are the topics about the imminent referendum on the change of some articles of the Constitution.

Table 8 Development of the occurrences in the storytelling of the Jobs Act

2014		2015		2016	
Tag Cloud 1		Tag Cloud 2		Tag Cloud 3	
Lemmas 1	Occurrences 1	Lemmas 2	Occurrences 2	Lemmas 3	Occurrences 3
Jobs Act	28	Renzi	5	Jobs Act	12
Sciopero/ Strike	11	Crescita/ Growth	3	Referendum	11
Renzi	8	Lavoro/Work	3	Pd	10
Marce/ Marches	6	Banca/Bank	3	Renzi	10
Camusso	5	Sindacati/ Unions	2	Lavoro/ Work	7

Source: 177 articles from corriere.it (December 2014-2015-2016).

These kinds of observations find strength and further confirmation in the cataloguing which has been performed on the tags (or narrative frames) used by *corriere.it*. Framing is one of the most important operations of reader orientation, because it has the double function of accompaniment and guidance in the construction of media meanings (Bryant and Oliver 2009). In other words, it is thanks to the frame that we are able to contextualise and to have an idea about the content we are using. However, in the case under examination, the editorial policies seem to privilege an extremely focused framing on the "exogenous" factors of the reorganisational process rather than on the "endogenous" ones. In fact, in 2014, "current affair" articles (36.7%) related to the protests prevailed over those concerning the "economy", which are the great majority in 2015 (52%) and those about "politics", which make up more than half the *corpus* in 2016.

Hence, the average reader risks having to ask him or herself if the change in the employment policies is an economic process, a political one or a "simple" current affairs episode. The Jobs Act probably contains all these tags, including the one associated with "cultural" factors, but the strong imbalance (Graph 3) between the narrative frames adopted not only during the three-year period, but also during just one year, could suggest a really explicit absence of narrative contextualisation capable of disorienting the reader.

Graph 3   The Jobs Act between narrative choices and contextualisation (2014-2016)

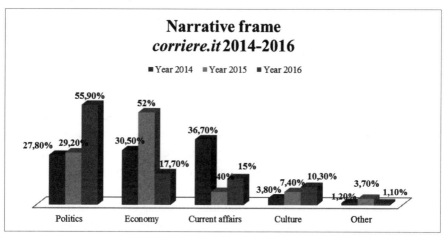

Source: 177 articles from corriere.it (December 2014-2015-2016).

If we consider the *people engaged in the storytelling*, it is necessary to bear in mind that the measure comes from an initiative of the PD (Partito Democratico - Democratic Party), yet the underrepresentation of the members of the other parties seems to reveal the newspaper's lack of pluralism. The name which comes up the most often in the three-year period is Matteo Renzi (21 times in 2014, seven times in 2015 and 45 times in 2016), followed in 2014 by Susanna Camusso (who appears in seven articles thanks to the general strike), Giorgio Napolitano (at the time President of the Republic and the only "impartial figure of the narration', six presences), Giuliano Poletti, Labour and Social Policy Minister in Renzi's Government (5) and Cesare Damiano, a member of the PD (4).

The *scenario* changes very little in 2015, when Maria Elena Boschi, at the time Minister for Constitutional Reforms and Relationships with the Parliament (3), Pier Carlo Padoan, Minister of Finance (3) and Giuliano Poletti (3) are only counterposed by Silvio Berlusconi (3). The same situation presents itself the following year, when Silvio Berlusconi (6) is the only one (not) to balance the presence of the PD politicians Giuliano Poletti (11), Roberto Speranza (10) and Enrico Rossi (4).

Indeed, favouring one position over another in a controversial scenario as the one we are referring to, tips the balance in favour of one of the sides engaged, creating in the readers an unbalance in the perception of the situation. This trend is confirmed also when analysing the presence in the texts of stakeholders/bodies/organisations: the PD is always at the top of the pyramid in terms of presence (eight in 2015 and 34 in 2016), with the exception of 2014, in which the Government party is in third place (20), leaving space to the unions CGIL (30) and UIL (21), cited because of the previously mentioned strike.

It is the case to underline that the observations made so far on the possible "distortive' effects of the overrepresentation of some personalities/organisations compared to others, derive not only from the study of the quantitative data collected. Also, the qualitative analysis of the articles on *corriere.it* provides a representation of the Jobs Act all but mild and non-confrontational. For this reason, we have good reasons to affirm that the positioning in favour of the PD to the detriment of the other positions creates a sort of monism of the points of view expressed. Such an unbalance in citing the personalities engaged probably would not have pushed us to these considerations if the narration of the reorganisation of the labour market had been characterised by a rather neutral style. Instead, the Jobs Act even in the month of its approval (December 2014) is generally presented in a heated way.

First of all, reading the articles published in December, we notice how it is almost difficult to understand the content of the amendments (which receive relatively little attention), exactly because the rhetoric of political polemic prevails even over the analysis of the economic, employment, social or cultural repercussions of the reform itself. In principle, we can affirm that the storytelling in 2014 is of two levels: an attack on the reform is always followed by its defence; praise is followed by criticism. The field where the battle takes place is far from being neutral from the point of view of the political formations. Even in the articles indicated with the tag "Economy" the controversies and the party attacks are more than a simple political background and, when we are not talking about a party against another party, there are unions and enraged unionists. Thus, the storytelling seems quite tense and, even if we cannot talk about an explicitly negative position (but neither of a positive one), the emerging representation is one of conflict and hostility. The Jobs Act is a controversial topic which creates tensions rather than dialogue between the social actors engaged.

This "battle between the parties" makes it hard for the reader to understand if we are referring to efficacious decrees or not. The various points of view expressed in the articles, rather than conferring balance and impartiality to the narration, provide only a series of "famous (sometimes factious) opinions", which strengthen the previous opinions of the audience in terms of opinions developed in the past and of party "ideologies". To this "war" scene we can add the protests which brought the general strike of December 12.

December 2015 is a period of little interest to the topic. Yet, we have to recognise that the 27 articles published during this period reveal a change in the trend compared to the year before. Even though political and union polemic continue to be there, a year is a long enough period of time to be able to start looking at the effects of the reform. The storytelling is more relaxed, and the data (rather fluctuating and negative in the case of women) on the employment situation in the country gradually gains space inside the articles. What remains is the inability to provide an image of the effectiveness of the Job Act which is not filtered through the various social parties engaged (Government party, opposition and unions). The employer organisations, such as *Confindustria* e *Confcommercio*, are instead almost absent. They appear in the storytelling in a poorly significant way – the peak of presence of *Confindustria* is reached in 2016 with only four occurrences.

On the other hand, in December 2016, the data about the effects of the application of the "new" employment policies forces *corriere.it* to change its narrative style. The dissatisfaction with the introduction of a conspicuous number of vouchers and a 30% decrease in the open-ended contract hiring in Tuscany (article of December 29, 2016), and the increase of dismissals without a valid reason in Apulia (December 27, 2016) are only some of the most significant examples showing a shift in the representation of the Jobs Act towards decisively negative levels. At the gates of 2017 it is not difficult for the reader to start believing in the ineffectiveness of the labour market reform wanted by Matteo Renzi. The political *querelle* loses weight and the issue is mainly brought forward by the "victims" of the Jobs Act: women (unemployed and underpaid) and young people (unemployed, ready to migrate, fired and exploited), who for the first time take on a central role in a debate which until that moment had seen them only marginally engaged.

In an attempt to simplify the development of this topic, we can say that the "frame" adopted by *Corriere* is *dispute –> balance –> effects*.

If we try instead to make predictions on the modalities through which *corriere.it* is cultivating its users' orientations, we cannot but recognise how the continuity and the constancy of the presence of this topic are key factors to favour a correct metabolism of meaning in the public opinion. However, the imbalance in favour of a scenario of contestation as well as the overrepresentation of the PD members compared to those of other parties, risks creating a collective imagery that is rather unfavourable, if not even "schizophrenic" towards the Jobs Act. What implicitly emerges from the pages of *corriere.it* is the storytelling of a measure which on one hand, shines under the stars of contestation and little popular consent and on the other hand, needs "parental" protection (Renzi and the PD) to defend its effectiveness.

In conclusion, we need to point out the abuse of the rhetoric "we versus you". It is true that the use of conflictual languages and the clashes between political groups tend to favour the audience's adoption of a clear stance, but it is also true that in this case the stakes should not be the choice of being in favour or against the Jobs Act. The objective of the storytelling should be rather to accompany the readers towards an understanding of the ongoing mechanisms of change in the labour market.

The storytelling which has prevailed could generate a distorted idea of the public policies introduced to fight against the employment crisis, moving the attention away from the real issue (work) and towards the rivalry and the discussions between political parties. Hence, the common good risks being delegated to the second row. In this sense, it seems that *corriere.it* has unfortunately privileged the cultivation of public opinion in a different direction: that of the acceptance or not of one of the party or union positions. The collective imagery seems to have been diverted from the path opened by the reform itself towards the dead end of political debate and erected walls.

5. Conclusions

As the reader will remember, we moved from the hypothesis of verifying the communicative strategies examined to the prevalence of a polemic polarisation between those who defended the measures and those who relentlessly attacked them. The hypothesis has been fully verified. In substance, what we have examined is a lost occasion. The organisations engaged and the national press could have taken advantage of the occasion to move from the contents of the Jobs Act to make an important and significant step towards the economic growth of the country. This could even have become the occasion to reflect on the development model we intend to follow in future years. None of this took place.

Let's try to sum up the main results reached with the three *incipient explorations* regarding three important social players in the reform process just described.

The positions expressed are clear, as if we were describing a battle field. The CGIL is against the measure, their critical point lies in the abrogation of the article 18 which softens the restrictions the entrepreneurs are tied to in the case of a dismissal. The problem raised is that of the continuous erosion of rights, including the issues connected to social welfare nets and to public contracts, in a general process aiming at monetising the right to work. Incidentally, the propensity to solve problems using money is not new to entrepreneurs; we can remember the trend to monetise the healthcare service, when during the 60s and the 70s that topic was central in the dispute between politics and unions.

As to the communicative strategies, what is evident is that the CGIL looks beyond, to the *external* market of the parties engaged, while the employer organisations open a dialogue with the *internal* market of their own members. The greater number of events and initiatives organised by *Confindustria* and *Confcommercio* wish to strengthen the external communication, and therefore, the internal cohesion in order to present themselves united in front of the opponent that expresses a perspective irreconcilable with the position of both the employers and the governance (who strongly wanted the approval of the measures in parliament).

The expectations matured in and/or encouraged by the two employer organisations rely on the determination of a social scenario founded on the semantic triad "change-new-evolution". In the numerous events set up, almost exclusively in Northern Italy, they encourage the conviction that the model of increasing protection contracts has to necessarily bring a prevalence of open-ended contracts rather than fixed-term ones. As we mentioned above, however, this has not occurred. On the contrary, the latest data introduces elements of great concern. Inps data on the first three months of 2017 strengthens the trend ongoing since the end of the contribution reductions in the case of stable hiring. In the three months considered there were 322,000 new job positions, but the open-ended ones were only 17,000; in concrete, a tiny minority.

Yet the reform had created important and deep expectations among the organisations involved and even among common people. The proof of this is the fact that the *Corriere della Sera* deals a lot with the topic and gives a lot of space to the new measures. In 2014 the articles numbered 460, but also in 2015 the number was 447 and in 2016 still 407. For three years in a row the newspaper published one or more articles every day on the topic or on topics connected to the Jobs Act. The quantitative analysis shows how Italy – the political world and the population – considered the strategic importance of a measure which could have revived the labour market and employment in Italy. It could have limited the flow of qualified manpower that is leaving the country every year. In 2015 over 107,000 Italians left the country, of whom the majority was aged between 18 and 34: this is was stated in the report "Italiani nel mondo 2016" (Italians in the World 2016).

Instead, with reference to the qualitative analysis, we can observe great limits in the management of the topics concerning the potential the measure could have expressed, as if the task were to throw a stone in a pond and to observe the concentric circles which form on its surface. On the other hand, the newspaper pages show that what prevails is the rhetoric of political polemic and therefore a scenario of conflict and rivalry; to this we must add the dichotomy between "we" and "you", as if the labour market were a prerogative of one of the parties engaged. What happens is the shift of attention from the crucial and serious issue of unemployment, in particular of young people and women, to one or another political party, one or another economic organisation, one or another political perspective which sort of tend to take over the semantic field.

This is in concrete the reaction of the social partners to the application of the Jobs Act. From the study of the digital communication strategies it seems clear how the debate has focused on a "war of figures" and how there has been poor sensitivity to scientific approaches or at least to clarity in facing the topic. With the exception of marginal cases, the greater audience is a secondary issue. The possibility of investing in a constructive public debate, based on the sharing and spreading of the reform has not been a political strategy adopted by the players engaged. On the contrary, in this specific case, the so-called consultations with the social players were strongly limited by Renzi's Government. What is clear is the role play performed by each organisation. We can just notice how Italy, together with Greece, is the only country at present that has difficulty in getting over the economic crisis, while other countries have a GDP that is growing at a rhythm of 2% per year.

References

Ballistreri, Maurizio (2015): Il diritto del lavoro, i diritti sociali: nuovi paradigmi nella crisi storica dello stato-nazione, in: Revista de Estudios Económicos y Empresariales, 27: pp. 183-195, http://158.49.113.108/bitstream/handle/10662/4185/0212-7237_27_183.pdf?sequence=1

Bryant, Jennings/Oliver, Mary B. (Eds.) (2009): Media Effects: Advances in Theory and Research, New York and London: Routledge

Carrieri, Mimmo (2012): I sindacati, Bologna: il Mulino

Cella, Gian P. (1999): Il sindacato, Bologna: il Mulino

Feltrin, Paolo/Zan, Stefano (2015): Imprese e rappresentanza. Ruolo e funzioni delle associazioni imprenditoriali, Roma: Carocci

Fontana, Renato/Ferrucci, Martina/Nemmo, Erika (2016): I giovani italiani dopo la crisi economica. Smart o smarriti? in: Rivista di Studi Politici, 4: pp. 50-73

Gallino, Luciano (2012): La lotta di classe dopo la lotta di classe, Roma-Bari: Laterza

Guastella, Erminia (14/04/2015): Audiweb rilascia i dati di traffico "puri": ecco i veri numeri delle testate online, in: Il fatto Quotidiano, http://www.ilfattoquotidiano.it/2015/04/14/audiweb-rilascia-i-dati-traffico-puri-i-veri-numeri-delle-testate-online/1586236/

Lanzalaco, Luca (1998): Le associazioni imprenditoriali, In Gian Primo Cella & Tiziano Treu (eds) Le nuove relazioni industriali. L'esperienza italiana nella prospettiva europea, Bologna: Il Mulino

Licata, Delfina (2016): Rapporto Italiani nel mondo 2016, Todi: Tau Editrice, http://ced.uab.es/wp-content/uploads/2016/11/Sintesi_Rapporto-Italiani_2016_Reca%C3%B1o-i-altres.pdf

Jacobelli, Jader (2001): Politica e internet, Soveria Mannelli: Rubettino

Seghezzi, Francesco/Nespoli, Francesco (2017): Jobs Act, per un bilancio oltre la "guerra dei numeri", ADAPT, University Press, Working Paper n. 3

Vatta, Alessia (2007): Italy, in: Franz Traxler & Gerhard Huemer (eds): Handbook of Business Interest Associations, Firm Size and Governance. A Comparative Analytical Approach, London-New York: Routledge, pp. 204-229

Websites

ADESSO LO SAI - CGIL: http://www.adessolosai.it/

AUDIPRESS: http://www.audipress.it/visual_report/ CGIL: www.cgil.it

CISL: www.cisl.it

CONFCOMMERCIO: www.confcommercio.it

CONFINDUSTRIA: www.confindustria.it

CORRIERE DELLA SERA: http://www.corriere.it

IL FATTO QUOTIDIANO: http://www.ilfattoquotidiano.it/

INPS: https://www.inps.it/

ISTAT: http://dati.istat.it/

PRIMA ON LINE: http://www.primaonline.it/

UIL: www.uil.it

WIKI LABOUR IT: http://www.wikilabour.it/

The Best Offer: Monitoring and Analysis of Best Practices of the Centres for Public and Private Employment and University Orientation and Placement Services

Patrizio Di Nicola, Alessandra Fasano, Piera Rella and Ludovica Rossotti

This article reports the first results of a survey conducted regarding Public and Private Employment Offices, and the University Orientation and Placement Services within the region of Lazio. The objective is to understand the functioning of the orientation and placement and to identify the best practices exportable from one territory to another. On a methodological level, a quality analysis was carried out through in-depth interviews aimed at operators and managers of public and private employment offices. The functioning of the services in terms of: tasks performed by operators and managers, liaison with business matching between labour supply and demand, and type of contracts offered, were all analysed. To identify the best practices, we have monitored the services offered by the various employment centres, including universities, by comparing them with the quality standards set by "Italia Lavoro" (Italia Lavoro e Ministero del lavoro 2014). In addition, a map of exportable services from one territory to another was constructed.

It was discovered how the universities of Lazio could offer both curricular and extra-curricular internships for graduates and, to a lesser degree, labour brokerage. Differences between public and private universities were noticed which highlight how critical points for one become strengths for the other.

As far as the users and operators of private and public employment offices are concerned, a certain difficulty in investing in demand and supply has emerged, often leaving this hard task to interpersonal skills and knowledge of the job seeker, who sees, in the informal contacts, the main and most effective way to find employment.

1. Introduction

Unemployment, discouragement, precariousness and poor quality are the facets of labour in Italy today. Already present since the 1980s, these feelings were aggravated by the financial crisis of 2007. It is a worldwide problem, as evidenced by the increasingly alarmed ILO's documents (International Labour Organization) on the difficulties of young people to enter the labour market (ILO 2015). Looking at the economic and social transformations in the West as a result of globalisation, a complex society emerges, divided by conflicts between classes, territories, and generations; in this context, social actors privileged at least in terms of cultural capital (e.g. the graduates) seem to have more possibilities, but nevertheless they still have many constraints.

The last ISTAT (National Institute for Statistics) report (2016) reveals that young people in Italy are increasingly struggling to enter the labour market, thus remaining trapped in a process of economic dependence on the family. This problem does not only involve the most disadvantaged youths, but also the young qualified graduates are forced to fight against unemployment, overeducation and overskilling.

Starting from the 80s, the Italian labour market was involved in a long process of deconstruction of labour protection aimed at mitigating the 1970 Workers' Statute, a law that established a modern body of rules to protect the work of employees. The process of flexibilisation of work is established with law No. 863 of 1984, which established the training contract for young people (even though the young people who entered the companies possessed much more training than in the past) and provided the possibility of establishing the so called "solidarity contracts' aimed at reducing working time (and salary) in the event of a business crisis: a questionable application of the rule of "working less to ensure work for everyone' (Aznar 1994). In 1991 Law No. 223 reduced the restrictions on collective lay-offs due to industrial crises or restructurings. The Memorandum of Understanding of July 1993, introduced the idea that flexibility could contribute to increasing employment but, as noted by Luciano Gallino (2007), it introduced the idea that the work of human beings, in various respects, is simply a commodity. In 1995, the Pension Reform came up with the introduction of a minimum social security benefit for temporary workers, raising the figure of the "collaborator": a young woman, mostly female, who worked with a temporary contract mid-way between autonomous and dependent worker, for an average of seven months a year and a gross salary of 700 Euro (Di Nicola 2009). In 2013, temporary "collaborators" had grown up to one million units including over 100,000 in the public administration. However, the laws unanimously considered the hubs of flexible labour were published in 1997 (Law 196) which introduced interim work, further extending the possibilities of term employment, and in 2003 with the implementation of Law 30. A norm affected by a kind of "bulimia" of over 40 precarious contractual types.

This legislative production, rooted in a prolonged period of strong economic uncertainty for businesses and a reduction in public welfare spending, created the emergence of the labour market precariousness that still remains today. To say it very briefly, while emphasising "flexsecurity", the Government created a flex-insecurity system (Berton et al. 2009).

The economic crisis, in spite of the policies implemented to mitigate its effects, including those analysed in this paper, has also had negative consequences for education in Italy, which was weakened in one of its main functions, social lift, aimed at fighting inequalities and to guarantee equal opportunities (Cavarra et al. 2015). The crisis strengthens the familial and class background, which through informal networks promotes entry into the world of work. However, it is still difficult even for the most prosperous classes to choose the degree program according to their aspirations and to ensure the entry into the desired occupation: the problem of transition from training to employment in the labour market transversely affects a large part of the youth population.

For over a decade, Europe has been very confident on active policies and employment services (SPIs), as proved by the new European Social Fund Regulation 2014/2020, which continues to promote, among the different investment priorities, the modernisation of the labour market institutions (Bergamante and Marocco 2014). Increasing people's employability is also a response to the economic-financial crisis begun in 2007 and to this day still makes it increasingly difficult for the Government to provide protection and support policies (Ibidem 2014).

This article is structured as follows: after a brief exposure of the difficult transition (compared to what is happening in other countries) from education to work in Italy, we will focus on the analysis of job orientation and job placement services provided by Latium Universities, Public Centres for employment, private employment agencies and training organisations. The study was conducted through semi-structured interviews with operators, executives and users. The aim is to try to highlight, in addition to differences and similarities between different employment services, the best practices that can be exported from one territory to another.

In conclusion, the evaluation of the "TAPIC framework" (Meuleman 2008, Greer et al. 2016) will be applied, as far as possible, to define:

- **Transparency**: who knows how much about the decision-making process and the underlying reasons for actions? **(T)**
- **Accountability**: who can demand an explanation and sanction an action? **(A)**
- **Participation**: in how far can those affected by the decisions participate in the decision-making processes? **(P)**
- **Integrity**: are processes organised in a non-corrupt and institutionalised manner? **(I)**
- **Capacity**: does expertise on policy formulation, implementation and evaluation exist? **(C)**

2. The difficult transition training - work in Italy

The problem of transition to school-work is of great interest, especially now, where political decision-makers are faced with relentless unemployment. There are several studies and approaches proposed in this area, Raffe (2008) in particular summarises three of them. The first highlights how the different transition schemes, in the various countries, seek to face the new challenges of transformation due to globalisation, without losing their role. The second one refers to the transition, calling into question various social components: economic, social, labour market, production systems that in a different way, affect the transition system. The third approach includes theories on social stratification, the labour market, human capital, analysing, by means of segmentation models, distinct internal employment systems based on the role of markets (Raffe 2008).

Researchers of transition systems, found out that there are indeed differences between countries in processing and in the continuous transition outcomes, and they are systematically related to the characteristics of the national transition. This also helped policy-makers understand in detail their transition systems and their internal characteristics that differ from one country to another. This provided conceptual tools to analyse the transition of a country. It has been seen how the institution has a significant weight on the transition to school-work (Raffe 2008). Employment services have a secular history, swinging between local and national services, where they play a significant role as trade unions and employers' associations and still reflect the characteristics of different welfare regimes. In the Mediterranean regime, the employment services were created later and they are not very functional (Weishaupt 2011), and only in the "90s a transition from management to objectives was tried (Pastore 2013, 2015).

The role of Public Services for Employment (PES) is to reduce frictional unemployment due to double information asymmetry between those asking and those looking for work, but they can also affect the structural unemployment in the phases in which some jobs disappear through vocational training toward new qualifications (Shepherd 2013). This is especially true of countries with higher social mobility, while Italy unfortunately positions itself in the last places in the list of countries concerning percentage of young people completing tertiary education (Caroleo and Pastore 2011). This is associated with low social mobility, the consequence of which is a high intergenerational transfer of human capital and social status. From an international perspective, research shows that Northern European countries have the highest rate of social mobility, followed by the Central European countries with very similar percentages in comparison to the United States. In this scenario, Italy is among the last industrialised countries, just above Latin America, which among the 42 countries surveyed, is the one with the highest social immobility. This means that Italy has low educational mobility, not only among countries where university rates are low, as in Northern Europe, but also where these are higher than in the USA (Caroleo and Pastore 2011). Such a phenomenon is interpreted by Bratti et al. (2008), who explains how graduates come from poor families, and this is reflected by the little truth about equal opportunities in Italy, where the difference is more and more due to the familiar background rather than the education received (Caroleo and Pastore 2011).

One of the key points of the Lisbon European Employment Strategy was precisely the removal of these constraints. An objective that Italy is struggling to achieve despite the various reforms that seek to approach the dual education system already in force in Germany by introducing university training credits corresponding to 25 hours of work and the alternation of high school work in upper secondary schools.

3. The national contest

Recently, the Organization for Economic Cooperation and Development (OECD 2013) found that there is a lack of organisation among Public Services for Employment (PSE) that should be revised. However, it considers that public employment services at the community level, are the main tool for implementing active labour policies and should be coordinated, guided and funded by European Union. Obviously, there are territorial differences between the various countries, which on the one hand reflect the employment situation in individual labour markets and on the other the different ways to deal with the problem by different governments.

ISFOL (Institute for the Development of Vocational Training of Workers) elaborations on Eurostat data, about the trend of PES expenditure, in the period between 2008 and 2011, shows how in general some countries have increased their spending allocated for employment services, apart from a few exceptions: Ireland, Italy and Greece. In particular, as far as the share of PIL for labour services is concerned. In fact, the Mediterranean countries, in the face of high growth in unemployment are characterised by a very low investment, moving away from the European average: Finland is the country that invests the most, while Italy and Portugal are at the bottom of the ranking (ISFOL 2014).

This situation is re-emerging with regard to operators of Public Job Centres. Between 2008 and 2011, France, Germany, and England increased their investments, in the form of increasing the number of operators unlike Italy and Portugal, which reduced them instead. Specifically, Italy together with other Mediterranean countries shows a paltry share of spending per unemployed and a low availability of operators for each unemployed person.

Italy is distinguished by another element: the majority of the unemployed mostly apply to informal networks to find employment (80%) or even[1] directly to the firms (66.6%) (Bergamante and Marrocco 2014). This is an indication of how Public Job Centres in Italy country are still unable to counteract the difficult situation in which young people are situated.

---

[1] It was possible to choose more than one answer.

3.1 Territorial differences

Italy is known as a country with strong territorial differences in twofold senses: between metropolitan cities and small towns, between geographical divisions and between different metropolitan cities. Central Italy, where Lazio is to be found, is the place of our research. In 2015 it showed the population occupancy rate of those aged above 15 years, was 46.7%. It was ranked just below the North (49%) and lower than the South (33.3%), which had an employment rate of 20 points according to the European average (ISTAT 2015).

In such a difficult context of declining employment rates in the South, it is not surprising that the crisis has led to a drop in university enrolment and more generally, that education is weakened in one of its main functions of social lifting, aimed at counteracting inequalities and ensuring equal opportunities for all. Territorial differences are accentuated by the different operating modes of the regional services network. In 2015, ISFOL attempted to cite private individuals in the regional employment service systems. Only a few regions out of 20 provided lists and operating locations[2].

The latter placed on the geographical map of Italy shows strong geographical concentration in the North. Particularly in Lombardy (36.1%) and Veneto (25.9%) followed by Piedmont (12.7%) and Lazio (6.4%). However, there is also a concentration of operating venues in the Roman metropolitan area as well. In particular, the Public Job Centres are widespread (933 operating sites accounting for 44% of the total) and exhibit larger structures, as they have an average of eight deployed offices. These are followed by training institutions (31.8%), which have on average two deployed offices. A distant third are the agencies of employment with 7.7% of seats and then a third sector, non-profit entities (foundations, university schools), trade unions and employers' associations.

In order to make a difference in territorial diffusion the large Public Job Centres prefer the most favourable economic environment, but this also depends on a more mature mediation market as a result of precise regional policy choices.

---

[2] The census was conducted in 2015, when ANPAL (National Agency for Active Labour Market Policies) proposed standardising the regional accreditation criteria for private entities and to evaluate them ex post based on the efficiency and effectiveness of their work. The data given below is taken from ISFOL 2016, p.67.

4. Research design and methodology

The weakness of our labour market makes it essential to strengthen the liaison instruments between supply and demand, such as public and private employment services, because our country is among those that have devoted a residual share of investments to employment services. For some years, in addition to Public Job Centres and Private Employment Agencies, universities have also had the task of guiding and insert young people into the labour market. The aim is to protect those who come from the lower middle-class families, which tend to have more difficulties concerning insertion compared to those coming from upper class families, on equal merit.

The mother function of employment services consists of composing and managing a set of vast and complex intervention devices aiming at the support and guidance of individuals in the various transitional phases of their professional career path.

Today, these centres need to have processes and activities that can adequately support the many steps that characterise the professional lives of individuals and progressively achieve flexibility with significant security margins in the market, through the provision of customised advanced services capable to reduce people's stay in risky conditions of inactivity as much as possible.

The context in which the services operate are characterised by the economic and employment crisis, and from a regulatory and procedural point of view. The latter view experienced the effects of applying Law 2/2009 (urgent measures for family support, employment, employment and enterprise, and a redesign of the anti-crisis function of the national strategic framework and the process of territorial conciliation for the integration of passive and active policies).

With regard to universities more specifically, the role of being brokers was awarded in 2003 with the Biagi reform, with the purpose of favouring the inclusion of graduates in the labour market. A function to be played not in competition or in place of the Public Job Centres, but with specific goals, including non-profit placement (Garofano and Spattin 2011).

In this article, the state of the services is illustrated which concern: the Public Job Centres (PES), the Private Employment Agencies (PEA), the Training institutions (IF) and University Orientation and Placement Services (SOPU).

As far as the Public Job Centres, the Private Employment Agencies and the Training institutions, are concerned, the target is varied, while for the University Orientation and Placement Services, whose service is aimed at students, graduates from the Lazio University, who belong to the SOUL project: Sapienza, Tor Vergata, Roma Tre, Foro Italico, La Tuscia, LUMSA and LUISS (the latter just out of SOUL).

Job Soul, first called BLUS, is a project begun in 2008, which departed from the University of La Sapienza in agreement with the Lazio Region. Job Soul's aim is to create a network of universities that encourage graduates to enter the world of work through services provided in a different, but complementary manner to those offered by the various universities that belong to the network.

For this reason, it uses an online platform (www.jobsoul.it) in which the undergraduate or graduate student can enrol and bid independently on the closest offering to his or her skills.

Through the realisation of recruiting, career days, presentation events and job orientation, users of public and private employment offices have the opportunity to establish direct contact with companies and to know the professional world even before stating work or obtaining a university degree.

In this way, they can carry out work experience and internships, apply for Bachelor's Degrees or scholarships, and learn about working opportunities offered in Italy and abroad, from national and international companies and institutions.

Most public and *private* employment offices also use a placement site, where job offers and databases are uploaded and advertised, listing the different professional profiles of each user so that companies can find the most suitable candidate, for their own needs and vice versa. Each user can receive constant updates on job offers and look for the one that best suits their professional profile.

Placement, however, does not merely mean publishing the students' curricula to make it available to the companies. In addition to matching supply and demand, placement creates an indispensable network of cooperative and trustees without which the call for human capital would risk being purely rhetorical in nature, which lacks the necessary institutional channels for its effective exploitation.

In reality, two privileged witnesses[3] from the University of Sapienza and LUISS have distanced themselves from the definition of placement as the core activity of the public and private employment offices.

"... Because placement means that, you take a person "to place" and put him on the job market. This cannot be done by just anyone because if there is no demand, the placement is not possible. Then it says placement but it reads work orientation. So all our activities are based on how to write the curriculum and how to deal with a job interview ..." (Privileged witness of Sapienza).[4]

Therefore, a set of services designed to accompany students, undergraduates and graduate students in the transition from university to work, in order to make them aware of their skills and the path they want to undertake.

On the same line, the words of some managers and operators of the Public Job Centres.

"The purpose is to improve the employability of the person through the enhancement of his curriculum and his abilities so that he can actually find work. The name Public Job Centres is misleading" (Operator Public Job Centres Primavalle).[5]

In fact, as Public Job Centres, the training institutions conducting courses promoted by the region also have the aim of finding the in-services trainings, which theoretically may result in job offers.

The survey began in January 2016 and ended in the second half of May 2017, opening a path, which is still underway, to building evaluation indicators for measuring performance and quality of services provided by the universities of Lazio.

The survey was developed in 55 semi-structured interviews aimed at privileged witnesses, operators and users of university and work orientation services.

---

3 In qualitative sociological investigations, a privileged witness is one who possesses knowledge and for the role that he plays is a major subject for research (Gianturco 2004).
4 In Italian: "...perché placement significa che tu prendi una persona "to place" e la metti sul mercato, questo non lo può fare nessuno perché se non c'è una domanda tu il placement non lo puoi fare, quindi si scrive placement ma si legge orientamento al lavoro quindi tutte le nostre attività sono come si scrive un curriculum e come si affronta un colloquio di lavoro...". (Testimone Privilegiato Sapienza).
5 In Italian: "Lo scopo è quello di migliorare l'occupabilità della persona attraverso la valorizzazione del suo curriculum e delle sue capacità in modo che possa effettivamente trovare lavoro. Il nome Centro per l'impiego è fuorviante".

The scientific and organisational leaders of the various public and private employment office have been chosen as privileged witnesses.

As a survey tool, an interview track[6], with general questions asking the interviewee to deepen the functioning of the Employment Centre, has been used.

Specifically, it was requested to illustrate: the objectives pursued and the type of services offered, the tasks performed by operators and managers, the connection with businesses, the matching of supply and demand, the type of contracts offered, linking with other employment services and, last but not least, an assessment of how to improve the placement service. This has led to the identification of the best practices to be exported from one territory to another, and to identify the critical points that need to be addressed to reinforce employment services in Italy.

The results that emerged from the research and the best practices identified can be found in the appendix.

5. Public Job Centre and Private Employment Agencies for a first reading

5.1 Reputation issues

From the results, it emerges that users of Public Job Centres have enrolled because they are "forced" to be able to access job announcements or positions. Even once you have experience with the Public Job Centres the basic idea does not change.

To counterbalance that there is excellent work being done by the operators. From the interviewees' words, it emerges that there is a fundamental error regarding the function the Public Job Centres have to perform. In their view, the Public Job Centres have the precise aim of finding work, a task that took place in the past when the Public Job Centres were placement offices, now the law has changed as well as their mission. It is no longer a matter of following public classification, in which a job seeker would join, but to guide job seekers through specific training courses on how to write their own curriculum vitae.

---

[6] Track of interview is the tool used in the interviews in depth, consisting of orientate questions to ask the interviewee without foreseeing an answer as in the questionnaire.

A first step is to address the correct functions and objectives of the Public Job Centres so that trust in their work can return.

Another issue that has arisen is the lack of funds needed to follow all the practices carried out by the Public Job Centres, but above all the need to strengthen human resources, primarily because most of them are understaffed. Besides, resources would be used for training, which is not done in the workplace; this carries some serious consequences for the operator, who needs to stay updated; and for the user too, being unsatisfied with the services.

On the contrary, what operators need is a continuous upgrade considering the complex and difficult work they do. To improve the structure and service you need to invest in three steps:

- Continuous upgrades;
- Increasing the number of operators;
- More resources to advertise services and collaborate with companies.

A different picture emerges from users who have turned directly and indirectly to the Private Employment Agencies which are very precise, organised and available even if they offer low-grade jobs. So even when the job does not meet the needs of the person concerned, it is still perceived positively.

The reasons of different perception are various, primarily, as an operator of the Public Job Centres explained, Private Employment Agencies deal with professional figures who are very sought after on the labour market, on the other hand the Public Job Centres are flooded with people from less wanted categories, such as disabled people, immigrants and people with mental disabilities.

Operators are therefore forced to tackle different and complex problems and needs, with the little staff available. To address this situation, some centres refuse to advertise themselves, since the users are so many and it becomes difficult to handle them with little staff available. Moreover, Private Employment Agencies have a different internal management; they should not expect to receive "tasks from above" in order to move.

This is a problem, which constantly stalls the organisational machinery of the Public Job Centres, since they depend on the regions, and most importantly, they lost the important linkage to the specificity of the territory in which each Public Job Centres operates.

5.2 The importance of "word of mouth" to find a job

A theme that emerges from users across both Public Job Centres and Private Employment Agencies but also from the operators is Italy's difficulty in investing in mediation, often leaving this arduous task to the person seeking employment and who is therefore dependent on their interpersonal skills and knowledge. These people seeking employment may consider informal contacts as the main and most effective way to find work. As we have seen in detail in the analysis of the macro areas of "Italia Lavoro" it has emerged on several occasions that word of mouth is seen as the key to access work.

A topic that emerges from users of both Public Job Centres and Private Employment Agencies but also from the operators, is Italy's difficulty in investing in brokering, often leaving this difficult task to the relational and cognitive skills of the person seeking employment, seeing informal contacts as the main and most effective way to find work.

Workers of the Private Employment Agencies work in the same direction; particularly as an operator explains, who contextualises the situation in Italy, how the problem is between categorisation and passive policies, outside which people are left to their own devices.

"The Private Employment Agencies who deal with active policies, they see them as passive politics, but a passive politics are actualised because the user belongs a particular category. So if they look for work they have to pay an agency since they are not supported by the State aid in the research for job, is that understood?" (Operator of Private Employment Agencies).[7]

This is unfortunately an aging problem in Italy country where there is continuing difficulty in enhancing active labour policies. First of all, it is impossible to get the unemployed from one job to another through income support.

Consequently, in a framework where Public Employment Offices, Public Job Centres, Private Employment Agencies and University Orientation and Placement Services state that the contracts offered the most are fixed-term and internships, the first step to relaunch work it is to put people in the condition so they can find a job. This does not mean just investing in training that is likely to be "a parking

---

[7] In Italian: "Le agenzie per il lavoro che si occupano di politiche attive, le trattano sempre in connessione con una politica passiva, e la politica passiva si attua perché tu sei una particolare categoria. Per aiutarti a cerca lavoro devi pagare una agenzia perché non sei sostenuto dal pubblico in questa tua ricerca, ok?"

lot" for disadvantaged young people, or a flyer for a miserable career-free internship, but to provide the necessary services and tools.

This is not just about ending training itself, which is likely to be "a parking lot" for discouraged young people, or a flyer for a miserable career without progress, but to provide the necessary services and tools.

6. The Job Centres in southern Italy: A first look at strengths and weaknesses

The regional dynamic of welfare to work, that includes all the tools and regulations to facilitate job matching and to improve job placement, is different from one territory to another.

Concerning the Southern context, it is interesting to analyse the first finding of another survey conducted in Calabria and in Apulia Region on the role of the Public Job Centres (PES) to promote job matching (Fasano 2017).

In this study, some employees and coordinators of the PES are interviewed. The results obtained show that there are still old ways to see PES: for employers, they have more control functions, while for the unemployed people they have more functions of bureaucracy. In order to compare the different point of views (employees and coordinators of the PES, unemployed people, employers), it is possible to identify strengths and weaknesses of public employment offices (see Table 2).

Table 2   Strengths and weaknesses of PES from different point of views

	Strengths	Weaknesses
Employees and coordinators of the PES	• Orientation services; • Differentiated services according to different groups of jobseekers (young people, women, long term unemployed, dismissed adult people, immigrants, disabled, companies); • Skills audit.	• Deficit of human resources; • Services more orientated towards quantity than to quality; • Lack of ad hoc training for the needs of the unemployed; • No official network with Private Public Job Centres (PEA); • Weak support from the Labour Market Observatory.
Unemployed people	• Counselling; • Careers guidance; • Information about job regulations and law procedures; • Support for an individualised path to employment; • Support for writing a CV and a cover letter; • Promotion of unemployed people between companies.	• Lack of a real link between unemployed and companies; • Absence of tools to facilitate the search for a job (for example, public internet point); • Little clarity and transparency of information dissemination channels (for example, the PES do not have a specific web site and so they publish the job offers on different links); • No monitoring of the started job path.
Employers	• Preselection or selection of CV; • Promotion of stages; • Free services (compared to the PEA).	• Limited number of trainees recruitment (since the PES aims at hiring the unemployed people rather than promoting stages); • The mandatory protected persons hiring from the dedicated lists supplied by the PES (persons considered less productive).

Source: own elaboration.

Regarding the strengths, the PES are considered as good free counselling service suppliers and useful both for unemployed persons and employers.

Regarding weaknesses, the PES are not inserted in a good network of employment services, they are not well promoted and have a lack of human and economic resources.

In general, the services efficiency is linked to the skills of single operators or to isolated initiatives (i.e. the Recruiting Week organised by the Career Service Office of the University of Salento).

In light of the previous considerations, the Southern Italy Public Job Centres need, first of all, a process of coordination and transparency of their activities in order to improve the best practices of local welfare.

7. Final considerations

In the light of what emerged in the first results of the Public Job Centres, Private Employment Agencies and University Orientation and Placement Services, it can be seen that a dichotomy between private and public institutions exists, both for Public Job Centres vs. Private Employment Agencies, public and private universities and public and private training institutes. In both cases, the problem of little public-sector funding coupled with the reduced number of operators makes work difficult, reproducing those inequalities that reflect the current social economic situation in Italy. It has been seen that private university students have a larger range of services than public university colleagues have, and, at the same time placement service operators exist in a greater number in private universities

Similar situations occur in training institutions, where we find more problems than in public ones, which limits their ability in setting up courses for the weakest users. The same scenario is found in the comparison between Public Job Centres and Private Employment Agencies, where the latter boast more services and better qualified staff. Thus, we have students, both unemployed and job seekers, as A-series and B-series, where the essential goal of employment services is being missing, namely universal access to all services for work.

It is no coincidence that in Italy, where the percentage of NEETs increases, there is little confidence in Private Employment Agencies and University Orientation and Placement Services. The Young Guarantee Program has been a benchmark for all employment services with unified national rules and after initial difficulties, intervention spaces have been offered with appropriate funding for training bodies, Public Job Centres and Private Employment Agencies, especially to try and curb the high percentage of NEETs.

Both users and operators say that word-of-mouth continues to be seen as a strong channel when searching for a job, witnessing how the efforts made were not sufficient, and how young people increasingly move away from the policies implemented by the state.

However, it has been asked if the policies implemented have been useful in achieving the goal we are aiming for? In addition, from an analytical point of view, what is missing? The table below tries to summarise, as far as possible, the impact of active policies on young people, according to both the public and private sectors. Table 3 takes into account that a network comprising trade unions and schools involved in young people's insertion to work is poorly developed in Italy, although it would better match the "participation" criterion.

Table 3   Grid for analysing the governance of labour market and the functionality of different modes of governance

Mode	Quality Criteria				
	Transparency	*Accountability*	*Participation*	*Integrity*	*Capacity*
Hierarchy (H)	Low	Low	Medium	Low	Very Low
Market (M)	High	Medium	High	Low	Medium
Network (N)	Low	Low	Very High	Low	Medium
H+M	High	Medium	High	Medium	Medium

Source: own elaboration based on Meuleman 2008 and Greer et al. 2016.

As we can see, public-based systems guided by hierarchy and typical market players are unable to achieve fully satisfactory results, primarily because the two types of structures are unable to activate important network synergies. Therefore, the strategy, though not optimal that could improve the ability of the system to respond to young unemployed is a mixed presence of public and private structures on the labour market that develop collaboration rather than competition.

As Fitoussi says, referring to young people in Western countries, *"the more a resource is scarce, the more its value is high"* (Vesan 2016: 27), it becomes unimportant but it is necessary to invest seriously in them, without waiting for the youth to become too old for the policies to be implemented to benefit from them. Steps to be taken are many but all of them are in the same direction: to make the agencies employment more effective, by increasing the number and quality of training of operators, in order to give the centres the possibility to fully carry out their functions: not only the purely bureaucratic ones, but, above all, the tools necessary to guide people towards the labour market.

At the same time, the Private Employment Agencies' action is an integral part of the work done by employment agencies. This is necessary to avoid falling into public-private competition, because it leaves the latter more freedom of action and more funding at the expenses of the employment agencies and of their own reputation, damaging people who turn to them.

Strengthening a system-wide integration between public and private institutions, based on a collaboration aimed at making the person seeking employment the centre of the attention, countering the needs of everyone in order to counteract and not widen the inequalities.

Finally, but more importantly, expanding active and income support policies by providing, as it is the case in Germany, France and England (Perazzoli 2014), a series of measures to alleviate the difficult situation of an unemployed or job seeker: rent and bills reduction, and especially the introduction of a minimum income. Only users with the fullest of their physical and psychical faculties can profess active citizenship, thus gaining momentum and making their way into the labour market.

References

Aznar, Guy (1994): Lavorare meno per lavorare tutti. Venti proposte, Bollati Boringhieri, Milano

Bergamante, Francesca/Marocco, Manuel (2014): "Lo Stato dei servizi pubblici per l'impiego in Europa: tendenze, conferme, sorprese" ISFOL

Berton, Fabio/Richiardi, Matteo G./Sacchi, Stefano (2009): Flex-insecurity. Perché in Italia la flessibilità diventa precarietà, Il Mulino, Bologna

Bratti, Cecchi e De Blasio (2008): Does the Expansion of Higher Education Increase the Equality of Educational Opportunities? Evidence from Italy, Banca d'Italia, Roma

Caroleo, Floro E./Pastore, Francesco (2011): Talking about the Pigou Paradox. Socio-Educational Background and Educational Outcomes of AlmaLaurea, in: International Journal of Manpower, Vol. 33, No. 1, pp. 27-50

Cavarra, Roberto/Rella, Piera/ Rossotti, Ludovica/Bergamante, Francesca/Canal, Tiziana (2015): Il lavoro in crisi. Trasformazioni del capitalismo e ruolo dei soggetti, Aracne, Ariccia

Di Nicola, Patrizio (2009): I lavoratori atipici tra flessibilità e precariato, in: Di Nicola, Rosati (Eds.) Visioni sul futuro delle organizzazioni, Guerini, Milano

Fasano, Andrea (2017): L'incontro tra domanda e offerta di lavoro nel mercato del lavoro regionale pugliese, in AA.VV., Future in research. La sfida dell'Università del Salento, Tangram Edizioni Scientifiche, Trento

Gallino, Luciano (2007): Il lavoro non è una merce. Contro la flessibilità, Laterza Bari

Garofano, Tonia/Spattini, Silvia (2011): Rinnovato slancio all'integrazione tra politiche attive e passive nell'accordo Stato-Regioni per una nuova fase nella gestione della crisi, in: Bollettino Adapt 20

Gianturco, Giovanna (2004): L'intervista qualitativa, dal discorso al testo scritto, Guerino Studio, Milano

Greer, Scott L./Wismar, Matthias/Figueras, Josep (Eds.) (2016): Strengthening Health System Governance: Better policies, stronger performance, Maidenhead: Open University Press

ILO (2015): Global Employment Trends for Youth 2015

ISFOL (2016): Rapporto di monitoraggio sui servizi per il lavoro 2015, Fondo sociale europeo, Ministero del Lavoro e delle Politiche Sociali

ISTAT (2016): Rapporto annuale del 2016. La situazione del Paese, www.istat.it

Italia Lavoro e Ministero del lavoro (2014): "Mappa degli standard di qualità dei placement universitari", Formazione e Innovazione per l'Occupazione Scuola e Università, www. Italialavoro.it

Meuleman, Louis (2008): Public Management and the Metagovernance of Hierarchies, Networks and Markets: The Feasibility of Designing and Managing Governance Style Combinations, Heidelberg: Physica-Verlag

OECD (2013): Employment Outlook, OECD Publishing, http://dx.doi.org/10.1787/empl_outlook2013-en

Pastore, Francesco (2013): I servizi per l'impiego nell'ottica delle transizioni scuola lavoro. Un'analisi comparata, FORMEZ, Roma

Pastore Francesco (2015): The Youth Experience Gap. Explaining National Differences in the School-to-Work Transition, Physica Verlag, Heidelberg

Raffe, David (2008): The Concept of Transition System, in: Journal of Education and Work, Vol. 21, No. 4, pp. 277-296

Vesan, Patrik (2016): Reforming the unreformable. Path departures in labour market policies and the new course of Italian politics, in: Paper presented at the Italian Political Science Society Conference. Vol. 15

Weishaupt, J. Timo (2011): "Social Partners and the Governance of Public Employment Services: Trends and Experiences from Western Europe", ILO, Geneva, working document No. 17, May

APPENDIX

Results

To carry out the monitoring and subsequent evaluation of the services, reference was made to a map of quality standards built by Italia Lavoro[8] and the Ministry of Labour in collaboration with FIXO (2014).

Through a funnel process, a summary map of the service map was first created and then the services offered by each employment centre were identified and, where possible, included in the categories of Italia Lavoro (Tab. 1).

In addition to the description of what services are available in Public Job Centres, Private Employment Agencies, Training Institutes and University Orientation and Placement Services, the goal we have is to identify the best practice for each standard and particularly those that can be exported from one territory to another.

---

[8] Italia Lavoro, the former agency for Active Labour Market Policies (now replaced by ANPAL) involves 15 services, but the "technology transfer service" and "quality assurance service" have not been analysed as we did not have enough information to evaluate its presence in Lazio universities.

Table 1   Summary map of quality "Italia Lavoro": typology and services provided

Category	Service provided
1-Knowledge	Database companies and organisations
	Information on local labour market dynamics
	Information about the professional needs of companies also through meetings at companies
2-Communication	Website updated with information on placement services and career guidance
	Publication of an updated charter of placement services -map of services, facilities and operators
	Provide a public communication plan to promote the dissemination of services to students/graduates/firms
3-Marketing	Perform an analysis of the services offered by identifying the criticalities and strengths to be developed
	Individual meetings with businesses to promote the services offered
	Organise meetings of business presentation
	Regularly send e-mails throughout the year to promote activities
	Maintain stable relationships with businesses
4-Network and Participation	Plan and manage and develop stable relationships with public and private services
	Plan and manage and develop relationships between faculties, departments and research centres within the university
	Collaboration with disability services
5-Access	Internal signage is suitable for identifying services in multiple languages
	The presence of a billboard/bulletin board contains a service map
	Ensure different modes of access to services: direct, phone, portal, e-mail
	Distribute the workload among the staff members, communicate the timetables

6-Reception and information	Presence of a space equipped for waiting for users	
	Presence of a fully equipped space for post-consultation	
	Presence of a space equipped for the reception	
	Presence of a bulletin board for training and working opportunities	
	The service accepts requests for information by mail and responds within two days	
7-Custom design	Presence of a space for individual interviews	
	Appointment in five days	
	In the first interview, the service must provide a service agreement regarding the use of the servants and the obligations of the user	
	The service needs to make an analysis of the user's needs from experience, ability	
	The service must arrange with the user a custom plan	
	Provide user target definition to activate custom actions	
	Assign users that require a referring operator to establish a custom report	
8-Mediation of demand/supply	Updating staff requests also published online - spread of job opportunities	
	Provide matching application/supply tools	
	The service organises selection talks to be carried out by employers, schedules the calendar of meetings	
9-Training	To achieve information and training on job search techniques (CV processing ...)	
	Report to students and graduates the training opportunities offered by other subjects	
	Communicate through the web or mailing list the planning of organised training meetings	
10-Measures and tools	The service identifies an educational tutor designated by the university to ensure the quality of internships	
	Provide trainee information about the host company	

		Provide trainee with ongoing assistance even during the course of the business trip
		Monitoring and evaluation of apprenticeship and apprenticeship activities
		Evaluation together with the host company of the activities carried out
11-Technology Transfer Services		Favouring technologies transfer services
		Organise courses on the management and economic enhancement of research results by collaborating with academic structures
		Disclosure of the results of the research at the various offices of the university to define the actions to be carried out
12-Support for business creation		Organise three-four individual talks on self-entrepreneurial orientation
		Providing individual consultancy to assist users in the start-up and spin-off creation and development phase
		Organising initiatives for business creation
13-Staff Requirements and Skills		Service with at least two qualified personnel with appropriate skills
		Annual training and updating of staff
14-Monitoring and evaluation		Annual assessment and monitoring actions with periodic cadence
		Carry out an annual assessment survey of users, whether they are individuals and regarding businesses and customer satisfaction
		Make known and periodically publish data, information and reports on the services provided and the results obtained
15-Quality Assurance		Have a computerised archive of updated user data
		Adopt a quality assurance system and provide feedback on performance outcomes

2. Knowledge

In the first category of knowledge (Tab. 1) two services of the three provided by "Italia Lavoro" have been identified: to provide a database of companies and organisations and to carry out events in the company.

The first one is present in almost all universities, but Sapienza is the best because it was the promoter and has created a system that is self-feeding: the initial effort of contacting businesses has worked so well that it is now businesses and organisations themselves which contact the university.

A best practice that has already been exported to the various universities and has returned concrete results. The same cannot be said, unfortunately, for public employment centres and public training institutes, especially those from Lazio are paying for the chaos that they are experiencing in the transition from province to region. This has consequences for the managers and operators, regarding how much work they need to manage.

This means that the database in Lazio is centralised but still under definition, resulting in situations like those of the Public Job Centre in Tivoli, where software and software equipment are scarce.

The Public Job Centre in Fabriano represents a different situation, because the database was ingeniously constructed, using mail from compulsory communications on company recruitment. A best practice to advice on Public Job Centre's Lazio.

The Private Employment Agencies, having their own website manage the issue with more convenience and autonomy.

Instead, for corporate events, starting from University Orientation and Placement Services, which is a practice promoted by Sapienza, Tor Vergata and LUISS. The latter is characterised by being active on an international scale by meeting prestigious companies such as Google in Dublin or bringing students to visit the European Community. It must be borne in mind that unfortunately not all students have the economic opportunities to pay for such a trip, nor do all universities have funds from which they can draw. Therefore, this is a non-exportable service from one university to another.

Public agencies are very heterogeneous in nature. It goes from Monterotondo's Public Job Centre that boasts of having a loyalty to companies for 10-15 years, to the Tiburtino, Tivoli and Catanzaro's Public Job Centres who complain that there are few companies that come to them because they are not aware of public agencies activity.

A situation that can only be improved through a territorial animation by Public Job Centres, as the operators of the centres in Tiburtino, Cerveteri and Tivoli say. Unfortunately, what is missing are the economic resources and extra staff - *"We should have at least three times the staff that we have now"*[9] (Tiburtino's Operator Public Job Centres).

Singular, but true of the Italian approach to the labour market, are the words of Pomezia's operator who states that contact is mostly through word-of-mouth.

On the same line is the operator of the Colleferro Public Job Centres. He says that companies search by word of mouth to recruit staff and only when they do not find any in their circle do they turn to Public Job Centres. This is a widespread practice in Italy, especially in job search, as ISFOL data points out that 80% of people are searching informally to find employment (ISFOL 2015).

Colleferro and Trebisacce's Public Job Centres say that they have a very active collaboration, however it is always Fabriano's Public Job Centre which has an edge over the other centres by creating a blog through which the demands of many companies are taken into consideration.

In reality, as revealed by a Primavalle operator's Public Job Centre, it is provided by the Legislative Decree N°150 of 2015 that the Public Job Centre in order to create territorial animation by going to companies to promote services.

However, the problem is not the ineffectiveness of those who work in the Public Job Centres, but the slowness of those who govern all the agencies. As stated by one operator: "It is something about to take off. We are waiting for the Region to give the green light" (Public Job Centres Primavalle)[10].

As far as training organisations are concerned, they do not have events at the company, but Forma-Tec's operator states: *"Strategic knowledge of the labour market and strong networking capabilities have enabled us to offer businesses*

---

9 "Dovremmo essere almeno il triplo rispetto adesso" (Operatore Centro per l'impiego di Tiburtino)
10 "E' una cosa che sta per partire. Stiamo attendendo che la Regione ci dia l'input" (Operatore Centro per l'impiego di Primavalle).

immediately consultancy and integrated training services modelled on the reference context and managed in extremely flexible ways" (operator's Formatec).[11]

3. Communication

At the level of communication in general, all universities invest a lot even beyond the standards set by "Italia Lavoro" (Fig.1). We therefore have to point out interesting ways of delivery that can be safely adopted by other universities.

As far as the website is concerned, all universities except Tuscia keep it up to date. Tor Vergata also has the opportunity to apply for Bachelor's Degrees or scholarships, while Sapienza has a good communication strategy to attract users (teachers, students and businesses) by using social networks too.

The idea of the Foro Italico of making registration compulsory for everyone is ingenious with the purpose of making the service known and accompanied by a press review of particular events.

LUMSA is characterised by a special focus on the dissemination of NEET (not engaged in education, employment or training*)* services for job offers, including leaflets and flyers. Lastly, a major action is taken by LUISS; in order to reach more students and graduates, they use student representatives who move on other channels besides the canons.

The Lazio Public Job Centres have a "RomaLabour' institutional site. This is a platform where the various job offers are uploaded and the services provided are reported. According to the interviewees' words, it is not very effective as the name is less intuitive, people looking for work on the internet use words as "placement" or "employment centre", which do not address you to the proper website.

Also for this service, it is the insufficient economic resources which prevent realisation.

---

11 La conoscenza strategica del mercato del lavoro e la forte capacità di networking ci hanno permesso di offrire da subito alle aziende consulenza e servizi formativi integrati e modellati sul contesto di riferimento e gestiti con modalità estremamente flessibili" (Operatore Formatec).

"There was a time when they made little advertising, but now there is no more money! Therefore, they stopped. We do not even have any brochures to distribute. There are no funds."(Tiburtino's operator Public Job Centres).[12]

An assessment that even the users we interviewed share: "As far the service evaluation is concerned, *I would give it five points over ten, which is just sufficient enough, because services and communication should greatly improve their efficiency*" (as reported by a user of Primavalle Public Job Centres).[13]

There are those who seek alternative and customised solutions such as the Cerveteri Public Job Centre that through job advisers sends e-mails to sponsor services. Nevertheless, the operator says, to promote itself, that the main instrument to be known remains the "word of mouth", while the Velletri Public Job Centre uses the "door to door" model to get in touch with companies.

Instead, Fabriano's Public Job Centre is more advanced and has created a blog for communication with companies, with two distinct communication channels. A mailing list compiled based on the database of companies present in the territory to send communications to, and the other channel is a newsletter, used only by companies that have expressed interest in becoming a party to which newsletters about recruitment and regional competitions are sent.

Private Employment Agencies have a personal website that allows them to manage their services, as they deem appropriate.

Training institutions all have a website, and most also use social networks, especially Facebook. Interestingly, the proposal of the training institution "Formulatec" that has placed a dedicated page on its website where it is possible to send a spontaneous application, although it emphasises the importance of word-of-mouth.

4. Marketing

According to the standards of "Italia Lavoro" (Fig.1), the first factor in the Marketing category is to carry out an analysis of the services offered by identifying

---

[12] "C'è stato un momento in cui hanno fatto piccole pubblicità, ma adesso non ci stanno più soldi! E quindi hanno smesso. Non abbiamo nemmeno più brochure da poter distribuire. Non ci sono fondi" (Operatore centro per l'impiego di Tiburtino).
[13] "Gli darei 5 perché riguardo i servizi e la comunicazione dovrebbero migliorare tantissimo" (Utente Centro per l'impiego di Primavalle).

the criticalities and strengths to be developed. In particular, with regard to the criticalities, Sapienza indicated the shortage of funding to carry out the SOUL project and to stabilise the operators and Tor Vergata.

This latter aspect is a strong point for Tuscia, and the two private universities. The Foro Italico considers it necessary to improve the professional skills of the operators because they are the main actors regarding the efficiency of the service.

As far as the other marketing services are concerned, as with "international business meetings', LUISS is virtually the only one that also issues an EQUIS certificate. As already pointed out there is a resource problem for the exportability of this service.

There are no particular differences between universities for organising events with Italian companies (recruiting days, career days, business presentations) and maintaining stable relationships with businesses. Lastly, the interview simulation activity offered by LUISS, an easily exportable best practice, is also interesting.

Critical points, which are shared among all Public Job Centres, is the scarcity of resources in terms of workforce, so there is a need to increase the number of operators and the low level of economic support, both of which are fundamental to publicise and make the services offered known. Additionally, there is a shortage of training courses for users and workers themselves. In addition, managers and operators complain about the lack of systematic and clear information provided by the superiors. This forces them to deal with new issues without having adequate training and time to upgrade, as the chairman of the Monterotondo Public Job Centres says. This is also borne out by the users who, while underscoring the availability and friendliness of the operators, at the same time disclose the lack of knowledge of practices and laws.

On the same line, Private Employment Agencies complain about the variety of regulations in the 21 Italian regions, according to different cities, as claimed by a Seha Fresia director, who also underlines a scant cooperation with the Public Job Centres.

Similarly, Private Employment Agencies are critical of companies that are not always collaborative and they still use labour search tools that are outdated. An opposite view comes from the Private Employment Agency Adecco, who boasts of having different partnerships with companies.

In addition, Public Job Centres' names are considered not representative of reality, due to the low effectiveness in facilitating meetings between supply and demand. Randastad Torino's operator also states that Private Employment Agencies are seen as agencies that only provide temporary employment relationships.

This is also evident from our analysis whereby most agencies declare their business to be rooted in fixed-term employment contracts or internships.

The training institutions collaborate mainly with private companies, including cooperatives, for which they organise courses for the safety of employees. This takes places by a specific choice of working policy, which finances the training courses related to internship, for an eventual recruitment.

It should be noted that the public training institution also works with private companies, most of which are small businesses: "*With the onset of the crisis, the companies that contact us directly to offer jobs are declining ... The only ones to do so were only the shopkeepers in the area mainly in the field of aesthetics* "(operator of Adriatic training institution).[14]

Erifo also works in partnership with the public administration, in particular with the regions, facilitating access to European funds, a work that is undoubtedly precious.

5. Network and participation

Among the most relevant services in the network category and participation there is the collaboration with the Public Employment Offices that is practiced differently for almost all universities: with Sapienza and Roma Three sharing the same physical space, allowing a very close collaboration. Above all, Roma Tre employs most of the guidance services at the Public Job Centres. At Luiss, however, the collaboration is less strict: a Public Job Centre representative goes to the university once a week. As far as active labour policies are concerned, there is collaboration with the Lazio Region and all the universities in the National Guarantee Programs and Returns.

---

14 "Con l'inizio della crisi sono diminuite le aziende che ci contattano in maniera diretta per offrire posti di lavoro... Gli unici a farlo sono rimasti solo i negozianti della zona prevalentemente nel campo dell'estetica" (operatore Ente di Formazione Adriatico).

It is also important to network between universities. The SOUL project was born at Sapienza with the intention of joining forces through networking of multiple subjects to better enhance the skills of graduates and move into the tough world of work by promoting more services that are integrated and encouraging close collaboration to get work opportunities even in the most difficult cases.

A philosophy contrasted with that of private universities, where the services are destined only to their graduates, with whom it seems to argue the scientific responsibility of Sapienza that emphasises:

"Open service - better to compete than to compete .... We also offer services to students from other universities; here the problem is occupation of graduates not of graduates Sapienza"(scientific responsibility of Sapienza). [15]

Collaboration between Public Job Centres and university Orientation and Placement Services and the dissemination of the "Young Guarantee" program has reignited in many young people the desire to reactivate and consequently go to the Public Job Centres and this has definitely affected their services. For example, this has been the case with the EURES program, an international program whose administrative practices are entrusted to Public Job Centres.

Weaker cooperation with companies, which apart from the aforementioned Fabriano's example, in other Public Job centres is stalling to take off.

A program created by the Randstand employment private agency, that offers a characteristic service called PES, which is equivalent to active work policies: work orientation, job alternation, and youth liaison with traineeships, start-up and delivery work. A model that synergises the various programs and policies.

At international training programs involving only the two entities: Forma-tec ed Erifo which also define research institutions. However, Form-tec uses "a network of partners' (external providers, professionals, teachers, language schools or computing) to reach the firms for postgraduate placements.

Employment private agency, rather than being linked to the Youth Guarantee program they host trainees internally coming from the program.

An informal level is also the most abnormal training institution, AIESEC, we wonder if it is really a training institution or a fake non-profit organisation that it

---

15 "Servizio aperto - meglio collaborare che competere.... Offriamo servizi anche agli studenti degli altri atenei, qui il problema è di occupazione dei laureati non dei laureati Sapienza" (responsabile scientifico della Sapienza).

seeks to exploit of the employment difficulties of young university students, asking them money to do an internship.

Finally, the training institution in the province of Latina emphasises the importance of direct contact with companies: "We go to the company... because talking in person is different, furthermore we can give more information, and we try to establish a relationship of trust "(Training institution Sezze).[16]

The collaboration with Employment Job Centres takes place in a stable way only in combination with the public training institution, which recognises the importance of networking to better serve the users.

6. Access

This is the last category of organisational features for which "Italia Lavoro" are offered, which facilitates user access.

According to what operators and privileged witnesses have said, Tor Vergata, Sapienza, Foro Italico and Luiss use different services in addition to mail, including social networks such as Facebook or Twitter. It should be extended to other universities, as it is a service that is not difficult to apply.

However, as for the division of labour, all universities have operators sharing the workload, but Sapienza has thought of doing so based on thematic areas.

If a large university such as Sapienza manages to divide work into thematic areas, it should not be difficult to do so in other universities, except in those cases that have only two operators.

To profit from the services of the Public Job Centres, it is necessary to go directly to the Centre. It is possible to consult the services provided through the website but in order to bid for the offers it is necessary to go first to a Public Job Centre.

A procedure which might appear old-fashioned, but which in reality favours the contact with people the importance of being included and especially the activation of the subject in being able to discover his own attitude towards a career.

---

[16] "Andiamo in azienda...parliamoci chiaro di persona è diverso, a parte che gli possiamo dare più informazioni, ma poi cerchiamo di instaurare anche un rapporto di fiducia" (FB Sezze).

All those features that are lost when sitting alone in front of a computer to send curricula around, which are usually ignored. As it is the case for Private Employment Agencies who use their own website, the unemployed can sign up here for a job interview without having to go to the agency.

From the organisational point of view, therefore, active labour policies are not well organised, in fact, there is no clear definition of public and private tasks, such as those of different employment services, neither are they sufficiently funded.

7. Reception and information

Now we will illustrate how the user may or may not find it easy to use various services.

As far as the reception area is concerned, all universities, except the Luiss, have a reception desk, especially Sapienza, which has expanded into branches far away from the old campus, in which we find different employment services.

Sapienza together with Roma Tre are fortunate to share the spaces with the Public Job Centres, so they have the opportunity to cooperate closely by providing a 360-degree service. This is definitely a best practice but perhaps not of immediate feasibility.

On the other hand a very ingenious service which could be exported, it is provided by Luiss, as defined by the responsible of the university.

"An interactive calendar, a recently addition, where the students can sign up to different events by clicking directly on its date and choosing the events most interesting to them" (responsible of the University of Luiss).[17]

This is a modality, which can be found also on the website of Porta Futuro's Public Job Centres, which could be extended to other universities and employment centres.

Finally, all universities provide a response channel for users' different requests, with Tuscia declaring it will respond within five days (standard of Italia Lavoro provide a response within two days). The same cannot be said of all the agencies

---

17 "Un calendario interattivo, una cosa che abbiamo fatto da pochissimo, dove i ragazzi si possono registrare a degli eventi dedicati cliccando direttamente sulla data e sull'evento che è più interessante per loro e inserendo ovviamente quelli che sono i loro dati" (Responsabile dell'Università LUISS).

for work that are overloaded by administrative burdens and they are not always able to respond quickly.

Training organisations have multiple channels of communication with users, but only in the case of Capodarco do they offer real psychological support. However, if Forma-tec believes that it has "consolidated and efficient services" Erifo complains that the administrations involved in a training course constrain them too much, for example, already prepared users need to take too long courses: they do not allow for personalised design.

8. Custom design

Job quality standards in "Italia Lavoro" provide a customised project, a space for individual interviews and with a reference operator's program. In this field, more or less all the universities have fantasied in predicting interesting activities. The personalised interview at the University of Tuscia was done with a psychological help desk and at Lumsa with a job psychologist while the other private university aims to raise soft skills by inviting students to participate in volunteer activities during their studies.

It would be important for all universities to secure such activities that are difficult to export for economic or personnel shortcomings. Instead, easy-to-use best practices are the services offered by Sapienza on the differentiation of disciplinary activity, and by Lumsa and Tor Vergata, which aim to identify their reference target.

A service that would be important for all universities is the promotion of women, as Luiss does in conjunction with the VALUE D association, where women's managerial skills are strengthened. Finally, Tuscia in addition to providing psychological support, has also a desk-service for students who find it difficult to look for the right career path and when using the online services.

9. Mediation of demand/supply

As far as mediation between supply and demand is concerned, all universities publish job offers, except for Roma Tre, which calls for vacancy issues for the Public Job Centres. Besides it is <u>important</u> to pay <u>attention</u> to <u>the quality</u> of the employment offers published. A service mainly performed by the University of Foro Italico, through the scouting activity concerning the most interesting job demands for graduates. Almost all universities support companies by explaining how the platform works, but LUMSA also helps them submit a job request.

There are also three easy-to-export activities. The first concerns the monitoring of the company to check that the student is actually entrusted with the job for which he has been nominated; otherwise, the company is placed on a black list. The second is the control of advertisements published by Foro Italico and Tor Vergata to make sure it is not a brokerage agency and finally Tuscia claims that the company should interview all candidates who request it, so that everyone has an answer to their application.

For Public Job Centres in addition to the already mentioned blogs and databases of Fabriano, it is also worth mentioning the group paths activated in Pomezia and Portafuturo Public Job Centres that help to *"create the first network that is then the main thing to help you find work"*(Operator of Public Job Centres Pomezia).[18] This is because group paths are based on a series of seminars aimed at the same target of people who will find themselves for a period of time sharing the same difficulties and concerns as they look for work. When working groups are over, people often keep in touch while continuing to exchange job information.

In addition, another interesting service is provided by the Marino CPI, which carries out the pre-selection section in their premises to monitor the company's conversations.

10. Training

In the field of Education, all universities, except Roma Tre, offer users training services, which can be done in at universities. An example is found in Lumsa where the student is assisted by writing the curriculum to the role sought by the company. Just as in Tor Vergata's work, orientation seminars on how to look for work over the Internet and how to support an interview are offered. While, the University of Italic Forum, provides continuous counselling for the course of study and student preferences in anticipation of future professional choices.

---

18 "Creare il primo network che poi è la cosa principale per aiutarti a trovare lavoro" (Operatore CPI Pomezia).

The activities mentioned in this category can be carried out in all the universities in many Employment Centres and Private Employment Agencies.

Training is obviously the main activity of training institutions, which also carry out orientation activities and balance of skills, as well as treating the inclusion of disadvantaged people from a psychological and social point of view.

On the other hand, some job agencies do not only assist in finding work (like a training institution Conform, but also in job placement (Private Employment Agencies Speha Fresia) and finding temporary workers.

11. Measures and tools

This category includes all activities related to internships, one of the major ways of working at a university.

However, only a few universities offer some interesting services. For example, Roma Tre, Tuscia and Luiss provide the intern with information about the company and the tasks to be carried out. In addition, above all, Roma Tre and Lumsa have a trained apprentice assistant with the aim of helping the student organise themselves in the studio / work alternation (Lumsa) and to support trainees and companies with a front office (Roma Tre). Both services are important and should be adopted by all universities. Even more crucial is the final assessment of the apprenticeship by the student, the company and the academic tutor. Unfortunately, not all the universities succeed in doing so because of the organisational effort it requires, but it would be useful, as Roma Tre does, to send an email to the company by inviting it to compile a card to assess whether the graduate had the necessary skills and whether he was offered work afterwards.

In general, the Public Job Centres, are not expected to follow the user, because, the operators explain, the people who turn to the centre are so many that you cannot succeed in assisting them all, and also for companies it is an unnecessary administrative burden.

Different situations for traineeships, where it is required to send an informal assessment to see if the trainee is exploited, that is, if it actually carries out the job for which it has been applied. Only in the Marino's Public Job Centres, the evaluation is more structured since it is required both by the trainee and the company.

A best practice that should be exported to other Public Job Centres. This can only be done by enhancing the informatics part, still very weak in Public Job Centres.

Most Private Employment Agencies follow the user and at the same time ask for feedback from the company. Fabiano's Private Employment Agencies rank the most deserving users to understand which are the best for selection and presentation to the companies. The agency's work, therefore, is not limited to the matching of demand / supply, but continues through an on-the-job check on the worker, so he receives feedback on his work.

In general, the training institutions follow the trainee with a tutor. Only Formatec calls for a final evaluation through specific questionnaires, a practice that should be widespread.

12. Support for business creation

On enterprise creation, the only university offering services is Sapienza, which includes seminars on start-up and development. Being able to profit from your skills and the different years of study in a project is a further opportunity for those who have ideas but do not know how to develop them. It is therefore appropriate for other universities to equip themselves in such a way or at least to make known and recognise the service offered by Sapienza.

Form-tec is the only one that offers start-up services for an entrepreneurial initiative.

13. Staff Requirements and Skills

A diverse number of training methods emerges from research, in addition to differences in the number of operators. Universities where operators are all graduates: are Sapienza, Foro Italico and Luiss; the last two also boast operators who have also followed master students. The variety and mode of distribution of the services offered, points out that the acquisition of more study by the operators actually determines the difference in the services offered. However, this is not enough, it is also important to have initial and ongoing training. The only two universities where operators have received continuing education are Lumsa and Forum Italico.

Strengthening training of the operator is important if you want to be able to cope with the difficult working situation of our society. This also applies to the contractual framing that unfortunately for some of them is still a collaboration making it difficult to carry out the work itself and paradoxically risking it being placed under the same conditions as the users who are addressing it. Finally, it should be noted that if there are at least two operators per university as required by Italia Lavoro standards, six operators for a university such as Sapienza with over 100,000 students are not enough, when compared to much smaller universities.

As we have seen on several occasions, the limited staff also affects Public Job Centre. While the contractual situation is better than university Public Job Centres because they are all contracted for an indefinite period, having entered the competition several years ago. At the time of recruitment, high level qualifications were not required, although many practitioners, often in an autonomous way, did master or completed training courses to specialise. Instead, a Private Employment Agencies, have operators graduated and/or with a master. Furthermore, a Private Employment Agencies organises continuous training course for operators and organise a continuous training for the operators.

In training institutions, there is no precise figure for the presence of external operators and consultants in particular between the teachers: however, it ranges from six to 50 employees. Only in the case of Form-tec where there is a stabilisation policy, are there definite employee numbers.

Respondents and practitioners of training organisations, are generally female, graduated in psychology, and feel sufficiently prepared. A separate case is that of the coordinator of Erifo who devotes at least two to three weeks a year to training and design and research activities. He notes: *"To get to work here you have to have a master and you must master at least two languages"*.

14. Monitoring and evaluation

The last category considered, but certainly not last in importance are Monitoring and Evaluating Services: "Italia Lavoro" requires an annual assessment, starting from periodic monitoring actions. La Sapienza, in collaboration with the Ministry of Labour, has activated a project for the compulsory labour market analysis from 2012, as well as monitoring what companies are in contact with.

The University of Luiss instead makes constant tracking of results through its research institute.

This service alongside the production of reports produced in all the universities, which for the universities that deal with the Job Soul platform are semi-annual, with the only difference that Sapienza has published several reports with the Ministry of Labour who report the situation of their services since the SOUL project began.

The largest Italian university (Sapienza), has been engaged in this field for a long time and has a scientific manager of the project, therefore a professor, and this allows a better interweaving of the third mission[19] with that of research.

The Public Job Centres monitoring the work have often been taken up by different institutions and research organisations such as ISFOL. However, the lack of a unique national database makes partial analysis and comparison. It would be advisable to intervene as soon as possible in order to identify the various criticalities in a short time and to export virtuous models from one territory to another.

---

19 The third mission of university is: promote the diffusion of knowledge and technologies to contribute to the social, economic and cultural development of society. While the first two goals are training and research.

2. HIERARCHY AND MARKET AS DOMINANT GOVERNANCE MODES

The Importance of Governance in the Regional Labour Market Monitoring for Evidence-based Policy-making: Basque Country Case

Javier Ramos Salazar

1. Introduction

In relation to the governance model in the Basque labour market monitoring, according to the approach of Considine and Lewis (2003), we can situate it as a combination of typologies: hierarchy and network.

Hierarchy: the Basque Government is the competent entity in the definition and management of statistical operations on a population in relation to the activity, and administrative records that regulate labour activity (labour contracts, offers, job applications, etc.). Both informative contents are the main source of quantitative information on the labour market and the pillars of labour information policy. It is regulated by specific regulations and its data models are compatible with international classifications of activity and occupation. Its dissemination is public although access to disaggregated data (microdata) is restricted. At the same time, the government has an important function of producing qualitative information on different areas of productive activity and the labour market, mainly in the form of monographic reports with different frequency.

Network: the Basque Government negotiates and brokers interests between different actors in the development of quantitative-qualitative information of various natures: socio-labour context, groups, sectors, occupations, etc. This working formula is based on the participation of the government in the total or partial financing of this information. The manifestations of this collaboration are varied, from exclusive financing to the prescription of the contents and scope of the information to be elaborated, being able to be developed by mixed teams of public-private personnel. The identification of the themes to be developed can be promoted both from public and private initiative.

The five major dimensions of governance in the Basque Country's labour market monitoring that constitute the "TAPIC framework" (Greer et al. 2016) establish the following quality criteria:

- Transparency: the uses of public information sources, and their uses as an argument and justification in the different reports produced by entities, guarantee the principle of transparency in decision-making in the labour market. All the actors in the labour market access common basic sources.
- Accountability: decision-making on the determination of the information policy, its contents and its application depends to a large extent on the ownership of the necessary information or, if applicable, the capacity to finance its preparation. In this sense, it is the incumbent entities and / or funders that require explanations and approve or refuse the elaboration of different specialised information contents.
- Participation: in most cases information on the labour market has the role of an argument or justification for the decisions of related actions. We have developed formulas for participation and consultation in the construction of information models by the actors involved, public administration, collaborating entities in the execution of actions, companies specialised in the provision of information and communication services. Channels of suggestions and contributions between the actors involved are kept open.
- Integrity: the processes of obtaining and disseminating quantitative information (statistics and administrative records) are guaranteed, supervised by the administration and subject to their audits. Information of a qualitative nature or based either on objective evidence or, where appropriate, subjective expert knowledge may influence decision making and are not subject to public auditing.
- Capacity: satisfaction measurement systems are used to assess the quality and relevance of information products. Use monitoring systems are also used, especially when the information uses web dissemination formats.

The governance model for the employment policy in the Basque Country's labour market is conditioned by the state legislative framework (the Constitution, ordinary and organic laws, legislative decrees and regulations). The institutional set-up of the Spanish State, and the aforementioned legal system, significantly determines this monitoring and governance model in the Basque

Country. To summarise, it should be noted that we are in a sphere of competence applied to the management of the state legislation and the development of specific legislation and instrumental aspects embodying it.

Therefore, governance of the labour market in the Basque Country involves its application to:

- The employment policy;
- The Basque Employment System, of which the Basque employment network is a part of.

2. Employment policy

A "results/evidence-based" analysis of the employment policy and its main economic impacts has led us to consider that the solution of its main objective, the problem of unemployment, does not exclusively depend on employment policy, but rather jointly depends on policies of which it is a subsidiary: passive employment policies, job security provisions, work agreements, fiscal policies, macro-economic policy, etc. In turn, if the employment context does not lead to an increase in labour demand, the active employment policies (AEP) will simply redistribute the existing jobs.

It is very complicated to establish the impact that active employment policies have, beyond their labour insertion results, due to the different and sometimes conflicting directions that many of its effects take. This is a sphere where the labour market observatories must continue to delve into in order to support the decision regarding the type of employment policies to be used at any time and in any country.

Focusing on employment policy in the Basque Country, the Central Government has legislative competence regarding employment and the Autonomous Communities are responsible for its enforcement. The National Employment System (SNE) consists of the set of structures and measures to develop the employment policy. It is made up of the State Public Employment Service (SEPE) and the Public Employment Services of the autonomous communities.

The instruments used by the SNE are as follows:

- Spanish Employment Strategy. It is prepared in conjunction with the autonomous communities and the social stakeholders.
- Annual Employment Policy Plan. It contains the employment active policy actions and measures implemented by the Autonomous Communities and by the Spanish State to meet the goals set in the strategy.
- Information System of the Public Employment Services.

In this state framework, the Basque Country is implementing its employment policy in a "system" with different spheres of action.

3. Basque Employment System

The Basque Employment System is taken to be the set of structures, measures and actions needed to foster and develop the employment policy in the sphere of the Basque Country. It should be noted that this System is de facto and is not underpinned by a legal system that identifies it as such. Its functions are to:

- Apply the Basque Employment Strategy, through the Annual Employment Policy Plan, which will establish targets that allow the results and effectiveness of employment policies to be assessed.
- Cooperate with the SEPE by coordinating passive and active employment policies.
- Adapt LANBIDE, the Basque Employment Service, to the needs of the labour market.
- Inform, propose and recommend to the different Public Administration about issues related to active employment policies.
- Analyse the labour market in the different sectors of activity and territorial sphere in order to bring adapt employment policies to their needs.
- Set up and keep up-to-date a catalogue of services for the general public, which includes the common ones set by the SEPE and the specific added ones in the BAC, by always guaranteeing access on a level playing field to a free and public employment service.

This system pursues a series of objectives to determine governance:

- Establish the principles that must underpin the intervention of Basque public institutions regarding employment.

- Regulate the structures and instruments to foster and develop employment policies, and establishing mechanisms that allow the Basque public action regarding employment to be planned and coordinated.

4. Guiding principles of employment policy areas

- Comprehensive, local dimensions and overcoming territorial imbalances.
- Efficiency and effectiveness in the provision of services, guaranteeing their quality, being free and coordination of them.
- Social inclusion and cohesion.
- The effective level playing field when accessing employment, with a total absence of discrimination due to any condition or social or personal circumstance.
- Permanent dialogue with social stakeholders.
- Increase of the level of employment, of its stability and its quality.
- The proactive and preventive treatment of unemployment and personalised service.
- Universal access to active lifelong learning in order to improve professional skills and employability.
- Fostering business initiatives for self-employment and start-ups, particularly in the social economy.
- Ensuring an efficient system to deal with unemployment to guarantee coherence and maximum coordination between active employment policies and public economic benefits.
- The co-responsibility of people and companies.

5. Regulating the structures and instruments to foster and develop employment policies, and establishing mechanisms that allow the Basque public action regarding employment to be planned and coordinated

The Basque public institutions involved in defining, designing, implementing, monitoring and/or assessing employment policies are:

The General Administration of the Autonomous Community of the Basque Country. It exercises the following duties through the department responsible for the field of employment:

- Planning/managing employment policies in the Basque Country.
- Establishing and planning LANBIDE - Basque Employment Service's strategy.
- Preparing the Basque Employment Strategy.
- Proposing employment provisions to the Governing Board.
- Signing territorial or local agreements.

LANBIDE - Basque Employment Service. Managing employment policies, following the strategic planning and guidelines set by the Department responsible for the field of employment.

Provincial Councils and Local Authorities. Both institutions may implement measures to foster employment policies as part of the general employment plan.

These structures of the Basque Country use the following operating, organisation and coordination instruments:

- The Basque Employment Strategy.
- The Lanbide Strategic Plan.
- The Annual Employment Policy Plan.

These instruments in turn have guiding principles in order to function:

- Participation of the most representative trade union and business organisations.
- LANBIDE-SVE is tasked with implementing the active employment policies without prejudice to the cooperation principles that are established with other entities that will act under its coordination. The cooperation of those entities will be aimed at objective criteria of efficiency, quality and specialisation of the entrusted service provision (specified with the social partners).
- Quality in provision of services, fostering ongoing and permanent improvements of the public employment services to adapt to the needs of the labour market, and using new technologies to galvanise change with sufficient material and human resources allocated to ensure a personalised and specialist service for both the job seekers and companies.

Coordinated by LANBIDE-Basque Employment Service and according to the timeline established in the Basque Employment Strategy, the **Basque Employment Network** will include the set of material and human measures, whether public or private, aimed at facilitating the provision of employment services to the general public and Basque companies.

Within the Basque Employment Network, the Basque local and provincial institutions working in employment in the framework of the Agreement signed with LANBIDE, which sets out the terms and areas of the cooperation, will have the status of **cooperating entities.**

Within the Basque Employment Network, those entities that work in the sphere of employment policies and which have been previously authorised will have the status of LANBIDE **partner entities**, according to the established terms.

The authorisations for the partner entities that are part of the Basque Employment Network will establish the terms, areas and scope of the partnership. The funding to which they may be entitled for providing their services will be in line with what is envisaged in the applicable legislation.

These operating mechanisms and structures will underpin the participation of the stakeholders involved in the different components of the active employment policy. Table 1 in the annex explains the participation of the stakeholders in the different employment policies.

6. Specific aspects of governance in the monitoring and preparation of LMI

When monitoring and preparing LMI in the Basque Country, the governance model takes into account the participation of different agents involved in the information policy. Table 2 in the annex describes the different types of information in terms of their use in the labour market, products, final users, sources and format.

7. Final reflections related to the governance of employment policies and their monitoring system

In view of the governance structures and instruments in the Basque Country, the way the different stakeholders are coordinated and the specific aspects of the LMI, the following measures have been identified in order to improve governance:

- Importance of showcasing the information policy as an active employment policy (AEP).
- Need for the employment policy to be linked to the economic promotion policy.
- Relevance to link the AEPs with the general labour/social policies.
- Importance of fostering coordination between institutions.
- Lack of monitoring and effective assessment of the programmes.
- Need to foster the economic and social effectiveness of the money spent.
- Guidance and information: focal point of the AEP policy area.
- Desirability of a common register of participation in AEP. Fostering traceability.
- Desirability to set up a one-stop-window.
- Preferential policy measure groups.
- Need to tailor the policy measures.

References

Considine, Mark/Lewis, Jenny M. (2003): Bureaucracy, Network, or Enterprise? Comparing Models of Governance in Australia, Britain, the Netherlands, and New Zealand, in: Public Administration Review, Vol. 63, No. 2, pp. 131-140

Greer, Scott L./Wismar, Mattias/Figueras, Josep (Eds.) (2016): Strengthening Health System Governance: Better policies, stronger performance, Maidenhead: Open University Press

ANNEX

Table 1 Participation of the different stakeholders in the employment policies

EMPLOYMENT POLICY	BASQUE GOVERNMENT	LANBIDE	PROVINCIAL COUNCILS	LOCAL COUNCILS	BASQUE NETWORK
Guidance	Guidelines and planning of the Dept. of Employment.	Exclusive	No	B*	B
Training	Guidelines and planning of the Departments of: Employment, Education, Economic Development.	Programming and management NO implementation. Monitoring and assessment.	C*	CB, if it has its own structure	B
Information (includes prospecting)	B	Integration point of all information	B	B	B
Self-employment	Ensure the development of a one-stop-shop in this area in the Basque Government	Own programmes. Experimental projects	C	C & B	Specialist "Placement Agency" figure Self-employment
Training and Employment	Guidelines and planning of the Departments of: Employment, Education, Economic Development.	Programming and management NO implementation. Monitoring and assessment.	C	B & C	B
Job creation	Guidelines and planning of the Dept. of Employment.	Programming and management. YES implemented. Monitoring and assessment.	C	C	

EMPLOYMENT POLICY	BASQUE GOVERNMENT	LANBIDE	PROVINCIAL COUNCILS	LOCAL COUNCILS	BASQUE NETWORK
Specialist and general advisory service				C & B (own programmes and third-party programmes)	
Integral action		Own programmes. Experimental projects Funding		A*	A
Brokering	Guidelines and planning of the Dept. of Employment.	Exclusive	B	B	B

LEGEND:

A= Cooperation referred to a time period, based on a shared diagnosis and agreed division in the co-funding and in the activities to be performed by each institution (local and territorial agreements).

B= Cooperation during a time period which the Basque Government - LANBIDE sets for the activity to be carried out, along with the models, guidelines and protocols for action. The other entity, if it wishes to participate and has the sufficient and appropriate measures to do so, performs those activities and in exchange it receives funding according to set scales.

C= Complementary actions to those carried out by Basque Government - LANBIDE that will be coordinated by means of the mechanisms established, in order to avoid duplicates and efficiency losses due to the dispersion of resources in a same type of programmes or measures.

Source: own elaboration.

Table 2   Components of the information policy

INFORMATION TYPE	SUPPLIER/ HOLDER	USERS	FORMAT	PRODUCTS	USE IN LABOUR MARKET MONITORING
Labour force surveys	• EUROSTAT • INE • EUSTAT • BASQUE GOVERNMENT	• Public Administration LANBIDE • Stakeholders/ partners • Universities and social research centres • General public and companies	• Internet • Excel • Csv	• Tables prepared • Microdata • Press releases	• They are used as benchmark and context frameworks of the labour market • Lack of desegregation for their use in active employment policy • Not very representative microdata
Job offers information	• EURES • LANBIDE • PRIVATE WEBSITES • PLACEMENT AGENCY • SEPE	• General public and companies • LANBIDE • Stakeholders/partners • Universities and social research centres	• Internet • Questionnaires • CV	• Offers • Demands • Reports	• Lack of coordination • Clack of representativeness of the set of formalised contracts • Not standard formats. • Lack of skills approach
Labour Market	• EUROSTAT • INE • EUSTAT • MINISTRIES	• Public Administration LANBIDE • Universities and social research centres • General public and companies	• Internet • Excel • Csv	• Tables prepared • Microdata • Press releases	• Variables do not coincide with context statistics • Disperse frequency
Social Security. Registrations	• SOCIAL SECURITY	• Public Administration LANBIDE • Universities and	• Internet • Excel • Csv	• Tables prepared • Microdata	• Difficult to access original database • Basic source to analyse

INFORMATION TYPE	SUPPLIER/ HOLDER	USERS	FORMAT	PRODUCTS	USE IN LABOUR MARKET MONITORING
		social research centres			employment rate
Labour demand	• LANBIDE • PRIVATE WEBSITES • PLACEMENT AGENCY • SEPE	• Public Administration LANBIDE • General public and companies	• Internet • Excel • Csv	• Tables prepared • Press releases	• Main operation of unemployment situation/trends • Data quality can be improved • Lack of skills profiles
Contract register	• LANBIDE • SEPE	• Public Administration LANBIDE • Universities and social research centres	• Internet • Excel • Csv	• Tables prepared • Press releases	• Lack of skills profiles • Consultancy operation cuts • Can be harmonised with statistical operations
Skills	• CEDEFOP • LANBIDE • PRIVATE AND PUBLIC WEBSITES	• Public Administration LANBIDE • Stakeholders/partners • Universities and social research centres • General public and companies	• Internet	• Tables prepared • Press releases	• Lack of information at regional level • Disparity in qualifications • Lack of standards that can be harmonised: technology, organisation, economic
Job placement	• LANBIDE	• Public Administration LANBIDE • Stakeholders/partners • Universities and	• Internet	• University degree and VT qualification reports • Press releases	• Connection between the education system and labour market • Important guidance value. • Primary source of

INFORMATION TYPE	SUPPLIER/ HOLDER	USERS	FORMAT	PRODUCTS	USE IN LABOUR MARKET MONITORING
		social research centres • General public and companies			youth access to the J.M.
Prospecting	• CEDEFOP • LANBIDE • PRIVATE AND PUBLIC WEBSITES	• Public Administration LANBIDE • Stakeholders/partners • Universities and social research centres • General public and companies	• Internet	• Specialist websites	• Emerging situation Diversity of methodological contributions • Difficulty to make qualitative and quantitative models compatible
Sector reports	• MINISTRIES • CLUSTERS • SEPE • UNIVERSITIES	• Public Administration LANBIDE • Stakeholders/partners • Universities and social research centres • General public and companies	• Internet	• Reports	• Response to non-unified strategies • Apply non-unified methodologies • Contemplate the HR chapter heterogeneously
Labour market Context	• MINISTRIES • LANBIDE • SEPE • UNIVERSITIES	• Public Administration LANBIDE • Stakeholders/partners • Universities and social research centres	• Internet	• Reports	• General • Not uniform • Do not provide an assessment • Do not put forward operating proposals

INFORMA-TION TYPE	SUPPLIER/ HOLDER	USERS	FORMAT	PRODUCTS	USE IN LABOUR MARKET MONITORING
		• General public and companies			

Source: own elaboration.

Employment Support Project in Bosnia and Herzegovina

Željko Tepavčević, Siniša Veselinović and Zvjezdana Jelić

1. Introduction

Bosnia and Herzegovina (BiH) is a small middle-income country with a population of nearly 3.8 million. Despite a period of successful recovery following the war in the 1990s, the country has yet to create the basis for sustainable economic growth. The growth performance has been of a mixed nature in recent years. After a relatively strong annual economic growth rate of 5.5% during 2005-2008, the global financial crisis has negatively affected the BiH economy resulting in an economic downturn in 2009 and 2012. Although the country saw the start of a recovery in 2013, when the growth reached 2.4%, the progress was interrupted by floods in May 2014. Early estimates suggest that the growth resumed in 2015 and 2016 driven by the manufacturing industry and services.

The structure of governance in BiH is rather complex. The country consists of two entities, the Federation of Bosnia and Herzegovina (FBIH) and the Republika Srpska (RS) with a high level of autonomy, and the Brčko District of BiH (BDBiH). The governance structure of the two entities is asymmetric. While the RS is subdivided only into municipalities (65 in total), the FBiH is subdivided into ten cantons, each with its own executive, legislative and judicial powers. Each canton is further subdivided into municipalities. In 1999 the Brčko District of BiH, a separate territory and administrative unit with its own government, was added to the structure of BiH.

Making progress in reducing poverty remains a challenge for BiH. The poverty level in BiH in 2011[1] stood at 15% of the population, just like in the previous four years (2007-2011). Although the poverty incidence in 2011 was similar at the country and entity levels, it is far higher in rural areas at 19% as compared to 9% in urban areas. High unemployment and inactivity rates represent a major challenge to the ability of entity governments to reduce poverty. Employment is one

---

[1] The latest available HBS (Household Budget Survey) is from 2011. Relative poverty threshold is set at the level of 60% of the median consumption per equivalent adult at the level of BiH. In this way, the poverty threshold in 2011 in Bosnia and Herzegovina was set at BAM 416.40 per month for a single-person household (RL: relative line 1).

of the most important factors in exiting poverty. Only 12% of people in employment are poor as compared to 22% of the unemployed.

In 2015 the BiH Council of Ministers and the governments of the RS and the FBiH officially adopted the **Reform Agenda**, a mid-term plan of structural reforms which represents a broader consensus among the Council of Ministers and entity governments on the key priorities for economic and social development aimed at pushing BiH towards a more sustainable growth path. The progress in the implementation of the Reform Agenda will corroborate the country's application for the European Union (EU) membership. When the public sector spends close to 50% of the gross domestic product (GDP), securing efficiency in public expenditures is of critical importance. At the same time, increasing formal employment will increase fiscal revenues through income tax and reduce the burden of health insurance, social contributions and other government transfers.

Such efforts are important for ensuring efficient use of public resources towards faster economic growth, poverty alleviation and joint prosperity. The Reform Agenda has recognised the importance of addressing the issue of high unemployment and inactivity in BiH. Structural reforms in BiH can be considered successful only if they are able to create new jobs and economic opportunities.

As such, the Reform Agenda has identified a broad set of employment-related policy reforms. First, concrete reforms have been identified towards enhancing business environment for the existing and new businesses. Although the Labour Code has been amended as part of the Reform Agenda, this is only the first step on the path of planned reforms. Both entities also plan to adjust their respective labour taxes and contributions with the aim to facilitate – not discourage - formal employment in the private sector while at the same time providing protection to workers. Second, the Reform Agenda has recognised that health insurance should be detached from unemployment registration in order to reduce the motivation for "informal work" (the work in the "grey economy") and to reduce the administrative and fiscal burden on public employment services (PES). The entity governments are working on this issue by trying to find an administrative solution first, that would be followed by a longer-term financially sustainable solution, such as extending health insurance to include the poor and vulnerable groups, and not only the unemployed. Third, it would be important that the secondary and tertiary education curricula, as well as the adult education system, were adjusted to the needs of the private sector and that they provided workers/job seekers with the relevant set of skills. Finally, social assistance programmes should be reformed so as to encourage work. It is important to say that institutional capacities of public employment services (PES) are low and in need of strengthening which will enable them to effectively intermediate between labour supply and demand, assisting the unemployed to find employment and companies to find qualified individuals who can meet their needs. The presence of strong PES and active labour market policies (ALMPs) is of paramount importance for the support to the Reform Agenda, as they will serve as a tool to alleviate potential negative effects that the forthcoming reforms might have on employment.

2. Sectoral and Institutional context

Poor labour market outcomes and an incomplete transition to a market economy remain the major problems in BiH. Recent analysis has confirmed the presence of low activity and employment rates and a high level of unemployment. In 2016, the unemployment rate of people aged 15 and older stood at 25.4%, which is one of the highest unemployment rates in the region[2]. An even bigger concern is a low activity level, which currently stands at 43.1%. BiH is affected by a deep problem of structural unemployment. 84.1% of the unemployed seek employment for more than a year, which suggests deep structural problems in the labour market with large share of job seekers not having the skills required by jobs offered by employers or being trapped in informality.

The Reform Agenda has identified a range of priorities to improve the labour market outcomes in BiH, from improving the business climate to taxation and education reforms. The Employment Support Project in BiH focuses on some of these priorities, *i.e.* on improving the results in the field of employment through increasing the effectiveness and the range of active labour market policies (ALMPs) and enhancing the intermediation services of PES in BiH. Strengthening the effectiveness of ALMPs and intermediation services provided by PES is of key importance in alleviating the difficulties in the labour market arising from high job/worker search costs, providing support to job seekers in faster transitions to

---

[2] Source: Agency for Statistics of Bosnia and Herzegovina (2016), Labour Force Survey 2016, preliminary results.

(formal) employment. Effective ALMPs increase the ability of governments to cushion economic and employment shocks and they are particularly important as an effective tool for those who will have to make transitions into new jobs as a result of structural reforms that are part of the Reform Agenda.

Experiences of other countries in employment promotion suggest that the provision of efficient intermediation services that respond to demands of the private sector and potential job seekers are crucial for a well-functioning labour market. BiH has yet to address this challenge. This will require ensuring appropriate human resources, knowledge and tools – including ALMPs – for PES in order to be able to reorient towards modernising their job intermediation services. BiH is currently short of qualified "employment counsellors" and administrative staff and the services are mainly provided on a face-to-face basis with little use of electronic platforms or automation. Significant human resources are used for administering health benefits and issuing different certificates to the registered unemployed. The second major problem is that a twice as many people are registered as unemployed than the actual number[3] which suggests that many of those in informal employment or inactive people register with PES, although they are not seeking support in finding employment. Many of the registered unemployed register to become entitled to certain rights, such as free health insurance or certificates for various local programmes and services. This puts a significant administrative burden on PES and prevents them from directing their resources to the real job seekers. Given the limited staff capacity, the only way to provide better public support in employment is to modernise the way the PES are managed and increase their efficiency.

---

3 Difference between the Labour Force Survey (LFS) data and administrative data on persons registered with public employment services as "unemployed".

Figure 1 Organisation of public employment services in BiH

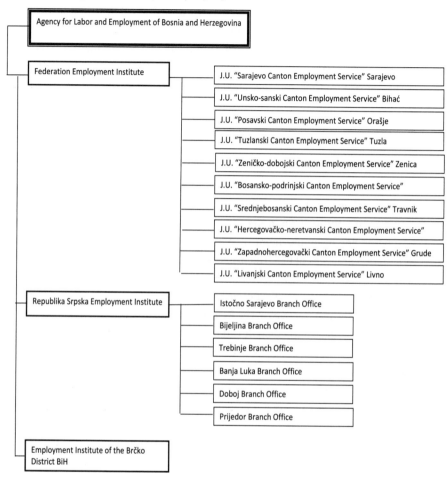

Source: own elaboration.

Governments of both entities have expressed explicit interest in reallocating the resources to measures that maximise the promotion of employment in the formal sector and reduce employment in the "grey economy" (informality) and inactivity. In the light of some previous positive experiences, the entity governments in BiH are most interested in expanding wage subsidy programmes, on-the-job training, providing support to self-employment and entrepreneurship, promoting the formalisation of small businesses and increasing employment in agriculture and agribusiness, as well as pursuing the reforms that increase the effectiveness of PES intermediation services. The chosen modality of this project with a share of results-based financing will enable the entity governments to implement the necessary reforms in the field of ALMPs and intermediation services, while ensuring that the largest part of resources is focused on support through ALMPs.

3. Project objectives

The primary objective of the project is to increase employment in the formal sector among the target groups of registered job seekers. The project will achieve this through financing a range of ALMPs, providing support to the strengthening of employment mediation and modernising the monitoring and evaluation practices of PES. The proposed project will contribute to the country's key objectives of stimulating employment in the private sector and reducing unemployment in BiH. The BiH Council of Ministers and entity governments have elaborated these objectives in the Reform Agenda for 2016-2018[4] and its accompanying implementation plan. It is directly connected to job creation under the focus area "Creating Conditions for Accelerated Private Sector Growth" and it will also contribute to the focus area "Increasing Public Sector Efficiency and Effectiveness". The project will directly contribute to job creation by providing financial incentives to formal employment in the private sector, increasing employability (i.e. enhancing employment outcomes such as access to employment, job retention rates or employment over a longer period of time and wages) of job seekers and improving intermediation services provided by PES. To that effect, the project will provide services to unemployed job seekers, in particular to selected groups identified as rather far away from the labour market (such as long-term unemployed, those aged 40 and above, those with secondary education or less, women and other socially and economically disadvantaged groups), as well as work experience to youth aimed at increasing their employability and job prospects. The total amount for the implementation of the project will be about EUR 50 million. The loan will be shared between the two entities, the RS

---

4 This Reform Agenda also constitutes the basis of advisory and financial support to BiH from the European Commission, European Bank for Reconstruction and Development, International Monetary Fund and the World Bank Group, as well as a range of bilateral donors.

and the FBiH, in different proportions: the total amount of the loan for the RS will be EUR 21 million and for the FBiH EUR 29 million.

4. Project beneficiaries

The direct project beneficiaries are selected groups of job seekers and private employers participating in ALMPs. The Ministries of Labour and PES of both entities will also benefit from the project as it will enhance their management practices. Through ALMPs and other PES services, the project will target youth, women and specific vulnerable groups such as long-term unemployed, those with secondary education or less and other disadvantaged groups at higher risk of being unemployed or jobless due to different constraints. All registered unemployed actively seeking PES services will benefit from the improved PES.

5. Project components and results indicators

The project will have two components:
- Support to employment promotion;
- Support to management systems, monitoring and communications.

Both components are relevant for the achievement of the results, given that they are mutually complementary and reinforce each other. The monitoring will be done by tracking two results areas:
- Results area 1: Increased formal employment among target groups of registered job seekers in the private sector through improved ALMPs and
- Results area 2: Increased formal employment among target groups of registered job seekers in the private sector through improved intermediation in employment.

Figure 2 Link between project activities and results

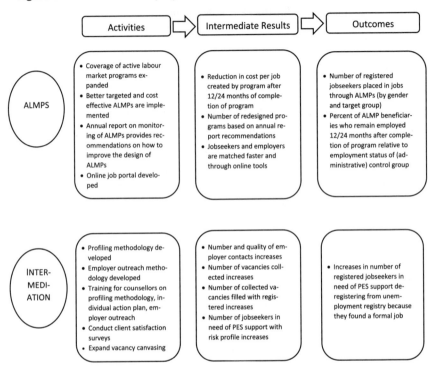

Source: own elaboration.

The achievement of project results will be measured by the following indicators:

- Number of active job seekers removed from the unemployment register because they found formal employment in the private sector;
- Number of registered job seekers (youth and vulnerable groups) placed in jobs in the private sector through ALPMs (total number and by target groups);
- Percentage of ALMPs beneficiaries remaining in employment as a result of their participation in ALMPs 12/24 months after programme completion relative to employment status of the control group from administrative data.

6. Sources of indicators and their link with key decision-makers

Given the complexity of the BiH constitutional set-up and the responsibilities which individual levels of authorities have in the field of employment, the mechanism of project approval was the responsibility of the state and entity authorities, namely:

- BiH Council of Ministers;
- FBiH Government;
- RS Government.

In the process of defining project activities, consultations were made with the state and entity-level institutions that were not directly involved in the implementation of the project (BiH Ministry of Civil Affairs, the Labour and Employment Agency of BiH, BiH and entity-level Ministries of Finances).

At an entity level, the project implementation will be the responsibility of Ministries in charge of labour and employment, namely the RS Ministry of Labour and Veterans Affairs (MoLVA) and the FBiH Ministry of Labour and Social Policy (MoLSP). These institutions will be responsible for monitoring and reporting to the World Bank. The sources of indicators and principal mechanisms for the implementation of project activities are PES in the FBiH and RS.

In the FBiH, the FBiH PES will be responsible for the implementation of ALMPs that will be financed by the project. The specific arrangements to be applied may differ for each ALMP and that will be indicated in public calls and instructions given to the cantonal PES. The MoLSP will be in charge of project monitoring, verification of the achievement of the DLIs as reported by the FBiH PES and in accordance with the reporting to the World Bank. A Project Committee will be put in place to supervise the implementation of the project to which the MoLSP will submit quarterly reports on the progress made in achieving the objectives and project indicators.

In the RS, the entity-level PES will be responsible for the implementation of ALMPs to be financed by the project. The MoLVA will be in charge of project management, verification of the achievement of the indicators and results as reported by the RS PES and in accordance with the reporting to the World Bank. The MoLVA will also supervise and guide the adoption of improved methodologies and the improvement of the monitoring system, including commissioning evaluations. Before the project becomes effective, a dedicated team of MoLVA representatives will be appointed and put in place to monitor the project implementation. A Project Committee will also be put in place to monitor the project implementation to which the MoLVA will submit quarterly or biannual reports on the progress made in achieving the results and project indicators.

Figure 3   Institutions participating in the project and mechanism of project implementation and results

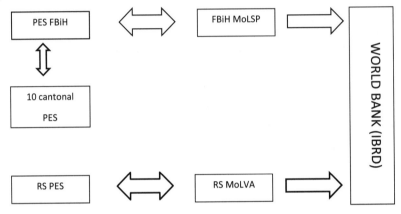

Source: own elaboration.

Hence, the project has defined that entity ministries responsible for the field of employment will be the official project holders and supervisors of the achievement of project indictors, while entity PES will be in charge of the implementation and results and they will also be the sources of information and indicators. The monitoring and evaluation of the results will be the responsibility of the RS MoLVA and the FBiH MoLSP. The information on the implementation of ALMPs and delivery of other services will come from relevant entity-level PES which will then be included in biannual reports to be submitted to the Project Committee – the IBRD. It should be mentioned that the outcomes indicators primarily focus on the placement of job seekers and PES performance, and not on the private sector companies, although these companies will be the beneficiaries of ALMPs. This is because the revenue-related outcomes, the survival of companies etc. are subject to changes in the macroeconomic situation, which is not under the direct control of the project and it would be difficult to attribute it to project activities. During the implementation period, the responsible entity ministries and entity

PES will conduct evaluations of at least four different ALMPs. The evaluations will use the administrative data and they will rely on econometric techniques to build the control group with similar characteristics to those of the beneficiaries of ALMPs, in order to measure the net impact of ALMPs (in terms of employment outcomes). The data will be taken from the administrative databases of relevant PES.

Table 2   Link between project activities and results under first component

Activities	Intermediate results	Outcomes
• Better-targeted and cost-effective ALMPs are implemented • ALMPs coverage is expanded	• Reduced costs per person employed through the programme 12/24 months after programme completion • Annual report on programme monitoring by individual subgroups (age, gender, target group, local office) with recommendations for improved targeting or programme design • Number of redesigned programmes based on recommendations of annual report	• Increased number of registered job seekers placed in jobs through employment support programmes (by gender and target group) • Increased number of youth placed in jobs through employment support programmes • Increased number of disadvantaged job seekers placed in jobs through employment support programmes • Percentage of ALMPs beneficiaries who remain in employment as a result of their participation in ALMPS 12/24 months after programme completion relative to employment status of the control group
• Services for employers	• Increased number of contacts with employers • Increased number of collected vacancies • Increased number of collected vacancies filled with registered job seekers • Client/employers' satisfaction – increases over time or remains at a high level	• Increased number of registered job seekers in need of PES support who have been deregistered because they found formal employment
• Services for job seekers	• An improved central database for case management of registered unemployed put in place • Number of counsellors certified with new methodologies of case management increases • Number of job seekers in need of PES services with risk profile increases • Number of job seekers in need of PES services with individual action plans increases (total and by risk categories)	

Source: own elaboration.

Support to Management Systems, Monitoring and Communications, which is key for PES will support effective project monitoring and provide finances to strengthen the management system in order to monitor ALMPs and employment services, as well as to develop and implement an effective communications strategy targeting job seekers, employers, policy-makers and the entire population. It will create a basis for the collection of evidence and lessons necessary to improve ALMPS and intermediation in employment during the implementation period. It will finance the enhancing of the IT system to:

- Enable data exchange among labour offices and other institutions;
- Offer online services;
- Monitor services delivered to job seekers and employers;
- Introduce/monitor the performance of labour offices and;
- Monitor and disseminate labour market trends.

This implies the connectivity of all offices to an upgraded IT system that will enable data exchange with other relevant institutions for the verification of job seeker status and basic data (e.g. social assistance, recipients of agricultural subsidies, etc.). This component will finance and ensure a strong communication and outreach strategy in order to plan, prepare and disseminate the information on project resources, activities and results through multiple channels to job seekers, employers, policy-makers and the general public. It will also finance the evaluation of the process and impact of the selected ALMPs and/or institutional measures to be implemented by entity PES and Ministries of Labour, as well as beneficiary surveys. In the RS, a randomised control trial impact evaluation of selected programmes will be conducted.

Figure 3   Link between data and project objectives

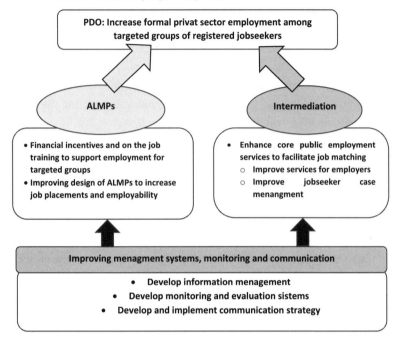

Source: own elaboration.

The sources of indicators for project implementation are exclusively ALMPs in the FBiH and RS, namely:

Federation of BiH:

- **Increasing employment through ALMPs** – 6,000 young persons placed in jobs, 15,000 disadvantaged persons placed in jobs;
- **Improving ALMPs design to increase employment** – design of one programme modified;
- **Increasing employment through job placement** – 30,000 job seekers in need of support profiled and with individual action plans stored in database;
- **Improving the management system and monitoring** – Online job portal with annual publications of trends in place.

Republika Srpska

- **Increasing employment through ALMPs** – 4,800 young persons placed in jobs, 11,200 disadvantaged persons placed in jobs;
- **Expanding the number of redesigned ALMPs to increase employment** - design of one programme modified;
- **Increasing employment through job placement** - 20.000 job seekers in need of support profiled and with individual action plans stored in database;
- **Improving the management system and monitoring** - Online matching tool in use.

The project investment and results are expected to generate a long-term impact in respect to labour market outcomes, given that they will help the entity governments achieve their objectives of improving the labour market performance and increasing the private sector employment in BiH. The selected results will be included in PES annual activity plans and budgets as they represent the crucial part of the core activities of the Ministries of Labour/PES. Therefore, the results are expected to be sustainable to a large extent, given the results-based approach and the project design. Once the economic transformation of BiH is done, and in particular, once the public sector reform has been completed, the range of ALMPs is expected to decline and/or consolidate as an adjustment to a better economic environment. It is also important that disbursements will only be made after the agreed objectives have been achieved, both for ALMPs and for delivery of public employment services. Therefore, the design and results-based mechanism are expected to enable a process of change with long-lasting effects.

The project is expected to have many positive social and economic impacts, such as enhancing employment, entrepreneurial skills and self-employment of inactive groups, in particular youth, low-skilled people, long-term unemployed and vulnerable groups. Through diversification of measures and improved targeting based on unemployment profile (e.g. long-term unemployed, low-skilled youth, women, those above the age of 40, and those with university degree) the improved ALMPs are expected to contribute to successful employment by improving the matching of job seekers' qualifications and employers' needs. Improvement of PES services for employers and job seekers is anticipated to increase PES staff competencies to provide better counselling services and individualised support to job seekers. Focusing attention on the intake/registration and counselling, i.e. spending more time in face-to-face contact is considered to be of particular importance in an environment where more than 40% of job seekers have been unemployed for more than five years and are considered to have slim chances of finding a job. Increase and diversification of counselling services and employment programmes will be of key importance in overcoming the disillusion that prevails in the country due to low employment opportunities.

7. Concluding remarks

The Employment Support Project in Bosnia and Herzegovina is a loan arrangement between BiH and WB aimed at increasing formal employment in the private sector among the target groups of registered job seekers. The Project will have two components:

- Support to employment promotion and;
- Support to management systems, monitoring and communications.

The types of programmes to be supported under the first component include the following: wage subsidies, on-the-job training and self-employment. The aim will also be to enhance delivery of core employment services, i.e. services for job seekers and services for employers until ultimately achieving the improved labour market outcomes and contributing to growth of formal employment in the private sector. This component will support effective project monitoring and provide finances to strengthen the management system in order to monitor ALMPs and employment services, as well as to develop and implement an effective communications strategy targeting job seekers, employers and policy-makers.

In the FBiH and RS, dedicated project teams under the FBH Ministry of Labour and Social Policy (MoLSP) and the RS Ministry of Labour and Veterans Affairs (MoLVA) will administer the funds, monitor and report on the implementation of project activities and the achievement of results, commission evaluations of selected ALMPs, and implement the selected activities. In the FBiH and RS Project Committees will be put in place. The most important institutions in the implementation of the project are: Ministries of Labour and public employment services of both entities that will ensure timely implementation of activities and the achievement of results. Dynamism of project financing will depend on project results for which indicators have been defined. Both the project implementation and the sources of indicators will be the responsibility of PES in BiH that will report to their relevant Ministries of Labour. The Project guides the activities related to enhancing job intermediation services for employers and job seekers. Enhancing job intermediation is important for labour market efficiency as it helps increase the speed and quality of matching. Efficient PES assists job seekers, especially the vulnerable groups, in finding and retaining their jobs.

References

Agency for Statistics of Bosnia and Herzegovina (2016): Labour Force Survey 2016. Preliminary results, online: http://www.bhas.ba/ankete/LFS_saopcenje%20BOS.pdf

Agency for Statistics of Bosnia and Herzegovina (2011): Household Budget Survey in BiH for 2011, online: http://www.bhas.ba/saopstenja/2014/BHAS_HBS_BH_dv5-2.pdf

BiH Council of Ministers, FBiH Government, RS Government, Brčko District BiH Government: Reform Agenda 2015-2018

Labour and Employment Agency of BiH, Federal Employment Service, RS Employment Service, Employment Service of Brčko District (2016): Review of Employment Policies in BiH for 2016

Labour and Employment Agency of BiH, Federal Employment Service, RS Employment Service, Employment Service of Brčko District (2017): Plan for Labour Market Policy Guidelines and Active Employment Measures in Bosnia and Herzegovina in 2017

World Bank, International Bank for Reconstruction and Development (2017): International Bank Project appraisal Document on a proposed Loan in the amount of 50.00 million EUR to Bosnia and Herzegovina for the Employment Support Project, online:

https://www.gtai.de/GTAI/Content/DE/Trade/Fachdaten/PRO/2017/01/Anlagen/PRO201701305000.pdf?v=1

Modelling Scenarios for Securing Skilled Healthcare personnel: Confronting Shortages in Skilled Personnel with Data-driven Participatory Strategies

Lisa Schäfer, Oliver Lauxen and Melanie Castello

1. The status quo and some projections

Due to demographic change, the coming years will see a strong increase in the number of elderly people in Germany. The oldest age groups will constitute an increasing percentage of the population. Since the elderly are in greater need of assistance in many spheres of life, the increase in this portion of the population will lead to an increased demand for healthcare and other services. According to official care statistics, the number of residents in nursing homes in Germany rose by 20,000 between 2013 and 2015 (Statistisches Bundesamt 2017). Home care services even provided care to 76,000 more elderly than just two years ago (Statistisches Bundesamt 2017). The inpatient cases in the hospital sector also show an increase of 450,000 from 2013 to 2015 (German Federal Statistical Office 2016). It is likely that these developments will show further increases and lead to a rise in demand for nursing personnel.

The forecasts for people in need of long-term care for 2030 vary between 2.95 and 3.36 million (SVR 2009), and for 2050 between 3.5 and 4.7 million (Nowossadeck 2013). These calculations are valid if they are considered in light of the reduced risk of being in need for long-term care, also referred to as "compression thesis" (Doblhammer et al. 2006, Rothgang et al. 2009, Statistische Ämter des Bundes und der Länder 2008, Wahl and Schneekloth 2008). A number of studies indicate that it may be nearly impossible to cover the increased demand for health care services (which goes along with an increased number of elderly in need of care) with skilled personnel (Burkhart et al. 2012, Ostwald et al. 2010, Pohl 2011, Zika et al. 2012). Depending on different scenarios, a shortage of between 125,400 and 464,000 certified nurses (full-time equivalents) is to be expected for the year 2030. Apart from this, existing data already shows shortages of registered nurses in most parts of Germany (Federal Labour Office 2015, Castello et al. 2017a, Isfort et al. 2016, Lauxen and Castello 2016). Vocational education and training (VET) is a central strategy for securing skilled labour. The extent of vocational education and training for registered nurses (RN) and other healthcare occupations is regulated under the authority of the 16 Federal States in Germany. Since the training facilities for registered nurses are usually under the sponsorship of one or several hospitals, the entire process is part of overall hospital planning. It is important to note that these procedures often lack transparency (DKG 2014). The future demand is often defined as "on call" by German state governments, based on estimations of healthcare providers themselves. Therefore, the capacity of vocational education and training is often adjusted according to the priorities and goals of the training providers. Budget constraints call for a better approach to planning. Beyond this, vocational education and training is not the only strategy for securing skilled personnel; on its own it will be insufficient to cover the increased demand.

Which measures have the most potential for securing skilled personnel? – In the German Federal State of Rhineland Palatinate (RLP), labour market monitoring was implemented in 2002. Besides planning the capacities of vocational education and training, the ongoing initiative includes further measures for securing skilled personnel. Indeed, scenarios are being developed for all occupations for which there are shortages. This important component of the monitoring process is presented in this article. Section 2 gives an overview of the initiation of the monitoring procedures. In section 3, the method for modelling scenarios for securing skilled personnel is outlined. In section 4, a draft version of the scenario for securing registered nurses is described. In chapter 5, we show which governance structures and -mechanisms come into effect. The review ends with a brief outlook in chapter 6.

2. The monitoring process in Rhineland-Palatinate

The RLP-monitor uses methods developed by the European Network on Regional Labour Market Monitoring to support evidence-based healthcare workforce forecasting and planning (Larsen and Mevius 2007). Based on a demand–supply model connected to population growth and needs, the current labour market situation is being analysed. In addition, forecasts up to 2030 are being calculated (Castello et al. 2017a, 2017b). In an overall view of current and future labour market situations, it becomes apparent how large the shortage is and will be.

The target figures for the measures of the scenario are based on the calculated shortage. The first phase in the monitoring process is called *diagnosis* (see Table 1).

Table 1   The monitoring process in RLP

Monitoring-phases	Key questions
Diagnosis	• Is there a current shortage of skilled personnel? • Will there be a shortage of skilled personnel in the future? • How large is the shortage of skilled personnel in total (present and future)?
Strategy	• Which measures hold the best potential for securing skilled labour? • What are the target figures for the different measures for securing skilled labour? • Which participants can make which kinds of contribution? • How can the specific measures be executed?
Evaluation	• Have the objectives been achieved? • If not: how can this be adjusted?

Source: IWAK 2017.

Based on the diagnosis, a strategy to avoid the forecasted shortages is being developed. A strategy is defined as a cluster of single measures with specific objectives. The first step is to explore the potential of each measure differentiated by occupational group. The most promising measures will be presented as a scenario for securing skilled personnel. The next step is to implement those measures. From the scenario, we can derive how many skilled personnel need to be trained in the future. Since most health professionals in Germany are trained in hospitals, part of this process involves consulting with hospitals to negotiate demand-based and realistic target figures for training for the next five years. The accompanying evaluation then takes place during the implementation process. The process, beginning with new projections, should be repeated every five years.

The monitoring process includes three occupational clusters, namely nursing professions/occupations, therapists, and assistant health professions/occupations (Castello et al. 2017a). The focus is primarily on three-year training programmes, with both basic practical as well as academic training included in the monitoring process. Basic and academic qualifications are included in parts of the monitoring process.

The way the monitoring process is devised in Rhineland-Palatinate is quite interesting, because the whole process – from diagnosis via setting objectives to planning and implementing measures – takes place in an interconnected setting between the state government and stakeholders in the healthcare professions and institutions. This monitoring process is now emerging as a complex governance tool. As Kuhlmann et al. (2016) describe, *"the novel aspect of the model is an integrated, procedural approach that promotes a "learning system" of governance based on three interconnected pillars: mixed methods and bottom-up data collection, strong stakeholder involvement with complex communication tools and shared decision- and policy-making"* (p. 3). Stakeholder involvement has thus been integrated in the process from the beginning. Stakeholders serve on a board consisting of the key players in the healthcare occupations: representatives of professional associations, labour unions, employers' associations, health insurances, labour administration, researchers, and representatives from the state government. They give professional impulses and bring their expertise, for instance by validating preliminary results or evaluating data. Therefore, regular board-meetings, workshops and other events, but also many individual conversations, take place.

The Institute for Economics, Labour and Culture (IWAK), Centre of Goethe-University Frankfurt/Main, has been assigned by the Ministry for Social Affairs, Labour, Health and Demography (MSAGD) of Rhineland-Palatinate to conduct most parts of the monitoring process. Analysing the present and future labour market situation and establishing target figures for scenarios for securing skilled personnel or readjusting the training capacities in the process of hospital planning was supported by publicly funded projects.

3. Methodological approach

In this section, we show how our project is developing the scenario for securing a sufficient number of registered nurses. The focus of the article is on registered nurses, although further nursing professions like elderly care nurses exist in Germany. The development of a "diagnosis", which means the analysis of the current and future labour market situation (see chapter 3.1), is the foundation for any further steps. The scope of the shortage of skilled personnel is determined in this first step. We then offer an overview of all measures for securing skilled personnel (see section 3.2 above). The development of the scenario itself needs to be conducted in several steps, which includes feedback from the board.

3.1 Diagnosis as a foundation: analysing the current and future labour market situations

A common base of knowledge and an understanding of the challenges are crucial to ensuring joint action by all stakeholders. Labour market data show the large size and scope of the current and future shortage of skilled personnel. To generate the necessary data, relevant studies are being conducted regularly in Rhineland-Palatinate (Bieräugel et al. 2012a, Bieräugel et al. 2012b, Castello et al. 2017b, Ministerium für Arbeit, Soziales, Gesundheit, Familie und Frauen, Rheinland-Pfalz 2008).

For measuring the current and future labour market situation, a demand-supply model is being used. The supply is defined as skilled workers who are available on the labour market and who can fill vacancies in hospitals, nursing homes, home care services and other healthcare facilities. This involves the sum of graduates from vocational education and training as well as academic graduates, unemployed skilled personnel and persons with recognised qualifications from abroad. The data for the supply-side can be generated with data from public statistics. There exists no data for defining the demand, which is understood as the number of skilled personnel that has been sought in healthcare facilities. Hence, a survey needs to be conducted in all healthcare facilities. By matching demand and supply for registered nurses over the period of one year, surpluses or shortages can be quantified (for further information see Castello et al. 2017a). The most current available numbers are for the year 2015. In total, 1,801 registered nurses were available on the labour market, while there were 2,943 vacancies.

The mismatch amounts to a shortfall of 1,142 registered nurses (Castello et. al 2017a). This gap corresponds to 5% of the current workforce (24,994 registered nurses).

The demand-supply model is also being used for forecasting the future labour market situation, though demand and supply are defined differently here (Castello et al. 2017b). The current workforce is the basis for the forecast. The workforce will be reduced gradually because skilled personnel will reach retirement age and therefore leave their positions (replacement demand). Unemployed skilled personnel are also part of the forecasted supply and will be affected in the same way. On the other hand, the supply-side is repopulated by graduates and persons with recognised qualifications from abroad. The total supply for the occupational group of registered nurses in the year 2025 is projected to be 27,222. Yet the forecasted demand of 27,823 is higher. The basis for this figure is also the current workforce, which is updated by additional demand due to demographic changes. In addition to the current lack of 1,142 nurses, this figure will rise by 602 by the year 2025. This adds up to a total shortfall of 1,744 registered nurses, if measures for securing skilled personnel are not taken (see Table 2). The mismatch of 1,744 is the target figure for these measures, and they must be extensive enough to cover the forecasted gap.

Table 2   Supply and demand of registered nurses in Rhineland-Palatinate (n=number of individual nurses)

	Supply	Demand	Balance of supply and demand
2015	1,801	2,943	- 1,142
2025	27,222	27,823	- 602
Total			- 1,744

Source: Castello et al. 2017a, Castello et al. 2017b.

3.2 Measures for securing skilled personnel (strategy)

There have been multiple attempts to bundle measures for securing skilled personnel conceptually (see for instance Kroezen et al. 2005). Within the monitoring process, IWAK focuses on measures to close the gap of skilled personnel that has been forecasted. The impact of those measures can be recorded quantitatively or simulated in the forecasting model. A distinction should be made according to four categories of measures. Different measures are assigned to each set.

Table 3   Categories of measures and measures for securing skilled healthcare personnel

Fields of measures	Measures
1. Vocational qualification	• Enhancing vocational education and training • Reducing dropout rates • Upskilling • Demography resistant vocational education and training
2. Activation	• Activation of the hidden reserve • Mobilisation of the unemployed
3. Mobility	• From other states • From abroad
4. Retention	• Extension of weekly working hours • Extension of working lifetime • Increase of the period of employment (net)/ reduction of the period of suspended employment (paternal leave, sabbaticals for instance) • Reduction of occupational changes

Source: IWAK 2017.

The first category, "vocational qualification", includes the most crucial measure for securing skilled personnel, namely enhancing vocational education and training. Another measure is increasing the number of graduates who will be available on the labour market by reducing dropout rates. The third is upskilling. In the healthcare sector this applies, for instance, to unskilled nursing staff or nursing assistants who can be upskilled as registered nurses. Some German states, including Rhineland-Palatinate, have specific upskilling programs to achieve this. Another measure is referred to as demography resistant vocational education and training. The objective here is to keep the training figures steady, although the number of young people (with the majority of trainees being young people) is declining (see chapter 3.1).

The second category of measures is about activating skilled personnel. This refers to the unemployed but also to the hidden reserve, which is defined as skilled personnel who left their professional career at some point in time but have not entered a new occupation.

The objective in the third category, "mobility" is to recruit skilled personnel from other German states or from abroad.

In the fourth category, "retention", the focus is on skilled personnel who are currently employed in health and elderly care facilities. Many of these are employed on a part-time basis (Becka et al. 2016), have long suspension periods in their occupational trajectories (Joost 2013), change their field of occupation (Pilger and Jahn 2013, Schaade 2013, Wiethölter 2012) or leave professional life before reaching the statutory retirement age. By improving working conditions and finding better ways of reconciling family and professional life, the part-time employment rate, the number of people who change occupation, and the extent of interruption periods could be reduced. The workforce would therefore prolong the period of employment for this population.

3.3 Elaborating scenarios for securing skilled personnel

In theory, all of the measures for securing skilled personnel named above could make a contribution to minimising or even eliminating the projected gap of 1,744 registered nurses. However, which measures are most promising? How much potential do they offer? IWAK has been awarded a public contract to present a first draft of scenarios for securing skilled personnel by combining different measures based on valid data.

At first, a range of statistics were examined and time series were analysed to explore developments which could possibly be maintained. An increasing part-time employment rate, for instance, could be an indicator of further developments in this matter, likewise gradually increasing the retirement age. Since the status quo regarding the number of graduates, the number of people who change their occupation, and the average retirement age was projected to be maintained in the forecast for 2025, these are also the key levers that can be adjusted for modelling scenarios for securing skilled personnel. Maintaining linear trends is different from maintaining the status quo because some components vary, such as the number of forecasted graduates or the number of recruited foreign-trained nurses. Therefore, it is possible to simulate the number of skilled personnel that can be gained with each measure within the forecasting model.

Beside these quantitative simulations, qualitative estimates also should be taken into account. From numerous workshops and over 40 expert interviews over the last few years, a great deal of information is available. Hence, we are aware of the barriers in different health professions and of which measures are most effective for securing skilled personnel (see Bieräugel et al. 2012b, Dalichau and Lauxen 2017, Lauxen 2015a, Lauxen 2015b). Such information has also been taken into account. As a result, a cluster of measures for all health professions with a forecasted gap of skilled personnel was compiled and visualised within a scenario for securing skilled personnel (see chapter 3). A workshop of experts was held at the Ministry for Social Affairs, Labour, Health and Demography in November 2016. First drafts of the scenarios were presented and discussed in occupation-specific working groups. Numerous background assumptions, databases and trends were also presented. Some of the working groups expressed the need for extensive modifications. They made suggestions on how to develop and improve the scenarios. IWAK examined those advancements more closely and continued developing the scenarios in consultation with the ministry. The advanced scenarios will go through a final coordination process with the board, which is planned for summer 2017.

4. Scenarios for securing registered nurses (RN)

For the occupational group of registered nurses, four measures within the scenario for securing skilled personnel are the most promising (see Figure 1): demography-resistant vocational education and training, reducing occupational changes, extension of the professional lifetime and intensifying mobility for foreign-trained nurses to Rhineland-Palatinate. With these measures, 86% of the gap of 1,744 registered nurses could be covered. Hence, 14% remain unfilled. The databases and objectives for these four measures for securing skilled personnel will described shortly. This scenario was discussed in autumn 2016 during a workshop comprised of experts. About ten people formed a working group on the occupational group of registered nurses. The group consisted of headmasters, nursing managers, and representatives of professional associations.

Figure 1   **Draft of a scenario for securing skilled personnel**

Category	Percentage
Demography resistant VET	23%
Occupational change rate	6%
Working lifetime	42%
Mobility foreign-trained nurses	15%
Not covered yet	14%

Source: IWAK 2017.

4.1 Demography resistant vocational education and training

Within the forecast of the labour market situation in 2025, the number of prospective graduates of vocational and professional training for registered nurses was calculated. The starting point was the year 2015, which saw 926 graduates in Rhineland-Palatinate. In our forecasting model, the 2015 figure was used as a basis but included a correction factor: because the age group of 15-29 year-olds, which comprises the largest percentage of trainees, will in fact decrease continuously until 2025, according to forecasts for population development of the State Statistical Office Rhineland Palatinate, the number of prospective graduates in our projections was reduced accordingly (Castello 2017b). If it were possible to maintain the number of graduates up through 2025 at 926 despite demographic changes, then 404 additional graduates could be gained. This would constitute an increased supply of skilled personnel and 23% of the gap would be covered. According to the experts who discussed the scenario at the workshop, this is indeed realistic, if the vocational education and training for the profession could be made more attractive. This could be achieved, for instance, by fostering better working conditions in hospitals and improving the image of care professions in general.

4.2 Reducing occupational changes

In our projection model, we assume that not all of the prospective graduates will remain in the profession. Some of them will not be available on the labour market. Studies of the Institute for Employment Research (IAB) (Pilger and Jahn 2013, Schaade 2013, Wiethölter 2012) established a quota of graduates, observing that they leave the profession of registered nurses within five years of graduation. Instead, this population pursues further education to qualify for a management position, to take a teaching position, or to start over with an unrelated educational track. For our forecast model, a quota of occupation changers was set at 18%. For this scenario, we suggest reducing this quota to 16% by encouraging retention in the field. Specifically, by 2025 113 additional graduates would be available on the labour market. In this way, 6% of the projected gap would be covered.

In the opinion of the experts who attended the workshop, better working conditions are the key to improving retention among registered nurses. If working conditions could be improved (through reliable work schedules, sponsored child care, etc.), it would be possible to reduce the rate of occupational changers even more than suggested within the scenario.

4.3 Extension of professional lifetime

The age distribution of registered nurses in Rhineland-Palatinate has been recorded in the projection model. In the field of long-term care public data was available, while the age distribution for nurses working in hospitals was recorded through the employer survey in 2016. The data reveals that almost one third of the employees are older than 50. This means that many of the currently employed nurses will not be available on the labour market in 2025. To determine an average retirement age, the employers were asked for the age at which their staff has usually left work in the last five years. As a result, an average retirement age of 60 years was observed, which is significantly lower than the statutory retirement age in Germany. Within the projection model it was calculated how many nurses will leave the workforce by 2025 based on this retirement age (60). If it were possible to raise the average retirement age by one year, 736 additional nurses would still be on the labour market in 2025. Thus 42% of the forecasted gap would be covered.

According to the experts (the members of the board, as described above), a later retirement can only be achieved by fostering better working conditions. This refers to age-equitable workplaces and in-house health management in particular.

4.4 Intensified mobility for foreign-trained nurses

In 2015, 264 foreign-trained nurses had registered for professional recognition of their certificates in Rhineland-Palatinate. In the projection model, an annual immigration of 264 nurses up through 2025 was projected. However, the total number of recognition of foreign certifications has increased continuously since 2012. The figures went up from 92 in 2012 to 160 in 2013 to 189 in 2014 (Dalichau et al. 2017). If annual immigration were to reach 296 instead of the projected 264, then a total of 256 additional registered nurses could be gained in Rhineland-Palatinate by the year 2025. Thus 15% of the forecasted gap would be covered.

In the opinion of the experts who discussed the scenario in the workshop, this objective is realistic. To make it workable, though, a sufficient number of German language courses and adequate training periods in healthcare facilities would be required.

4.5 Interim conclusion and next steps

By increasing the retirement age and keeping the current figures for vocational education and training steady despite demographic changes, a large part of the forecasted gap can be covered. Other measures, such as activation of the unemployed or reducing the part-time employment rate, have less potential in this occupational group. The figures for the unemployed are low, anyway (Castello et al. 2017b), and the part-time rate for registered nurses has even increased between 2010 to 2015 – from 52% to 54%.

The remaining gap of 14% could probably be covered by enhancing vocational education and training, reducing the rate of occupation changers even more, or by a moderate decrease in the rate of interruption of professional employment.

For the latter measures, better working conditions are crucial. Mobility of personnel from other countries may hold a higher potential than expected within the scenario.

Subsequent to the workshop, IWAK reviewed the suggested modifications and revised the scenarios in consultation with the ministry. New drafts will be sent to the members of the board in summer 2017. Thereafter, the board will have the chance to give feedback and consent to the final versions of the scenarios.

The implementation of the proposed measures will begin thereafter, also with the involvement of the stakeholders. In 2012, a formalised administrative structure that connects top-down (represented by the Federal Government) hierarchical governance and bottom-up network governance through a board of stakeholders and subordinated working groups was developed, the so-called "*Fachkräfte- und Qualifizierungsinitiative Gesundheitsfachberufe*" (Kuhlmann et al. 2016, Ministerium für Soziales, Arbeit, Gesundheit und Demografie Rheinland-Pfalz 2013). Within the scope of the initiative, the measures are being developed, implemented, monitored and evaluated.

5. Types and dimensions of governance in the construction of scenarios for securing skilled personnel

This section concerns the types and dimensions of governance in the construction of scenarios for securing skilled healthcare personnel. Governance in this case is understood as a generic term for all patterns of handling interdependencies among states, as well as among public and social participants (Benz et al. 2007). This applies to typical hierarchically influenced patterns, as well as to strongly market-organised or participative patterns.

The governance perspective enables us to analyse structures, mechanisms and interdependencies between individual, collective or corporative participants in political processes, such as the construction of scenarios for securing skilled personnel (Benz et al. 2007). Hence, it describes the targeted control of developments with regard to all parties involved. Greer et al. (2016) propose five dimensions of governance:

- *Transparency* is how and to what extent decisions and their motivations are made known;

- *Accountability* is explanation and sanction – who can effectively demand an explanation and sanction an action?
- *Participation* is the participation of those involved in and affected by the decision-making process.
- *Integrity* is the establishment of ethical, institutionalised processes.
- *Capacity* is policy capacity, the availability of expertise in policy formulation, implementation and evaluation. (adapted from Greer et al. 2016: 106).

The question remains how to evaluate each of these in order to secure skilled personnel for the health professions in Rhineland-Palatinate.

5.1 Transparency

Who knows how much about the decision-making process and the underlying reasons for actions? –The decision-making process and the underlying reasons for decisions are often opaque to various stakeholders. Transparency about a course of action for developing the scenarios and the results thereof has been created by numerous project reports. These are readily accessible on the Internet and are being disseminated over several mailing lists. Those reports can be used by regional participants by adapting the scenarios, which are specific to Rhineland-Palatinate, for regional planning purposes. Since it is known that reports containing large amounts of data are not used on a regular basis, we developed several options for communication. For instance, the members of the board were consulted to validate the assumptions on which the scenarios are based. There also was a board meeting to consent on the final versions of the scenarios. And finally, the professional public at large was invited to the workshop of experts in November 2016, where the development of the scenarios was the main issue.

Nevertheless, the participation of several participants in the process has a different scope. Not all of the information is included in the reports or communicated publicly. Therefore, IWAK, the ministry, and the members of the board have more information than the professional public at large which is due to the complexity of our monitoring procedures. Despite the attempt to create maximum transparency, some members of the board are overwhelmed by the complexity of the entire monitoring process, as well as by the methodology of constructing the scenarios. IWAK was informed about this by some board members. In order to address such unsatisfactory tendencies, in the current phase we have been implementing more opportunities for exchange than was previously the case. For instance, several meetings were held with individual board members outside the formal meeting framework. Within these meetings it was possible to explain the methodology and interim results, and to discuss occupational specifics.

Furthermore, an online portal was developed in spring and summer 2017. On this platform, information about the monitoring process and specific results are presented and can also be discussed. The portal is also another channel of communication between the ministry, stakeholders, and practitioners. The opportunity to conduct surveys and short ad-hoc polls is also provided.

5.2 Accountability

Who can demand an explanation and sanction an action? There are no clear rules about this. On closer inspection, it becomes clear that either policy-makers as well as the involved stakeholders could thwart or even end the process of developing projections and scenarios for healthcare personnel staffing. So far there have been no moves to do so. That is possibly because both parties know that they depend on each other. The stakeholders are needed to develop realistic objectives and implement measures for securing skilled personnel. Policy-makers cannot implement measures for securing skilled personnel on their own. Since the exchange between policy-makers and practitioners in the health professions has been the norm for several years in Rhineland-Palatinate, the following should be clear to all involved participants: first, the activities of the ministry are supported by real-world practice. Second, reforms must be disseminated and ultimately implemented by practitioners. That said, stakeholders need policy-makers to provide personnel and financial resources. Therefore, a balance of power is a given at an informal level, which helps to keep the process open and fact-based.

IWAK has the role of an intermediary between policymakers and stakeholders. We need the support of stakeholders to interpret and assess data, but contractually, IWAK is accountable to the ministry. The funding creates a relationship of dependency for IWAK.

5.3 Participation

To what extent can those affected by decisions about healthcare personnel planning participate in the decision-making processes? Participation is conceptually embedded in the RLP-monitor, and the stakeholders' inclusion through the board is institutionalised. Members of the board participate in the process of evaluating data and trends. They also take part in setting objectives for the scenarios. At various points in the process, it is necessary to ask experts for their interpretations when there are gaps in the data. Members of the board can either be involved directly as experts, or they can name others we can contact. They become part of the policy-making process and influence developments in the field through this support. The approval of the scenarios for securing skilled healthcare personnel takes place in board meetings and thus must be by majority consent.

It should also be considered that not all of the participants who are ultimately affected can be involved in the entire process. The vast majority is represented by stakeholders of the board. Nevertheless, workshops and presentations that are open to the broader population of healthcare professionals are offered as well, at which the results and next steps in the process are presented and discussed.

5.4 Integrity

Are processes organised in an ethical and institutionalised manner? From our point of view that is the case. There are no signs of corruption or unethical behaviour. The risk is reduced because most parts of the process are institutionalised, but ultimately there is no independent control. In theory, members of the board could provide false information in pursuit of their own interests. Policy-makers also might have their own agenda as well and influence the process. In the narrow sense of the word, either policy-makers or IWAK could be corrupt, whereby ethical standards would be violated. Additionally, checks and balances within the organisations would have to be bypassed or undermined. Also, the board serves as a corrective mechanism; the comparative perspectives of the different occupations among stakeholders and policymakers have a controlling effect. This blocks the ministry or any individual stakeholder from pursuing a particular, self-interested position. Furthermore, positions must be made public, discussed and legitimated. Nevertheless, truly testing the integrity of the procedure may be impossible.

5.5 Capacity

Is expertise on the formulation, implementation and evaluation of policy available? This can be operationalised, for instance, through formalised structures to connect top-down and bottom-up decision making (Kuhlmann et al. 2016). The Ministry for Social Affairs, Labour, Health and Demography of Rhineland Palatinate has the capacity for and desires this type of monitoring. The ministry provides considerable personnel and financial resources for implementation by financing projects, whereby IWAK analyses the current labour market situation, generates forecasts, or elaborates scenarios for securing skilled healthcare personnel. Employees of the ministry are assigned to carry out projects or organise board meetings. On the other hand, the level of available resources always depends on the budget situation. Scarce budget resources raise the risk that the process will not be continued. Furthermore, political priorities can shift over time. Otherwise the ministry or rather their representatives have installed a culture of open dialogue, which makes this type of implementation possible. Even under a change in the political landscape it would be difficult to go back to a less databased and less dialogue-orientated situation. In addition, the ministry facilitated the large pool of secondary data that was made available in Rhineland-Palatinate. These data can be used in the monitoring process. Official school statistics, for instance, are quite a bit more extensive compared to other German states.

5.6 Summary

The Ministry for Social Affairs, Labour, Health and Demography of Rhineland Palatinate is responsible for and bears the costs of the development of scenarios for securing skilled healthcare personnel. Thus, the procedures for doing so are influenced by typical hierarchical governance structures. Policy-makers provide the framework for the procedures. As a result, both IWAK as the executive body and the stakeholders of the board are bound by this framework. Nevertheless, the procedure is characterised by the strong involvement of the stakeholders, which is institutionalised for the most part. To this extent, hierarchical (H=hierarchy) as well as participative (N=network) modes of governance ensue. Transparency, participation, integrity and capacity are rather high, while accountability can be rated as rather low (see Table 4).

Table 4   Types and dimensions of governance within the construction of scenarios for securing skilled healthcare personnel

Mode	Quality Criteria				
	Transparency	Accountability	Participation	Integrity	Capacity
H+N	rather high	rather low	rather high	rather high	rather high

Source: IWAK 2017.

6. Conclusion and outlook

In conclusion, the specifics that come into effect for elaborating the scenarios for securing skilled healthcare personnel in Rhineland-Palatinate will be summarised. Compiling target figures for measures undertaken to secure skilled healthcare personnel is part of a complex monitoring process. It was implemented based on labour market research in order to better match demand and supply developments in the labour market. The strong involvement of all stakeholders has been institutionalised, and numerous communication platforms and feedback loops have been set up. The aim is to reduce the overall costs of policy implementation and enable innovative healthcare workforce governance through a sort of "learning system of policy-making" (Kuhlmann et al. 2016, p. 7). The basis of this is a reciprocal culture of respect and trust, the acceptance of a division of labour, the willingness to embrace change and a creative drive. Problems can and should be identified to make new challenges apparent and facilitate the collaborative search for solutions to those challenges.

Apart from stakeholder involvement, the utilisation of labour-market and educational data plays an important role for elaborating scenarios for securing skilled healthcare personnel. A major part of the modelling process is based on such data. Especially important are data about the current and prospective labour market situation, which was generated in the beginning of the monitoring process and created a common understanding of the situation. These data are the starting point for subsequent decisions.

The role of IWAK is important for elaborating the scenarios we have described here. As an independent academic institute, it acts as an intermediary between state policymakers and stakeholders among the professional public. For constructing the scenarios, a wide repertoire of social-scientific methods are employed. This is important because the data available in Germany, as well as the institutional settings of the German healthcare system, are quite disparate and fragmented. The connection between quantitative statistical data and qualitative expert information provided by the various stakeholders thus adds valuable knowledge about the development of the different health professions and the potential for different measures for securing skilled healthcare personnel (Kuhlmann 2016). This is particularly helpful since monitoring of the situation in Rhineland-Palatinate takes place on a relatively small scale. Region-specific information is needed which is often not available through official statistics. For example, a head of school may be able to provide specific information about where the graduates are placed, or a nursing manager mighty provide information about the potential or recruiting foreign-trained nurses in the region.

All things considered, the scenarios are just one step in the monitoring process. They need to be finalised in collaboration with the ministry and the stakeholders. Objective targets must be agreed on. To achieve these aims, specific measure would need to be implemented. This represents considerable effort for everyone involved, such as policy-makers, organisations and schools, etc. Experiences in the monitoring process indicate that these objectives can be achieved: Within the last several years, steps taken have included extending the capacity of vocational education and training, increasing the number of apprentices, and attracting more foreign-trained nurses to Rhineland Palatinate (Dalichau et al. 2017). Therefore, the orientation of scenarios for securing skilled healthcare personnel with the participation of all relevant stakeholders can contribute to avoiding the forecasted gap of 1,744 nurses in the year 2025.

References

Becka, Denise/Evans, Michaela/Öz, Fikret (2016): Teilzeitarbeit in Gesundheit und Pflege. Profile aus Perspektive der Beschäftigten im Branchen- und Berufsvergleich, in: Forschung aktuell, No. 4

Benz, Arthur/Lütz, Susanne/Schimank, Uwe/Simonis, Georg (2007): Einleitung, in: Benz, Arthur/Lütz, Susanne/Schimank, Uwe/Simonis, Georg (Eds.): Handbuch Governance. Theoretische Grundlagen und empirische Anwendungsfelder, Wiesbaden: VS Verlag für Sozialwissenschaften, pp. 9-24

Bieräugel, Roland/Demireva, Lora/Larsen, Christa/Lauxen, Oliver/Papke, Jan/Metzenrath, Anke (2012a): Branchenmonitoring Gesundheitsfachberufe Rheinland-Pfalz. Ergebnisse aus dem Landesleitprojekt „Fachkräftesicherung in den Gesundheitsfachberufen", in: Berichte aus der Pflege No. 17, Ministerium für Soziales, Arbeit, Gesundheit und Demografie Rheinland-Pfalz

Bieräugel, Roland/Demireva, Lora/Larsen, Christa/Lauxen, Oliver/Papke, Jan/Metzenrath, Anke (2012b): Gutachten zum Fachkräfte- und Ausbildungsbedarf. Ergebnisse aus dem Landesleitprojekt „Fachkräftesicherung in den Gesundheitsfachberufen", in: Berichte aus der Pflege No. 18, Ministerium für Soziales, Arbeit, Gesundheit und Demografie Rheinland-Pfalz

Bundesagentur für Arbeit (2015): Der Arbeitsmarkt in Deutschland – Fachkräfteengpassanalyse: http://statistik.arbeitsagentur.de/Navigation/Statistik/Arbeitsmarktberichte/Fachkraeftebedarf-Stellen/Fachkraeftebedarf-Stellen-Nav.html, last accessed on 8 March 2017

Burkhart, Michael/Ostwald, Dennis A./Erhard, Tobias (2012): 112 – und niemand hilft, Frankfurt am Main: PricewaterhouseCoopers AG Wirtschaftsprüfungsgesellschaft

Castello, Melanie/Lauxen, Oliver/Schäfer, Lisa (2017a): Branchenmonitoring Gesundheitsfachberufe Rheinland-Pfalz 2015. Ergebnisse aus dem Landesprojekt „Branchenmonitoring und Ausbildungsbedarf Gesundheitsfachberufe Rheinland-Pfalz 2015", in: Berichte aus der Pflege No. 30, Ministerium für Soziales, Arbeit, Gesundheit und Demografie Rheinland-Pfalz

Castello, Melanie/Dalichau, Dirk/Lauxen, Oliver/Schäfer, Lisa (2017b): Gutachten zum Fachkräftebedarf in den Gesundheitsfachberufen in Rheinland-Pfalz. Ergebnisse aus dem Landesprojekt „Branchenmonitoring und Ausbildungsbedarf Gesundheitsfachberufe Rheinland-Pfalz 2015", in: Berichte aus der Pflege No. 31, Ministerium für Soziales, Arbeit, Gesundheit und Demografie Rheinland-Pfalz

Dalichau, Dirk/Lauxen, Oliver (2017): Regionale Workshops zur Steigerung der Ausbildungszahlen in den Pflegeberufen in Rheinland-Pfalz. Abschlussbericht, under review

Dalichau, Dirk/Lauxen, Oliver/Larsen, Christa (2017): Stand der Umsetzung der „Fachkräfte- und Qualifizierungsinitiative Gesundheitsfachberufe Rheinland-Pfalz 2012-2015" (FQI), Berichte aus der Pflege No. 29, Ministerium für Soziales, Arbeit, Gesundheit und Demografie Rheinland-Pfalz

DKG (Deutsche Krankenhaus Gesellschaft) (2014): Bestandsaufnahme zur Krankenhausplanung und Investitionsfinanzierung in den Bundesländern: http://www.dkgev.de/media/file/21337.Bestandsaufnahme_Januar_2014.pdf, last accessed on 2 March 2017

Doblhammer, Gabriele/ Westphal, Christina/ Ziegler, Ute (2006): Pflegende Angehörige brauchen mehr Unterstützung. Bedarfsprognosen zeigen Anstieg häuslichen Pflegepotenzials in Deutschland bis 2030, in: Demografische Forschung Aus Erster Hand, Vol. 3, No. 4, pp. 3

Greer, Scott L./ Wismar, Matthias/Figueras, Josep/Vasev, Nikolay (2016): Policy lessons for health governance, in: Greer, Scott L./Wismar, Matthias/Figueras, Josep (Eds.): Strengthening health system governance: better policies, stronger performance, Maidenhead: Open University Press, pp. 105–125

Isfort, Michael/Rottländer, Ruth/Weidner, Frank/Tucman, Daniel/Gehlen, Danny/Hylla, Jonas (2016): Pflege-Thermometer 2016. Eine bundesweite Befragung von Leitungskräften zur Situation der Pflege und Patientenversorgung in der ambulanten Pflege, online: http://www.dip.de/fileadmin/data/pdf/projekte/Endbericht_Pflege-Thermometer_2016-MI-2.pdf, last accessed on 8 March 2017

Joost, Angela (2013): Altenpflegekräfte länger im Beruf halten. Chancen, Potenziale und strategische Ansätze, in: Bundesgesundheitsblatt, Vol. 56, No. 8, pp. 1112–1118

Kroezen, Marieke/Dussault, Gilles/Craveiro, Isabel/Dieleman, Marjolein/Jansen, Christel/Buchan, James/Barriball, Louise/Rafferty, Anne Marie/Bremner, Jeni/Sermeus, Walter (2015): Recruitment and retention of health professionals across Europe: A literature review and multiple case study research, in: Health Policy, Vol. 119, No. 12, pp. 1517-1528

Kuhlmann, Ellen/Larsen, Christa (2015): Why we need multi-level health workforce governance: Case studies from nursing and medicine in Germany, in: Health Policy, Vol. 119, No. 12, pp. 1636-1644

Kuhlmann, Ellen/Lauxen, Oliver/Larsen, Christa (2016): Regional health workforce monitoring as governance innovation: a German model to coordinate sectoral demand, skill mix and mobility, in: Human Resources for Health, Vol. 14, No. 71, online: http://rdcu.be/m4Ul, last accessed on 2 March 2017

Larsen, Christa/Mevius, Marco (2007): The importance of communication for the success of regional labour market monitoring, in: Larsen, Christa/Mathejczyk, Waldemar/Schmid, Alfons (Eds.): Monitoring of regional labour markets in European states. Concepts–experiences–perspectives, München: Hampp Verlag, pp. 70–81

Lauxen, Oliver/Castello, Melanie (2016): Die Arbeitsmarktlage für Altenpflegefachkräfte im zeitlichen Vergleich – Ergebnisse aus dem Hessischen Pflegemonitor, in: Pflegen, No. 1+2, pp. 6-10

Lauxen, Oliver (2015a): Problemlagen und Handlungsansätze – Bericht aus der Arbeitsgruppe „Assistenzberufe". Abschlussbericht im Rahmen der „Fachkräfte- und Qualifizierungsinitiative

Gesundheitsfachberufe 2012-2015", online: http://www.iwak-frankfurt.de/wp-content/uploads/2015/10/Bericht_Assistenzberufe_final.pdf, last accessed on 2 March 2017

Lauxen, Oliver (2015b): Problemlagen und Handlungsansätze – Bericht aus der Arbeitsgruppe „Therapeutische Gesundheitsfachberufe". Abschlussbericht im Rahmen der „Fachkräfte- und Qualifizierungsinitiative Gesundheitsfachberufe 2012-2015", online: http://www.iwak-frankfurt.de/wp-content/uploads/2015/10/Bericht_Therapeutische_GFB_final.pdf, last accessed on 2 March 2017

Ministerium für Arbeit, Soziales, Gesundheit, Familie und Frauen, Rheinland-Pfalz (2008): Abschlussbericht Branchenmonitoring Pflege Rheinland-Pfalz 2005/2006, Institut für Wirtschaft, Arbeit und Kultur, in: Berichte aus der Pflege Nr. 7, online: https://msagd.rlp.de/fileadmin/msagd/Gesundheit_und_Pflege/GP_Dokumente/Berichte_aus_der_Pflege_25.pdf, last accessed on 2 March 2017

Ministerium für Soziales, Arbeit, Gesundheit und Demografie Rheinland-Pfalz (2013): Vereinbarung zur Fachkräfte- und Qualifizierungsinitiative Gesundheitsfachberufe 2012-2015, Berufsfeld Pflege, in: Berichte aus der Pflege Nr. 25, online: https://msagd.rlp.de/fileadmin/msagd/Gesundheit_und_Pflege/GP_Dokumente/Berichte_aus_der_Pflege_25.pdf, last accessed on 2 March 2017

Nowossadeck, Enno (2013): Demografischer Wandel, Pflegebedürftige und der künftige Bedarf an Pflegekräften, in: Bundesgesundheitsblatt, Vol. 56, No. 8, pp. 1040–1047

Ostwald, Dennis A./Ehrhard, Tobias/Bruntsch, Friedrich/Schmidt, Harald/Friedl, Corinna (2010): Fachkräftemangel. Stationärer und ambulanter Bereich bis 2030, Frankfurt am Main: PricewaterhouseCoopers AG Wirtschaftsprüfungsgesellschaft

Pilger, Carmen/Jahn, Daniel (2013): Gesundheitswesen in Baden-Württemberg. Struktur und Entwicklung der Beschäftigung, in: IAB-Regional Baden-Württemberg, No. 01/2013

Pohl, Carsten (2011): Demografischer Wandel und der Arbeitsmarkt für Pflege in Deutschland: Modellrechnungen bis zum Jahr 2030, in: Pflege & Gesellschaft, Vol. 16, No. 1, pp. 36–52

Rothgang, Heinz/Kulik, Dawid/Müller, Rolf/Unger, Rainer (2009): GEK-Pflegereport 2009. Schwerpunktthema: Regionale Unterschiede in der pflegerischen Versorgung, Schwäbisch Gmünd: Schriftenreihe zur Gesundheitsanalyse, Band 73

Schaade, Peter (2013): Gesundheitswesen in Hessen. Die Beschäftigung boomt, in: IAB-Regional Hessen, No. 01/2013

Simoens, Steven/Villeneuve, Mike/Hurst, Jeremy (2005): Tackling Nurse Shortages in OECD Countries, in: OECD Health Working Papers No. 19

Statistisches Bundesamt (2016): Gesundheit. Diagnosedaten der Patienten und Patientinnen in Krankenhäusern (einschl. Sterbe- und Stundenfälle) 2015, Wiesbaden: https://www.destatis.de/DE/Publikationen/Thematisch/Gesundheit/Krankenhaeuser/DiagnosedatenKrankenhaus2120621157004.pdf;jsessionid=88E7E2ADEC36EE64A913535892D47FFE.cae3?__blob=publicationFile, last accessed on 2 March 2017

Statistisches Bundesamt (2017): Pflegestatistik 2015. Pflege im Rahmen der Pflegeversicherung. Deutschlandergebnisse, Wiesbaden: https://www.destatis.de/DE/Publikationen/Thematisch/Gesundheit/Pflege/PflegeDeutschlandergebnisse5224001159004.pdf?__blob=publicationFile, last accessed on 2 March 2017

Statistische Ämter des Bundes und der Länder (Eds.) (2008): Demografischer Wandel in Deutschland. Heft 2. Auswirkungen auf Krankenhausbehandlungen und Pflegebedürftige im Bund und in den Ländern, Wiesbaden

SVR (Sachverständigenrat zur Begutachtung der Entwicklung im Gesundheitswesen) (2009): Koordination und Integration - Gesundheitsversorgung in einer Gesellschaft des längeren Lebens. Sondergutachten 2009. Kurzfassung, online: http://www.svr-gesundheit.de/fileadmin/user_upload/Gutachten/2009/Kurzfassung-2009.pdf, last accessed on 8 March 2017

Wahl, Hans-Werner/Schneekloth, Ulrich (2008): Hintergrund und Positionierung des Projekts MuG III, in: Schneekloth, Ulrich/Wahl, Hans-Werner (Eds.): Selbständigkeit und Hilfebedarf bei älteren Menschen in Privathaushalten. Pflegearrangements, Demenz, Versorgungsangebote, 2nd Edition, Stuttgart: Kohlhammer, pp. 13-54

Wiethölter, Doris (2012): Berufstreue in Gesundheitsberufen in Berlin und Brandenburg. Die Bindung der Ausbildungsabsolventen an den Beruf: Ausgewählte Gesundheitsberufe im Vergleich, in: IAB-Regional Berlin-Brandenburg, No. 03/2012

Zika, Gerd/Helmrich, Robert/Kalinowski, Michael/Wolter, Marc Ingo/Hummel, Markus/Maier, Tobias/ Hänisch, Carsten/ Drosdowski, Thomas (2012): In der Arbeitszeit steckt noch eine Menge Potenzial. Qualifikations- und Berufsfeldprojektionen bis 2030, in: IAB-Kurzbericht, No. 03/2012

Challenges for Albania Regrading Improving the Labour Market Information System and Labour Market Governance from Hierarchy to Market to Network Governance

Neshat Zeneli

1. Abstract

The labour market policy of the Republic of Albania in terms of design (preparation, issue identification, formulation and approval), programming and budgeting, implementation, monitoring and evaluation does not have a long history (1993-ongoing). The influence and presence of the hierarchy model is very high besides the support of different programs and projects through bilateral and EU programs. Still, there are a lot of key issues to be addressed.

The most important issues to be addressed in this paper are:

- The labour market structure on a national, regional and local level in Albania and the availability of labour market information and how this information is used for policy-making and monitoring/evaluation in terms of input, output, outcome and impact.
- The mode of governance of the labour market in Albania and challenges to change from hierarchy governance to market and network governance.

The main aim of this paper is to perform a complete and thorough analysis of the actual situation of the labour market information system and labour market governance in Albania and to propose conclusions and recommendations that will improve both the labour market information system and labour market governance. A change from hierarchy governance to market and network governance is needed, because a good and standardised labour market information system can help in making the right policy decisions and good governance of labour market policy means more employment, more stability, more social inclusion in society.

2. Introduction

Good governance[1] in general terms and good governance of labour markets are some of the key issues in ensuring sustainable employment and development. Good governance is more imperative in transition countries such as Albania and the other Western Balkan countries, to align them with the standards of the European Union as soon as possible. The study of governance is also concerned with the structure of decision-making and policy implementation in a distinct system (Greer et al. 2016: 3).

For the purpose of this paper the decision-making and policy implementations of the labour market policy in Albania will be analysed in a complete and thorough manner through a logical framework approach, starting with:

- A description of the current situation of the labour market information system[2] and;
- A description of the governance mode of the labour market policies.

The research questions raised in this paper are:

- Does the labour market information system in Albania fulfil the standards of an optimal labour market system?
- What kind of governance mode (hierarchy, market or network mode) is used by the labour market policy-makers in Albania?

The final aim of this paper is to do a complete and detailed analysis of the actual situation of the labour market information system and labour market governance in Albania, to propose conclusions and recommendations that will improve both the labour market Information system and labour market governance, because good governance of labour market policy means more employment, more stability, more social inclusion in society.

---

1 Governance has been defined as "directing, guiding or regulating individuals, organizations, or nations in conduct or actions" (Lynn 2010: 67).
2 Labour market information includes any quantitative and qualitative information and intelligence on the labour market agents in making informed plans, choices, and decisions related to business requirements, career planning and preparation, education and training offering, job searches, hiring, and governmental policy and workforce investment strategies. (IOM-International Organization for Migration2011-Best practices for the improvement of the Labour Market Information Systems).

3. Description of the situation

The labour market information system and governance of labour markets in Albania, is not yet at the heart of the political agenda. These two concepts are elaborated in the policy documents as follows.

The first one was designed in July 2012 in the policy paper titled: "Developing a Labour Market Information System in Albania" commissioned by the GIZ VET program in Albania in cooperation between GIZ/ Vocational Education and Training Program and the Former Ministry of Labour, Social Affairs and Equal Opportunities (now the Ministry of Social Welfare and Youth).

The second one was developed in the National Employment and Skills Strategy, 2014-2020, designed by the Ministry of Social Welfare and Youth, approved by the Decision of Council of Minister Nr. 818, date 26.11.2014, in the fourth part of the policy objective of the strategy titled: "strengthening of the governance of the labour market and qualification systems"

Based on the INSTAT online publications of the Republic of Albania (www.instat.gov.al) that have improved a lot from 2007-2016, it has actually become easier to retrieve official data and conduct analyses regarding some of the key indicators of the labour market such as: (un-)employment rate, youth (un-)employment rate, employment by economic sector, employment by status of work etc.

The description of the situation based on a comparative approach is done for the last three decades and started with 1992 as the first year after the collapse of the communist regime and 2007 has been selected as the first year of the application of the Labour Force Survey in Albania. All data after 2007 makes reference to Labour Force Survey. The data of 1992 and 2000 make reference to administrative data.

For more details on labour market data for Albania 1992-2016, please see Table 1 below.

Table 1 Population, employment and unemployment in Albania from 1992 to 2016, divided by sector

Nature of employment	1992	2000	2007[3]	2010	2016
Working age population	1,849,000	1,939,000	2,105,961	1,800,606	2,374,391[4]
Total Labour Force	1,489,000	1,283,000	1,382,464	1,358,029	1,364,948
Employed	1,095,000	1,068,190	1,197,684	1,167,376	1,157,177
Employed in the public sector	614,607	191,166	185,000	185,000	164 635
Employed in the private sector non-agriculture (administrative data).	60,000 or 5.5%	116,024 or 10.8%	229,900 or 24.5%	229, 900	412,473 or 39.6%
Employed in the agricultural private sector (administrative data).	38%	71%	57.7 %	42.1%	46.1 %
Jobseekers/unemployed	394,000[5] or 26.5%	215,000 or 16.8%	184,780[6] or 13.5%	190,653 or14.2	207,770 or 15.6%
Youth unemployment (between 15-29 years old)	n. a	n. a	19.8%	22.5%[7]	28.9%

Source: INSTAT, Republic of Albania, The Statistical Yearbook 1991-1999, 1993-2001,2010-2014, and Labour Force Survey 2007, 2010 and 2016.

Another important element of the labour market information system is the analysis of the skills and qualifications of the people by investigating the vocational education and training (VET) systems as well as the university education system (in terms of quantity and quality) based on agreed upon standards. The student enrolment data from Albania between 1990 -2016 offers the following insights.

---

3 In 2007, INSTAT started the Labour Force Survey, based on international standards set by EUROSTAT.
4 From 1992-2010 the working age was defined as between 15-64 and in 2016 the working age was defined as 15-year-olds.
5 Jobseekers registered in the public employment offices.
6 The data on unemployment from 2007-2016 makes reference to the Labour Force Survey. The data from 1992 2000 are administrative data reported by registered jobseekers in employment offices.
7 Age group 15-29 years old for 2007, 2010 and 2016, this is different compared to EU member countries where the working age group for youth unemployment is 15-25.

After the collapse of the former communist regime, all the former upper professional schools (agriculture profile) of the rural area were transformed into upper secondary general schools in 1992. This process resulted in a drastic diminution of the rate of enrolment in professional schools, from 59% (or 123,137 students) in 1991 to 19.5% in 2015 (or 27,267 students). The number of students enrolled at university increased by nearly six times between 1990-2016, rising from 27,641 students in 1991 to 162,544 students in 2015. For more details regarding quantitative data on enrolment and graduation for pupils and students for upper general secondary, upper professional and university level between 1991-2015, please see Table 2.

Table 2   Evolution of enrolment and graduation of students in Albania
1990-2015

		1990-1991	2000-2001	2010-2011	2014-2015
1.	Total of students enrolled at private and public universities[8]	27,641 22,059(FT[9])	40,859 23,704(FT)	134,877 88,439 (FT)	162,544 111,663 (FT)
1.1	Total of students enrolled at private higher education institutions (universities)	n. a	n. a	27,375	24,134
1.1	Females	n. a	n. a	55.3%	57%
1.2	Total of students graduated from university	4647	4618	22,814	29,504
2	Total of students enrolled in upper secondary schools	205,774	108,178	150,134	140,042
2.1	Students enrolled in general education schools	82,637	91,786	131,437	112,775
2.1.1	Students graduated from general schools	12,635	16,337	35,553	34,927
2.2	Total of students enrolled in vocational educational schools	123,137	16,387	18,697	27,267
2.2.1	Pupils graduated in Vocational Education Schools	18,999	2,506	4,801	4,702
2.2.2	Female	9,715	856	1,858	1,349

Source: INSTAT, Republic of Albania, Statistical Yearbook 1991-1999, 1993-2001, Ministry of Education and Sport, Statistical Yearbook 2012-2013, and 2014-2015.

Another key element of the comparison between different education systems in different countries is the student's enrolment and graduation according to the

---

[8] The first private University in Albania opened in 2002, New York University of Tirana and in 2016 there were 27 operational private Universities. Public Higher Education Institutions (Universities) in 2016 in Albania number 15 in the main cities as Tirana with eight, Shkodër with two, Korçë, Elbasanë, Durrës, Gjirokastër and Vlorë with one University for each city.
[9] Full-time.

standards of the ISCED (International Standard Classification of Education of UNESCO) which is composed of:

Ten education programmes with their respective code:

- 0-Early childhood education, 1-Primary education, 2-Lower secondary education, 3-Upper secondary education, 4- Post-secondary non-tertiary education, 5-Short-cycle tertiary education, 6- Bachelor's or equivalent level, 7-Master's or equivalent level, 8-Doctoral or equivalent level and 9-Not classified elsewhere, and;

Nine broad groups and fields of education with their respective code:

- 0-General programmes, 1-Education, 2-Humanities and arts, 3-Social sciences, business and law, 4-Science, 5-Engineering, manufacturing and construction, 6-Agriculture, 7-Health and welfare, 8-Services.

For more details on the broad groups of education field in Albania for the years 2005-2010, 2015 please see Table 1 above and Graph 1 below.

Graph 1   Graduated students in universities in Albania based on the broad group of fields of education (2005, 2010 and 2015)

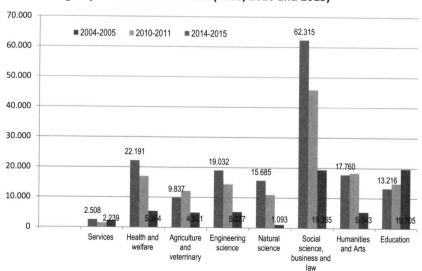

Source: Ministry of Education and Science- Albania-Statistical Yearbook on Education 2012-2013, and 2014-2015.

The figures on enrolment in Albania from 2005-2015 based on broad groups and fields of education show that the education system is not in line with the main economic sectors such as agriculture and services. The rate of enrolment in natural science is also very low compared to other fields of education.

Quality assessment of the vocational education training (VET) and university systems in Albania, related to one of the most important indicators of quality assurance[10] (employment rate after the finishing of the education system and utilisation of the education skills received in the labour market), is not yet functional. Different pilot reports have been done through projects and programs such as the Cards VET III program by the European Union in June 2009, titled: "tracer study on the graduates from the technical vocational educations schools", or the GIZ VET program in June 2014 titled: "pilot tracer system in Public Vocational Training Canters of Tirana and mobile vocational training canter of north east of Albania".

Some improvements are available in terms of information on the providers of the vocational training schools and public vocational training centres such as www.shkp.gov.al, the website of the Public Employment Service. There, information regarding the locations of ten public vocational training centres and the provided courses is available and on another website www.vet.al, information on legislation and regulation of the VET system in Albania can be found, such as the typology of profiles offered by the professional vocational schools in the country.

The weak point of this information is that it is not very functional for the follow up and matching process in the labour market. There is no interconnection at the local level between public employment offices and the list of graduates by profession at the end of the academic year. This interconnection could be very useful for the intermediary acting between the employers that need skilled workers and the employment advisers that guide and help graduates integrate into the labour market.

---

10 Recommendation of the EU Parliament and Council from the 18th June 2009, on the establishment of a European Quality Assurance Reference Framework for Vocational Education and Training.

4. Analysis of the current situation of labour market information system in Albania and users of LMI

The labour market information system is not yet at the heart of the political agenda. The first political document on this issue was published by GIZ-Albania - Vocational Education and Training Program in cooperation with the Former Ministry of Labour, Social Affairs and Equal Opportunities (now the Ministry of Social Welfare and Youth), in July 2012 titled: "Developing a Labour Market Information System in Albania".

Legal and Institutional context: the concept of the labour market information system is regulated in a legal framework, the promotion employment law nr. 7995 of 20.09.1995, amended in 1999, 2002, and 2006. For more details on LMI framework in Albania see Box 3. below.

Box 1 Legal framework in Albania on labour market Information[11]

> **I: Law No. 7995, 20 September 1995: "For Promotion of Employment "**
>
> **Article 23-Employer obligations**
>
> Every employer reports to the public employment office every three months regarding:
>
> - The number of employed people and a list with their names and;
> - The most important activity of the company, for example an increase in employment, a stable situation or a decrease in employment etc.
>
> **Article 24-Employment office**
>
> Every employment office reports to the General Director of National Employment Office regarding:
>
> - The number of jobseekers employed after searching for a job in the public employment office with the respective attached list;
> - The number of employers and institutions that the public employment office has contacted and has relations with in the local area where the employment office is operational;
> - The number of job vacancies according to profession, level of education and qualification requested;
> - The number of layoffs and expected bankruptcies and;
> - The number of people/jobseekers trained by profession, education, age and gender.

---

[11] Box 1 is a synthesis of the legal framework elaborated by the author after analyzing the available legal framework in Albania.

II: Decision of the Council of Minister on Labour Market Information in Albania No. 94, 2 April 1998
This decision gives responsibility and competences to the Ministry of Social Welfare and Youth to: • Collect and elaborate statistical information on the labour market and social protection and;   • To use it for analyses and forecasts of the labour market.   • After that the Ministry of Social Welfare and Youth has to approve the final report of the forecast of the labour market and send it to all ministries and public institutions at the central level.
III: Law No. 9180, 5 February 2014: "For official statistics"
The law "For official statistics" defines all the responsibilities and competences of INSTAT of the Republic of Albania for the publication of official statistical data for the public and for all State Institutions such as the Parliament, the Prime Minister Office, for business and economic associations and for research and academic institutions etc.

Source: Law No. 7995, 20 September 1995: "For Promotion of Employment" of the Republic of Albania, Law No. 9180, 5 Februar 2014: "For official statistics" and Decision of the Council of Minister on Labour Market Information in Albania No. 94, 2 April 1998.

The current situation of the labour market information system: in order to conduct a detailed analysis of the current situation, this part of the paper will analyse the currently available labour market information, the shortcomings still inhibiting an optimal[12] labour market information system and offer a proposal for moving forward. The LMI in Albania is provided by many actors, but the most important ones are: INSTAT, the Ministry of Social Welfare and Youth, the National Employment Service and the Ministry of Education and Sports. The majority of the information is provided by INSTAT. From 2012 onwards INSTAT has improved its offering of online publications (www.instat.gov.al) in general and for labour markets specifically. A detailed analysis of the typology of the available information from the key actors will be provided in Table 3 below, including frequency and comments.

---

12 The data foundation for an optimal labour market information system is classified by the W.F Upjohn Institute for Employment research into six categories: 1) core labour force and market data, 2) demand data, 3) occupational supply, 4) occupational characteristics, 5) education and training information, and 6) crosswalks and linkages across different data sets.

Table 3 The key sources of LMI in Albania

I	INSTAT	Frequency	Comments
1.	Census of the population	Decennial	The last one is from 2011.
2.	Labour Market	2007-2011 annually 2012-2016, quarterly & annually	The reports are published and public. Very good foundation for doing analysis at a national and regional level. **Weak point:** The data does not reflect the local level (61 one new municipalities).
3.	Business register	Every year	The last one is from 2016. Are public and published. The data are available also at the local level and this is very important for doing analysis at the local level.
4.	Census of agriculture entities	Every four years	Is supported by the Government of Sweden.
5.	Labour Cost Survey	Every four years	The last one was published in 2013.
II	**Ministry of Social welfare and Youth**	Frequency	Comments
1	Different strategies	Every 5-6 years	National Employment and Skills Strategy 2014-2020, National Action Plan for Youth 2015-2020 and National Strategy for Social Protection 2015-2020 etc. **Weak Point:** no evaluation report available or published for the users –individuals/ intermediaries including employment specialists, counsellors, government officials and business etc.
2	Annual Report	Every year	**Not available** There are some monitoring reports but no updated ones, the latest one is January-September 2015[13].
III	**National Employment Service**	Frequency	Comments

---

13 www.sociale.gov.al, date of access 2 June 2017.

1	Statistical Yearbook	Every year	The last one is from 2016. It offers good data on jobseekers, job vacancies, promotion employment programs, delivery and participants of vocational training courses.
			Weak Point: No data on promotion employment programs at the local level. This makes it difficult to study local approaches.
2	Skills Data Analysis	The last one is from 2014	A good foundation but not repeated every year and no ownership at the regional and local level.
			Weak Point: No ownership at the regional and local level.
IV	**Ministry of Education and Sports**	**Frequency**	**Comments**
1	Statistical Yearbook on Education.	The last one is from 2014-2015	Good basis for analysis but not useful for matching & intermediaries' institutions[14], whose aim it is to match the demand and the supply side.

Source: www.instat.gov.al, www.sociale.gov.al, www.arsimi.gov.al, www.shkp.gov.al.

Based on the above key sources of labour market information in Albania, I can argue that there is a good foundation for moving forward. In order to reach optimal standards in the labour market information system in Albania, work at an operational level and not only at a strategic level is needed, to close the most important gaps that are:

- Lack of local labour market information and analysis;
- Lack of structure and regular skills require analysis through a local/regional and national approach and dissemination of it;
- Lack of structured transparency on labour market information as per optimal standards in order to realise: "The establishment of a Labour Market Information System as an Inclusive activity and promotion of the culture of using the labour market information for all the categories of users at individual levels (workers, and students) at intermediaries level institu-

---

[14]. The forms of the labour market intermediaries (LMI)-matching workers to jobs are: placing workers in jobs (Public employment services (PES), Private employment agencies and for Temporary work agencies (TWA)-employing workers to place in a job with third party, Private employment agencies only. Eurofound(European Foundation for the Improvement of Living and Working Conditions), page 13 of the publication Regulation of labour market intermediaries and the role of social partners in preventing trafficking of labour 2016.

tions (public employment offices, private employment agencies), governmental officials at national and regional and local levels (Woods and O'Leary 2006: 23).

5. Analysis of labour market governance in Albania

In the last two decades (2000-ongoing), the different governments of Albania have not achieved the designed output terms of governance of the labour market, for ensuring a better employment situation, as designed in chapter three of the National Employment and Skills Strategy 2014-2020, titled "Strengthening the governance of the labour market and qualification systems" - wherein the outcome indicators and outputs are defined on pages 74-77.

The unemployment in general and the youth unemployment in particular are very high compared to the average of the EU countries. For more details see Graph 2.

Graph 2   Youth unemployment in the EU, Albania and Western Balkan of less than 25 years old

Country	2005	2010	2015
EU 28	19	21.4	20.4
Albania	20.1	30.5	20
Kosovo	70.5	55.3	57.7
Bos-Herc	62.3	57.7	62.3
Fyrom-MK	62.6	53.7	47.3
Montenegro	0	43.7	47.3
Serbia	47.7	46.1	43.2

Source: Eurostat, basic figures on enlargement countries 2016 edition.

The very high level of youth unemployment in Albania and Western Balkan countries makes the improvement of labour market policies and labour market governance imperative. This is achieved through the use of best practices from EU countries, through the improvement of policy design, policy implementation, policy evaluation and the governance of the labour market and qualification systems, with the final aim being to ensure better employability for all categories, including the young people, besides the level of qualifications that they have.

Analysis of the situation as per policy documents: for details regarding the strategic priority of strengthening the governance of the labour market in Albania see Box 2 below.

Box 2 Strategic priority 2014-2020 for strengthening the governance of the labour market

> Five strategic priorities approved with deadlines ranging from 2014-2020:
> - Reforming the financing and governance of the labour market and VET systems, through the creation of an employment and skills development fund, the creation of an autonomous structure for development and oversights of Vocational Education and Training (actual National Agency for Vocational Education and Training of Albania), strengthening the role of the National Labour Council that exists and through the creation of a new professional body called the National Council for Employment and Vocational Education and Training (VET) etc;
> - Development and implementation of an Albanian Qualification Framework through the establishment of the sectoral committee as per experience of the European Union countries;
> - Improving the quality of labour market information for ensuring effective governance including funding;
> - Modernising the legislative framework of VET;
> - Legislation on mobility and labour market governance is in line with the EU Acquis.

Source: National Employment and Skills Strategy 2014-2020, chapter 3 policy objectives and main outcomes for employment and skills development, pp. 74-77.

The strategic objectives for strengthening governance of the labour market are programmed as per timeline of the National Employment and Skills Strategy 2014-2020, in 80%[15] of the cases for 2014-2020 and this makes it difficult to follow up and evaluate the output and outcome indicator as defined in the Strategy 2014-2020: "labour market and qualification systems are well governed and use the financing and human resources in a transparent and effective manner."

---

[15] Syntheses of the author's analysis. From a total of 15 timeline deadlines for each subjective, twelve of them are deadlines for 2015-2020, and only one deadline is for a specific year, 2015.

If we do the analyses of labour market governance in Albania based on two main indicators:

- Firstly, on the mode of governance (hierarchy, market or network) and on the principles/literature review of Greer et al. (2016) as per the TAPIC framework (Transparency, Accountability, Participation, Integrity and Capacity), and;
- Secondly, based on the Albanian strategic objective outcome indicator from the National Employment and Skills Strategy 2014-2020, which focuses more on the use of financing and human resources in a transparent and effective manner.

I argue that labour market governance in Albania is more hierarchy than market and network and the transparency regarding the use of finance and human resources is far away from EU and modern standards.

In terms of labour market governance, the hierarchic mode is the result of a lack of a structured and optimal labour market information system and this produces a hierarchic mode of decision making, based on individual policy-maker's perceptions and decisions. The hierarchic and in transparent mode of governance is a result of the ex-communist countries mentality and culture of governing. In order to improve the transition from a hierarchy mode to a market and network mode of governance, from 1995 onwards, improvements in the management of the main labour market institutions have been undertaken with the help of a legal framework. Different administrative tripartite boards for public institutions have been created e.g. for the National Employment Service, State Social Service or National Institute of Social Insurance etc. However, at any time the Minister is the chairman and the professionalism of the members of the board is not regulated by professional criteria, but is more a formal representation of social partners in the board mentioned above.

In this context, based on EU standards and on the best practices of the most developed countries on a European level, Albanian labour market governance regarding the governance of all public policies needs to be improved based on the principles of transparency, participation, accountability, and performance monitoring.

The labour market policy inputs in Albania are below European Union standards. The active labour market policy expenditure in Albania is very limited compared to the other EU countries. The 2016, and 2017 budget or funding available for active programs called promotion employment programs is 490,000,000 Albania Lek or 3.5 million Euros for each year (Budget of National Employment Service 2016, 2017 as approved by the government of the Republic of Albania).

The inputs in terms of human resources in the Public Employment Service in Albania are also limited compared to the other countries in the region or worse compared to other EU countries. More details on input in a comparative approach between Albania and some EU countries and Western Balkan countries can be found in Table 4 below.

Table 4 Human resources employed for public employment services in EU countries and Western Balkans

I	European Union Country	Total staff of Public Employment Service	Jobseekers registered	Ratio between advisers and jobseekers	Expenditure for active labour market policies
1	Germany	96,300 full-time staff	2,790,000	Around 80-100 jobseekers per adviser.	-
2	Austria	5831 staff (5231 full time)	354,332	Around 80-100 jobseekers per adviser.	-
3	France	53,000 staff full time	6,200,000	Around 150-200 jobseekers per adviser.	-
II	Balkan Countries	Total staff of Public Employment Service	Jobseekers registered	Ratio between advisers and jobseekers	Expenditure for active labour market policies
1	Slovenia	1100 staff	110,000	150-200 jobseekers per adviser.	Over 100 million Euro per year.
2	Croatia	1242 staff	285,906	250-300 jobseekers per adviser.	
3	Montenegro	332 staff (advisers are divided between advisers for jobseekers, for employers and for vocational training)	41,440	250-300 jobseekers per adviser.	Over 10 million Euro per year.
4	FYROM/ Republic of Macedonia	492 staff (63% of staff work in front office)	n.a	n.a	Around 10 million Euro.
5	Albania	323 staff (200 staff work in front office or 62%)	145,147		3.5 million euro.

Source: Annual Report of PES, Austria, Germany, France, Croatia 2015. Albania National Employment Service Statistical Yearbook 2015.

Besides the limited input for labour market policy in Albania, other sections also need to be improved:

- Improvements of transparency in the management of the available funding by providing annual reports on expenditures and participants by each local entity and not only at the national or regional level.
- Avoid the management of funds for active labour market policy at the central level, because in this way the role of local units is limited, since between 1999-2017, the approval of projects was done at the national level after a formal approval at the regional and local level. This approach produces a bureaucratic and hierarchic mode of governance.

6. Conclusions

In the last decade (from 2010 onwards) there has been an increasing focus on designing policy papers for the labour market information system and labour market governance.

Based on the fact that the labour market information system in Albania is not fully developed in an optimal way when compared to most developed countries, in order to reach optimal standards in the labour market information system some changes are needed. Work at an operational level and not only at a strategic level is needed, to close the most important shortcomings such as:

- Lack of local labour market information and analysis;
- Lack of structure and regular skills require analysis through a local/regional and national approach and dissemination of it. My proposal for a solution: the skills analysis for Albania needs to be done based on EU standards and other developed countries such as the UK model.
- Lack of structured transparency regarding labour market policy by expenditure. In order to fulfil this gap annual reports, need to be published for all expenditures by every local unit (based on the new territorial organisation- 61 municipalities);
- Lack of integration of labour market information and intelligence in the vocational education and training system;
- The integration of the labour market information system into a lifelong learning system, in order to realise: " The establishment of a Labour Market Information System as an Inclusive activity and promotion of the culture of using the labour market information for all the categories of users

at individual levels (workers, and students) at intermediaries level institutions (public employment offices, private employment agencies), governmental officials at national and regional and local levels (Woods and O'Leary 2006: 23).

Regarding labour market governance, besides the designated strategy document, a broader approach for the reform of the labour market in Albania is needed in order to fulfil and apply all the principles of good governance of the labour market.

Regarding labour market information, a lot has to be done to develop and use it for matching and anticipating skills through the five following steps: 1-Building a conducive institutional setting, 2-Data audit, 3-Capability building, 4-Analysis and 5-Dissemination and use of labour market information (ETF, European Training Foundation, Cedefop-European Centre for the Development of Vocational Training and International Labour Office, Geneva, Using Labour Market Information, guide to anticipating and matching skills and jobs Volume 1, 2016).

References

Arbetsförmedlingen (2015): Annual report 2015

Austrian Employment Service (AMS) (2015): 2015 at a Glance, online: http://www.ams.at/_docs/001_gb_2015_kurzbericht_en_2015.pdf

Bundesagentur für Arbeit (2015): Annual report 2015

Cards VET III Support to Vocational Education and Training Reform", Europeaid/125482, June 2009, titled: "tracer study on the graduates from the technical vocational educations schools"

Cedefop (2016): Labour market information and guidance, Luxemburg: Publications Office of the European Union, No.55, online: http://dx.doi.org/10.2801/72440

Employment Service: Yearbook Croatia 2015.

European Foundation for the Improvement of Living and Working Conditions (2016): Regulation of labour market intermediaries and the role of social partners in preventing trafficking of labour, Luxemburg: Publications Office of the European Union

European Training Foundation/Cedefop-European Centre for the Development of Vocational Training/International Labour Office (2016): Using Labour Market Information: Guide to anticipating and matching skills and jobs, Luxemburg: Publications Office of the European Union

European Training Foundation/European Centre for the Development of Vocational Training/International Labour Office (2015): the role of employment service providers: guide to anticipating and matching skills and jobs volume 1, Luxemburg: Publications Office of the European Union

Eurostat (2016): Basic figures on enlargement countries 2016 edition, Luxemburg: Publications Office of the European Union

Eurostat (2017): Key figures on enlargement countries 2017 edition, Luxemburg: Publications Office of the European Union

GIZ Deutsche Gesellschaft für Internationale Zusammenarbeit (2014): Vocational Education and Training (VET) program: pilot tracer system in Public Vocational Training Canters of Tirana and mobile vocational training canter of north east of Albania

Greer, Scott L./Wismar, Matthias/Figueras, Josep (Eds.) (2016 a): Strengthening Health System Governance: Better policies, stronger performance, Maidenhead: Open University Press

Instituti i Statistikës INSTAT: The Statistical Yearbook 1991-1999

Instituti i Statistikës INSTAT: The Statistical Yearbook 1998-2007

Instituti i Statistikës INSTAT: The Statistical Yearbook 2010-2014

Ministry of Education and Sport: Statistical Yearbook on Education 2012-2013

Ministry of Education and Sport: Statistical Yearbook on Education 2014-2015

Ministry of Social Welfare and Youth (2014): National Employment and Skills Strategy 2014-2020

National Employment Service: Statistical Yearbook 2016

Walsh, Kenneth / Muça, Mirela (2012): GIZ VET Program: Developing a Labour Market Information System in Albania, Policy Paper July 2012

Woods, James F./O'Leary, Christopher J. (2006): Conceptual framework for an Optimal Labour Market Information System: Final Report: Upjohn Institute Technical, in: Report Nr.07-022. Kalamazoo, MI: W.E>: WE Upjohn Institute for Employment Research https://doi.org/10.17848/tr07-022.

Websites

Arbeitsmarktservice Österreich: www.ams.at

Instituti i Statistikës INSTAT, Labour Market 2010, 2015, 2016: http://www.instat.gov.al/en/themes/labour-market.aspx

International Standard Classification of Education ISCED, published in 2012 by: UNESCO Institute for Statistics: http://www.uis.unesco.org

Ministria e Arsimit dhe Sportit: www.arsimi.gov.al

Ministria e Mirëqenies Sociele dhe Rinisë: www.sociale.gov.al

Pole Emploi (2015): Rapport annuel: www.pole-emploi.org

Portali i Arsimit dhe Formimit Profesional: www.vet.al

Shërbimi Kombëtar I Punësimit: www.shkp.gov.al

The Provision of Skills Information in Scotland and Its Governance – Skills Investment Plans and Regional Skills Assessments

Ronald McQuaid

1. Introduction

Much of the provision of labour market information and intelligence in Scotland is based on a clear set of multi-level policy frameworks, ranging from local and regional to Scottish, and sometimes, UK levels. Scottish policy is of interest in its emphasis on the process of creating and using skills information to assist economic growth and competitiveness and inclusive growth that tackles inequality. This paper considers some of the ways in which Scottish policies have sought to improve the provision and development of skills information through more effective use of different types of governance and different logics which help to improve the focus and underlying co-ordination of government agencies, employers and other actors.

The integration of policies is needed to support an effective and efficient skills development system. Although there are many definitions of governance, in this paper governance is taken to be the rules, norms and actions around the creation of some examples of skills information in Scotland, incorporating the authority, decision-making and accountability of how this information is created. Related governance systems are likely to be multi-level (supranational/national/regional/local agencies), multi-dimensional (seeking to integrate skills, training/educational demand and supply, economic development, business development policy areas) and multi-stakeholder (public-private-third sector and individuals seeking training) (see Heidenreich et al. 2014). Different variations in governance types may lead to differing results in different locations (Savini et al. 2015), so it is important to be clear about the types of governance that are used.

In addition, the types of institutional logic that influence organisational relations concerning skills information both affect, and are affected by, the types of governance used. Thornton et al. (2012) set out an institutional logics framework for considering inter-organisational relations. Of interest in the present paper are the logics for the system of inter-institutional relations including: *community logics* (local understandings, norms, and rules which may encompass employers' or employer bodies' understanding of the skills system); *professions* (common bodies of knowledge and expertise, criteria and standards of ways of dealing with dealing with issues, perhaps based on personal expertise which may vary greatly by topic or location); *state* (dependent upon public policies, administrative rules, legal competences etc.); *market* (where the operation of market exchange is seen as the appropriate and legitimate form of relationships); and *others* such as family and religion. While institutional logics are located at the supra-organisational level, in practice they are observed at the level of the individual or organisation. In the UK, market logics play an essential role mainly in the provision of training and further education services, including skills information (Fuertes et al. 2014). In general, the UK skills development systems are largely employer led (based on market institutional logic) (Page and Hillage 2006), although the provision of skills development services in terms of further and higher education is heavily government influenced.

The next section of this paper sets out the policy context for skills governance in Scotland and the issue of joint governance for economic development and skills agencies. Section 3 considers the sector provision of labour market information and intelligence and section 4 the spatial provision, by region. Finally, conclusions are set out.

2. Policy context and system wide governance

Scotland is a devolved nation within the UK with a population of 5 million. It has its own Parliament (re-established in 1999 after being dissolved in 1707) with responsibility for skills and economic development. However, the UK Parliament retains control over employment policy. The non-departmental public body bodies of Skills Development Scotland (SDS) and the Scottish Funding Council (SFC) are primarily responsible for skills and Labour Market Information delivery in Scotland (Dean 2015)[1]. SDS works closely, both vertically and horizontally, with: the 32 Scottish local authorities (downward) and the UK Government's Job Centre Plus (upwards); as well as with employers and individuals; and horizontally with other key departments and agencies (e.g. Scottish Enterprise and Highlands

---

[1] SDS and SFC also share a joint Skills Committee to facilitate joint working and offers advice to both organisations on the full range of post-school skills, workforce development and education issues. In addition the government's Scottish Qualifications Agency oversees school and vocational qualifications.

and Islands Enterprise, which are mainly responsible for economic development). SFC is responsible for the funding of post-school further education colleges and universities, including issues related to improving learning and teaching, supporting (university) research and greater innovation in the economy. In contrast to England, Scottish policy and SFC are aimed at greater integration of higher and further education.

Skills policies operate within the context of the government's strategic plans, in particular:

Scotland's Economic Strategy (Scottish Government 2015), which focuses on improving economically and environmentally sustainable economic growth and has goals of both increasing the country's competitiveness and tackling inequality (through prioritising higher investment and innovation, supporting inclusive growth and increasing internationalisation).

Scotland's Labour Market Strategy (Scottish Government 2016), which provides a framework that identifies and supports interactions between the labour market and wider social and economic policies that promote stronger inclusive growth (including issues such as a fair work, employability and skills, investment, innovation and promoting Scotland internationally).

Youth Employment Strategy (Scottish Government 2014) which seeks to implement the recommendations of a Commission for Developing Scotland's Young Workforce and has a target of reducing 2014 levels of youth unemployment by 40% by 2021.

In line with the government's general evidence and outcomes based approach, specific measurable targets with timescales have been set; these include the country being ranked amongst the top quartile of OECD countries for productivity, equality, sustainability and wellbeing.

The Economic Strategy and the other policy documents provide a context to guide the governance of different agencies, policies and programmes. However, given the interconnections between the policy areas, the governance of the joint system as a whole needs consideration[2]. Consistent with European Union (2010) strategies, there is a desire by the Scottish government to better integrate skills

---

[2] As OECD (2012) and Keep and Mayhew (2010) argue, improving the supply of highly qualified workforce will not in itself increase productivity, innovation etc., as there also needs to be investment of various types (physical, intellectual, workforce and financial) and employer demand for greater skills and their utilisation.

development with wider (more demand side) economic development; as a major employment problem is seen as a lack of demand for, rather than a lack of supply of, high skilled workers (Keep 2014). Indeed, skills and economic development were brought together in 1991 when the relevant agencies were merged into Scottish Enterprise, but this was not seen as being particularly successful and the skills function later split out to joint Careers, Modern Apprentices and other skills related services to form the new Skills Development Scotland in 2008. The alignment of the objectives and activities of different agencies, and of the skills and economic development support system in total is often difficult, with resulting inefficiencies and lower effectiveness than if there was closer, mutually reinforcing alignment.

The issues become more complex when the full skills and economic development support system is considered, including multiple actors (both users and service providers and others with a genuine interest in the issues). There can be problems of confusion among users (both individuals and organisations using the system), a range of different institutional logics being in operation, a lack of coherence, inefficiencies, duplication, limited effectiveness and tensions between geographical, sectoral and governmental levels as well as between private, third sector and governmental bodies.

The Scottish government has recently focused on how to set up a governance system to get agencies responsible to them to better work together, as well as to try to make the wider system operate more effectively. As a result, an Enterprise and Skills Review was set up to improve joint governance between the two main skills and two main enterprise support agencies; also taking account of other actors such as employers, trades unions, individuals and other bodies involved in these areas (often at different levels such as local or UK levels, but including complementary, "horizontal" areas such as transport or health) (Scottish Government 2017). Hence the governance explicitly incorporates multi-level (UK, Scotland and local), multi-stakeholder (employers, agencies, individuals) and multi-dimensional (skills, employment, transport etc.) (Fuertes and McQuaid 2016).

The Review's aim was "to ensure that our businesses, workforce, training providers, colleges and universities and young people all receive the joined-up support they need" (First Minister 2016), arguably encompassing various community, professional, state and market institutional logics, but arguably predominantly a largely state logic (and focusing upon the role of state agencies) with recognition of the role of the market. The Scottish Government (2017) proposes to set a new governance mechanism, to be operationalised through a Scottish high level Strategic Board that ensures each of the Agencies (mentioned above plus a new rural development agency in the south) knows the shared goals and aspirations of the whole system, with all activities of each agency contributing to these goals.

The goals for the skills and enterprise system are still to be agreed but will include innovation and high levels of aspiration, a focus on sectors with comparative global strengths and on building a future orientated skills infrastructure. The system will also focus on the skills needed for the economy, developing the appropriate skills among young people but also providing opportunities for up-skilling and reskilling for those who are working in industries which are rapidly being transformed by digital innovation. Upskilling and reskilling is particularly important in Scotland as there is a rapidly aging population structure and technological change, so upgrading the skills of existing, including older, workers are needed and will require changes to the skills system (Canduela et al. 2012, McQuaid et al. 2008). This also suggests an increased focus on the employers' role in increasing demand for higher skills and ensuring better utilisation of workforce skills.

However, a joint inter-agency governance mechanism is likely to affect the freedom of operation and governance of each individual organisation (although each is already formally subordinate to the Parliament and government). The core functions, statutory responsibilities of each individual agency are unchanged but their delivery has to be aligned by the Strategic Board (Scottish Government 2017: 9). This Strategic Board has five main aims:

- To improve the overall performance of the economy by ensuring that the whole Enterprise and Skills System delivers Scotland's Economic Strategy and supporting strategies, in all parts of Scotland.
- Through collective responsibility ensure hard alignment between agencies to drive improvement in Scottish productivity and better support business and users of the skills system.
- Hold agencies to account for performance against agreed measures.
- To actively engage with other agencies and bodies who support the economy with a view to increasing alignment and challenging others where collaboration is not happening.

- To deliver wider collective leadership, based on common culture and values, and which inspires and empowers delivery.

These illustrate various aspects of a governance system, including greater collaboration both between public sector bodies (and between them and employers and wider society), with the Board representing an external "force" (state institutional logic) of being able to hold the individual public bodies to account[3]. In addition, the role of bodies beyond the main government agencies are recognised and are to be influenced through leadership ability to challenge them if there is insufficient alignment. While this mainly suggests multi-dimensional and multi-stakeholder governance, the interaction with non-government and UK government agencies may include multi-level governance. Within the governance structure there will also be a role for regional partnerships to ensure better joint working at the regional level. While a prominent role is given to local authorities and the private sector (market institutional logic), other social actors (such as the Third sector or trades unions or user representatives) are not explicitly given significant roles, although they are likely to be involved in most cases. This focus on one set of non-governmental actors may reflect the need for an approach giving primacy to those other bodies most influenced, and likely to influence, by the successful operation of skills and enterprise system. Mechanisms for the voice and influence of individuals using the system need greater clarity (which might involve the incorporation of greater community logics).

In terms of skills alignment (p. 27), the two main bodies involved in funding provision and delivery (Scottish Funding Council and Skills Development Scotland) are to be more closely aligned through having a single set of strategic skills guidance from Government (encompassing state institutional logics); a Skills Committee of the Strategic Board, providing a joint decision making forum; a joint working team with a single director reporting to the two agency chief executives; and a jointly delivered skills planning and provision model (including the identification of skills needs in partnership with other actors, working with main skills providers to respond to skills needs, investment coordination, performance monitoring and management, and evaluation), encompassing professional logics. So there will be strong coordination between the skills agency, although there may be tensions and potential power struggles between the agencies and

---

3 Thomas Hobbes (1651), the 17th Century philosopher argued that it was difficult to develop co-operation, or a social contract, without a strong central authority.

the joint team that will need to be resolved. This is expected to better help individuals to develop their skills and also reskill and contribute to a more productive workforce and more efficient investment in human capital, as well as reduce skills gaps for employers. From an organisational perspective, it is expected to improve the efficiency and effectiveness of training providers including universities and colleges while reducing duplication. The effectiveness of the Board will depend to a large extent on the implementation and level of long term support across key actors, encompassing each of community, professional, state and market institutional logics, and the avoidance of unintended negative effects (such as potential feelings of disempowerment etc. among the wider set of decision-makers and staff in the agencies and the wider set of bodies).

3. Skills Investment Plans

Multi-stakeholder governance is particularly illustrated by the development of Skills Investment Plans (SIPs). Skills Development Scotland base their skills planning on a model (Figure 1) which roughly includes skills demand and supply factors, as well as main government agency intermediaries, and a clear role for data analysis. This analysis includes the creation of SIPs at an early stage of the model's operation, which is a sector based document produced by Skills Development Scotland on behalf of the Scottish Government, but is explicitly industry-led.

Figure 1 Scottish skills planning model

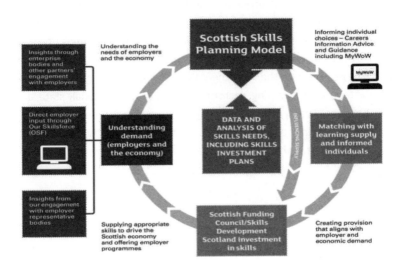

Source: Skills Development Scotland.

SIPs are sector based and eleven have been developed for key (government priority) industrial sectors in the economy (Table 1). They provide: a description of their skills challenges and opportunities; analyse key economic and labour market characteristics and trends in skills and qualification supply together with the perspectives of employers on major skills issues that are likely to influence the growth of the sector. In so doing they aim to help generate a better shared understanding by employers and the educational community of skills needs, however, the involvement of wider parts of the community or other issues are not always fully identified. SIPs are revised or refreshed regularly as the economy and skills needs and supply are dynamic.

Table 1   Skills Investment Plans 2011-17

Sector	SIP Publication
Energy	2011, refresh 2015
Food and Drink	2012 & 2017
Tourism	2013 & 2016
Finance	2013 & 2016
ICT & Digital Technologies	2015
Life Sciences	2015
Engineering	2015
Chemical Sciences	2014
Creative Industries	2015
Construction	2012
Early Learning and Childcare	2017

Source: based on SDS (2017a).

The process of developing SIPs clearly shows the multi-stakeholder dimensions of skills information and intelligence gathering and strategy development for the industry. The process includes: analysis of the sector and its future (involving economic development agencies); a review of the skills needs (involving multi-stakeholder sector skills councils); identifying priorities for skills to enable economic growth of the sector (involving private industry leadership groups); testing the views with the industry; assessing supply-side constraints (involving the skills agencies, SDS, SFC); ensuring buy-in from key actors for the strategy and actions; and the publication of the strategy. Together these are likely to encompass various components of community, professional, state and market institutional logics, arguably underpinned by a market logic.

The SIPs seek to explicitly emphasise skills policy as a driver of economic growth, and means to help in reducing youth unemployment, align skills provision to economic and employer demand and help in the development of Outcome Agreements with further education colleges (where the outcomes of colleges are agreed with their funders).

SIPs reflect different conditions and issues in different sectors. For instance, the ICT sector is estimated to employ 73,000 (29,000 in ICT & digital tech sector, 44,000 in other industries) and have up to 11,000 job opportunities potentially available each year. The process of developing the ICT and Digital Technologies SIP seeks to: validate and bring clarity to the scale and nature of the skills issues which face the sector; create direction and bring focus to the nature of the response required by the public sector and industry, on the priority skills issues identified; and provide a framework for public sector and private sector investment to develop skills provision to meet industry needs (SDS 2014). This SIP is chaired by a private sector CEO and is a collaborative public-private action, so clearly involves multi-stakeholder governance. The resulting main aims of the ICT SIP strategy are to: deepen the educational capabilities to produce and retain high-ranking performers; position the sector as a positive career destination for young talent; and foster a culture that supports exports, innovation and entrepreneurship. However, as Keep (2014) argues, employers may seek to influence SIPs so that the public sector or individuals pay for more training (a variant of "producer capture") and so may see SIPs as "bid documents" to further their own aims. Hence the importance of bringing in other bodies, such as trades unions and social organisations and local authorities who should have wider or more disinterested views. This may involve seeking to give a greater prominence beyond market logics.

4. Regional Skills Assessments

The multi-level governance and spatial availability of labour market information and intelligence is also important. Regional Skills Assessments (RSAs), initiated in 2014, are designed to provide a coherent evidence base on which to base future investment in skill development. They are based on existing labour market information and intelligence data sources, and public agency led (encompassing state and professional logics). However, RSAs were developed only after considerable consultation with different groups (using community logics). RDAs for different regions in Scotland are developed by Skills Development Scotland with the other related skills and economic development agencies and local authority bodies (Scottish Local Authorities Economic Development Group).

The purpose of RDAs include: supporting colleges (e.g. to develop their Regional Outcome Agreements with their funders); providing a framework for aligning SDS investment in individuals and businesses; assisting partners in planning their strategic skills investment; and supporting potential wider public and private investment. Eleven RDAs were developed for the main city regions and rural areas (for instance, Edinburgh and South East Scotland City Region (SDS 2016)) although not for Scotland as a whole (Thom and MacKay 2015).

RDAs cover a wide range of labour market information and intelligence, especially on future skills needs, including labour and skills demand, supply and skills gaps and shortages and other problems. They set out the background of the region in terms of forecasts and trends of employment, activity rates and Gross Value Added Regional performance and characteristics and provide a data matrix to assist users doing their own analysis at three different regional spatial units, with comparisons to Scotland and GB or UK (SDS 2017). Currently the data is based on 2016 with 117 social and economic indicators are used.

In terms of governance, this approach contributes to the development of new information and intelligence (for public agencies, employers and individuals) to more rigorously support governance rather than developing a governance system itself. For instance, considering multi-level governance, UK wide bodies are not particularly involved other than in providing comparative databases, while multi-dimensional governance is limited as wider non-government data sources of information are unlikely to be significantly included, although they may be added by others at later stages in their decision making, and the range of actors is limited for multi-stakeholder governance. However, this is unsurprising as the role of RDAs is not to provide a governance system but to support wider decision-making.

5. Conclusions

The Scottish Government set out a comprehensive system of frameworks within which skills and enterprise governance and policies are situated. In addition, there is a strong emphasis on more local or regional input, labour market information and intelligence development and action (showing explicit support for multi-level governance). The emphasis of policy development usually incorporates multi-level, multi-stakeholder and multi-dimensional elements (the latter supporting the integration of skills, training/educational demand and supply, and economic development). The problems of system wide governance, and limitations to inter-public body co-ordination and focus, have been explicitly recognised and a new system-wide governance structure proposed. Different elements of community, professional, state and market institutional logics are likely to be dominant in different components of the strategies (although community logics appear more limited in influence than the others), but it is argued here that different logics should be explicitly considered when dealing with skills development (rather than using logics to solely describe the current situation). The success of this governance structure will depend upon the close working of a range of key actors in its implementation in the future, and a clear view of the underlying institutional logic can help in this.

References

Canduela, Jesus/Dutton, Matthew/Johnston, Steve/Lindsay, Colin/McQuaid, Ronald W./Raeside, Robert (2012): Ageing, Skills and Participation in Work-Related Training in Britain: Assessing the Position of Older Workers, in: Work, Employment and Society, Vol. 26, No. 1, pp. 42-60

Dean, Andrew (2015): "Scottish Skills Planning Model" in Compendium of National and Regional Case Studies, VETS-EDS Project, pp. 48-62. (Accessed 31/7/17) http://www.regionallabourmarketmonitoring.net/veteds_outputs_2016_5.htm

European Commission (2010): Europe 2020: A European Strategy for Smart, Sustainable and Inclusive Growth. Luxembourg: Publications Office of the European Union

First Minister of Scotland (2016) Announcement 25 May 2016. Edinburgh. (Accessed 31/7/17) http://www.gov.scot/Topics/Economy/EntandSkillsreview

Fuertes, Vanesa/Ronald. McQuaid (2016): "Personalized activation policies for the long-term unemployed: the role of local governance in the UK", in: Heidenreich, Martin/Rice, Deborah. (Eds.) Integrating Social and Employment Policies in Europe: Active Inclusion and Challenges for Local Welfare Governance. Cheltenham: Edward Elgar, pp. 93-117

Fuertes Vanesa/Jantz, Bastian/Klenk, Tanja/McQuaid, Ronald (2014): Between cooperation and competition: the organisation of employment service delivery in the United Kingdom and Germany, in: International Journal of Social Welfare, Vol. 23 No. S1, pp. S71-S86

Heidenreich, Martin/Petzold, Norbert/Natili, Marcello/Panican, Alexandru (2014): Active inclusion as an organisational challenge: integrated anti-poverty policies in three European countries, in: Journal of International and Comparative Social Policy, Vol. 30, No. 2, pp. 180-198

Hobbes, Thomas (1651): Leviathan. New York: Collier Books, 1962

Keep, Ewart (2014): The Role of Higher Education within Broader Skills Policies, a Comparison of Emerging Scottish and English Approaches, in: Higher Education Quarterly, Vol. 68, No. 3, pp. 249–266

Keep, Ewart/Mayhew, Ken (2010): Moving beyond Skills as a Social and Economic Panacea, in: Work, Employment and Society, Vol. 24, No. 3, pp. 565–577

McQuaid, Ronald (2010): Theory of organisational partnerships-partnership advantages, disadvantages and success factors, in: Osborne, Stephen P. (Eds.) The New Public Governance: Critical Perspectives and Future Directions, London: Routledge, pp.125–146

McQuaid, Ronald W./Brown, Ross/Newlands, David (2008): Demographic Change and Economic Challenge: What Future for Scotland and other Small Countries? in: Scottish Affairs, Vol. 64, pp. 3-17

OECD (Organisation for Economic Co-operation and Development) (2012): Better Skills, Better Jobs, Better Lives: A Strategic Approach to Skills Policy. Paris: OECD

Page, Rosie/Hillage, Jim (2006): Vocational education and training in the UK: strategies to overcome skill gaps in the workforce, Discussion paper, Wissenschaftszentrum Berlin für Sozialforschung, Forschungsschwerpunkt: Arbeit, Sozialstruktur und Sozialstaat, Abteilung: Arbeitsmarktpolitik und Beschäftigung, No. SP I 2006-102

Savini, Federico/Majoor, Stan/Salet, Willem (2015): EPC Urban peripheries: reflecting on politics and projects in Amsterdam, Milan, and Paris, in: Environment and Planning C: Government and Policy, Vol. 33, pp. 457-474

Scottish Government (2014) Developing the Young Workforce: Scotland's Youth Employment Strategy. Edinburgh (Accessed 31/7/17) http://www.gov.scot/Resource/0046/00466386.pdf

Scottish Government (2015) Scotland's Economic Strategy. Edinburgh (Accessed 31/7/17) http://www.gov.scot/Resource/0047/00472389.pdf

Scottish Government (2016) Scotland's Labour Market Strategy. Edinburgh (Accessed 31/7/17) http://www.gov.scot/Resource/0050/00504798.pdf

SDS (2017a) List of SIPs. (Accessed 31/7/17) http://www.skillsdevelopmentscotland.co.uk/what-we-do/partnerships/skills-investment-plans/

Scottish Government (2017b) *Enterprise and Skills Review: report on Phase 2*. Edinburgh (Accessed 31/7/17) https://beta.gov.scot/publications/enterprise-skills-review-report-phase-2/

SDS (Skills Development Scotland) (2014) *Skills Investment Plan for Scotland's ICT & Digital Technologies*. SDS, Glasgow (Accessed 31/7/17) http://www.skillsdevelopmentscotland.co.uk/media/35682/ict___digital_technologies_sector_skills_investment_plan.pdf

SDS (2016) *Regional Skills Assessments: Edinburgh and South East Scotland City Region*. SDS, Glasgow (Accessed 31/7/17) http://www.skillsdevelopmentscotland.co.uk/media/42752/edinburgh-and-south-east-scotland-city-deal.pptx

SDS (2017) *Data Matrix User Guide*. SDS, Glasgow (Accessed 31/7/17) http://www.skillsdevelopmentscotland.co.uk/media/42829/data-matrix-user-guide.pdf

Thom, Graham/Mackay, Susan (2015): Some key issues for employment and skills planning in Scotland: a review of emerging evidence, in: Fraser of Allander Institute Economic Commentary, Vol. 39, No. 2, pp. 112-121

Thornton, Patricia H./Ocasio, William/Lounsbury, Michael (2012): The institutional logics perspective: A new approach to culture, structure, and process. Oxford: Oxford University Press

3. NETWORK RELATED TO MARKET AND HIERARCHY

(Regional) Labour Market Monitoring – Experience from Developing and Transition Countries

Sara Ennya, Heike Hoess, Uwe Kühnert, Pierre Lucante, Laura Schmid and Etleva Vertopi

1. Introduction

Labour market monitoring (LMM), and regional[1] labour market monitoring (RLMM) in particular, can play a decisive role in developing and transition countries in addressing employment constraints and labour market challenges, as well as in planning and implementing suitable interventions for employment promotion.

The Deutsche Gesellschaft für Internationale Zusammenarbeit (GIZ) has cooperated with developing and transition countries in the fields of Technical and Vocational Education and Training (TVET) and Active Labour Market Policies (ALMP) for many years. Despite this fact, labour market monitoring is a relatively new area of intervention for many partner countries. While (R)LMM activities in several Organisation for Economic Cooperation and Development (OECD) countries can look back on many years of experience, such projects are only recently emerging in developing countries and therefore also relatively new to German development cooperation. Nevertheless, several (R)LMM related activities exist today in a variety of bilateral development programmes implemented by GIZ to support public authorities, as well as private sector entities, in planning and implementing instruments of regional labour market monitoring. Most of these are in the Middle East and Northern Africa (MENA) region and in South East Europe (SEE). Indeed, many governments have come to recognise the importance of accurate, continuous and specific regional labour market information as a prerequisite for job creation, evidence-based policymaking and the alignment of the education system with private sector needs. As a result, while existing efforts are

---

[1] In this article, the term "regional" refers to the sub-national level, not a cross-country dimension.

still nascent, building strong labour market information systems with sound governance structures has become a priority within employment promotion agendas across MENA and SEE.

Given the priority of promoting employment and creating jobs across GIZ programmes in MENA and SEE, a GIZ working group named *"Linking Regional Labour Market Information (RLMI) with TVET and LM Policy Making"* was established in 2016. Under the auspices of GIZ, the working group gathers and analyses existing (best) practices in the MENA region and provides a platform for dialogue bringing together international experts on (R)LMM, international development practitioners and relevant GIZ projects working in that field. The goal of the working group is to transfer knowledge (e.g. on appropriate governance structures), encourage strategic debate, and identify links between RLMI and policymaking. This article is based largely on the previous work of the working group as well as on a stocktaking of eight RLMM initiatives (see 1.3), and reflects current practices, the main challenges, and needs for further assistance with regards to (R)LMM activities in developing and transition countries.

1.1 Framework conditions: Main influencing factors for (R)LMM

Any detailed description of (GIZ-supported) (R)LMM activities in developing and transition countries, their main challenges, success factors, and good practices cannot be assessed in isolation. Considering the complexity of the interacting processes within the labour market, it is not surprising that the development of (R)LMM in developing and transition countries is influenced by several contextual factors. These include elements specific to the countries under consideration here, as well as more generic factors also known from younger European (R)LMM history. In the context of international development cooperation, the following constitute the main influencing factors (see Figure 1):

Figure 1   Main influencing factors for (R)LMM in developing and transition countries

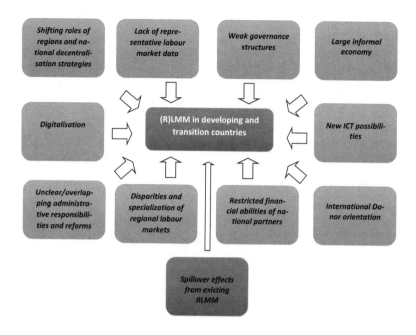

Source: GIZ.

Lack of timely and representative labour market data. Even developing and transition countries generate some type of labour market information, either deliberately or indirectly, through national surveys (e.g. census, labour force surveys, etc.) and various forms of administrative data that stem from running employment services, managing taxes or the educational system. However, while access to quality data at the national and (mostly) regional level is widespread in many OECD countries, this is not the case in the majority of developing and transition countries. If any labour market data exist, it often refers to labour supply only, suffers from a significant "time lag", and in some cases existing data is not made available to the public and key stakeholders. In most cases, representative data is based on periodic censuses with large time gaps, often carried out and financed by international donors like the World Bank. Moreover, sample sizes tend to be small and are therefore only representative for the national level, but have very low or no significance at the sub-national level.

Large informal economy. Nearly all developing countries have a large informal economy (i.e. unregistered firms and/or workers), which may reach 50% and more of the entire economic output. In SEE, the informal economy is primarily regarded as a "black market" and is therefore fought against, whereas in the MENA region the informal economy is more accepted. Given the informal nature of these economic activities, they are often not captured in official labour market data. Against this background, several cooperation projects in developing countries seek to gain more practical experience in developing and carrying out customised solutions for (R)LMM that take into account the informal economy.

Unclear and/or overlapping administrative responsibilities and reforms. Administrative reforms, such as governance reforms and/or public management reforms on national and/or regional levels, seek to provide better or additional public services. However, there typically remains a multitude of political and administrative players to deal with and this complexity and fragmentation in decision-making renders the implementation of LMM often more complicated than in OECD countries. Against this background, soft steering and coordination mechanisms should be more strongly incorporated into a governance toolkit of administration (Brzozowski et al. 2013).

Weak governance structures. In comparison to most European countries, many developing and transition countries appear to show weaker governance structures regarding Labour Market Information Systems (LMIS). Among the key contributing factors are:

- Lack of central administration to manage the system and/or lack of ownership. This is due in part because the responsibility for LMIS is often attributed to the agency in charge of statistics (usually, the National Institute of Statistics) that is, by definition, removed from policy and decision-making at the level of the line ministries (e.g. of education, health, infrastructure, or the economy);
- A fragmented institutional landscape with unclear and/or changing mandates and responsibilities, and potential competition between agencies (e.g. between National Statistics Agency, Labour Ministry, etc.); and
- Lack of coordination among producers and users of information, including the private sector, which is reflected in weak or no consultations on the

type of information needed and most appropriate ways to produce and analyse it.

Restricted financial abilities of national partners. From the development cooperation perspective, work has to be conducted in cooperation with the partner countries. This explicitly includes access to domestic resources for the implementation of labour market policies to provide co-financing for projects, and more importantly, ensure country ownership. However, developing and transition countries face financial constraints related to many policy areas. In particular, the topic of (R)LMM often lacks attention – and thus funding – from national resources, while donor-led efforts tend to be financially unsustainable. In Europe, many (R)LMM measures are financed with EU funds. When the funding runs out, the activities also come to an end. Thus, the issue of financial sustainability for (R)LMM seems to be a joint challenge between different regions in the world.

International Donor orientation. Even through international development cooperation is subject to change (e.g. due to a change in political priorities, reallocation of funds etc.), it can be regarded a success that much more funding has recently been allocated to labour market-related interventions in both the MENA and SEE regions. At the same time, requirements from donor countries for targeted allocation of these financial means have grown substantially. In this context, analysis of labour market trends and problems have become important, and will grow in importance.

Shifting roles of regions and national decentralisation strategies. Especially in Europe, the expert community seems to be in agreement that the increasing role of regions in policy and regulation has been a clear pull factor for (R)LMM and directly connected with the ongoing process of economic globalisation. Even though many developing countries will only experience these changes in the future, we are already seeing first indications of this trend, as exemplified by the case of Morocco in this article. Moreover, it is well accepted that larger economies in the region are not characterised by one big labour market, but that in-country differences can be substantial. Therefore, RLMM offers an innovative approach even when the decentralisation level is not yet very advanced. Governance structures that combine national and regional levels will become more important. Even if regional political levels are not responsible for this political area by law, these developments may lead to their bigger influence as labour market stakeholders. Under the pressure of globalisation, many regions feel encouraged to create and realise their own development strategies. To achieve this, small and medium-sized companies (SME) in particular have to cooperate more than ever as they find themselves embedded in economic clusters based on regional comparative advantage. Bigger regional companies become cluster leaders, and cooperation activities between companies, universities, training providers and other stakeholders emerge. These developments must be supported, steered, and regulated more and more by regions themselves. Even though most decentralisation efforts in developing countries have been implemented very carefully, there seems to be consensus that decentralisation can bring more transparency, will increase allocative efficiency, and can be a catalyst for regional growth and economic convergence by offering regional stakeholders incentives to engage in competition with other regions. Although it is currently not possible to predict decentralisation as a major trend for developing and transition countries, it seems to be plausible that this factor will become increasingly important in the future.

Disparities and specialisation of regional labour markets. Studies have shown that the economic disparities between EU member states have decreased since the 1980s, while in-country disparities (e.g. increasing polarisation and specialisation of regional economies) have grown in the same time period (Brzozowski et al. 2013). For developing countries, it can be expected that ongoing in-country disparities will also affect their regional labour markets, and potentially even more than within Europe. Reasons include, too little political attention to a balancing between different regions, and migration of younger people from underdeveloped peripheral regions to the main cities. Against this backdrop, more and more specific regional economic approaches have to be developed, putting a premium on sound information about the labour force in different regions.

New Information and Communication Technology (ICT) possibilities. Information and communication technologies in general, particularly the internet, are important tools to provide disadvantaged regions and target groups with access to information. The use of internet services is mainly influenced by socio-economic factors such as age, educational level, disposable income and the presence of children in families. Thanks to a young population[2], ICT-based tools are

---

[2] In some MENA region states in particular, the mean age of the national population is around 30-years-old or is even younger.

well accepted in many developing countries and could be integrated in (R)LMM tools and services. Due to methodological and technological progress, labour market data have become more standardised and timely. This can open up new opportunities for identification of specific regional needs and trends (Brzozowski et al. 2013). On the other hand, it is the apparent simplicity and nonchalance of new ICT that may create a new problem. Due to an overreliance on apparently simple and quick ICT solutions by political and administrative stakeholders in developing countries, it can be difficult to convince these stakeholders of the need to start with the foundations of (R)LMM such as defining LM indicators relevant to their region.

Digitalisation. Even though it is not presently foreseeable to what extent and how fast developing and transition countries will be affected by digitalisation, the process is already underway and will create additional chances and challenges for (R)LMM approaches. Digitalisation will affect all functions of a labour market monitoring system. Digital technologies can be used for building up, analysing, and maintaining heterogeneous and complex data stocks. They also open up new possibilities for generating real-time data (information function). Interactive technologies offer opportunities for systematically optimising the strong, person-oriented interactions between data producers, interpreters and users, while taking into account their different needs (communication function). In addition, digitalisation creates scope and increases opportunities for targeted action (action dimension). New tools could be used for ensuring that decision-making processes and actions remain participatory, and bottom-up developments can be systematically combined with top-down decision-making processes (Larsen et al. 2016).

Spillover effects from existing (R)LMM. Last but not least, spillover effects of good practices from (R)LMM examples in Europe to younger (R)LMM activities in developing and transition countries seem to become more significant. For instance, GIZ takes into account the entire range of such spillover effects: their contribution to the development of social capital at the regional level; their role as a starting point for networking and cooperation between stakeholders; and their role as a nucleus for evidence-based political decisions regarding decent work and stronger regional economies.

1.2 (R)LMM as an instrument of the GIZ integrated approach to employment promotion

Due to the complexity of employment promotion that requires a range of interventions in different areas, German Development Cooperation addresses employment promotion by using an integrated, multi-dimensional approach that focuses on the supply and demand sides of the labour market as well as on active labour market policies and matching instruments (see Figure 2).

Figure 2 The integrated approach to employment promotion of German Development Cooperation

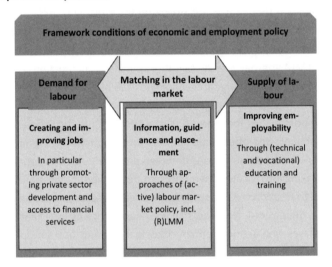

Source: GIZ.

In accordance with that approach, effective promotion of employment must focus equally on labour market supply and demand, and improve matching between them:

- **Creating productive and decent jobs.** Private sector development and business start-ups can increase demand for labour. Small and medium-sized enterprises (SMEs) are especially important in promoting employment-oriented private sector development because they provide the majority of jobs in many countries and are a major driver of innovation and competitiveness. To ensure that companies' growth and productivity gains actually generate employment, the GIZ approaches to private sector development aim to achieve long-term, structural impacts on employment.

- **Establishing effective labour market services, e.g. information and career counselling services.** The existence of productive jobs and qualified workers alone does not guarantee more employment if there is a shortage of labour market information and a mismatch between labour supply and demand. To improve job placement, GIZ is assisting partner countries to develop and apply active labour market policy instruments. This includes supporting labour market analyses, establishing (R)LMM systems, and providing advice on the conceptual development of career counselling, guidance and job placement services.
- **Promoting employability.** As labour market conditions are constantly changing, workers must maintain and develop their technical and social skills in order to remain employable. These include occupational qualifications, the ability to engage in dialogue with employers or job placement agencies. To increase employability, GIZ supports national partners' efforts to improve basic education, develop formal and non-formal technical and vocational education and training, and promote skills development schemes that are always geared towards labour market needs[3].

Although activities related to labour market monitoring are relatively new in the GIZ portfolio, (R)LMM activities can be seen as fully embedded in the GIZ integrated approach to employment promotion. Indeed, they are part of the frameworks' second pillar concerned with improving matching in the labour market. Often integrated in larger GIZ technical cooperation projects, activities related to (regional) labour market monitoring typically seek to:

- Understand labour market dynamics and implications for different stakeholders;
- Identify critical issues in the labour market;
- Provide objective empirical foundations and guidance for policy-making (e.g. for active labour market policy including vocational education and training);
- Guide targeting and programme formulation; and
- Monitor and evaluate impacts of policies and interventions and progress in labour markets[4].

---

[3]Cf. Deutsche Gesellschaft für Internationale Zusammenarbeit: https://www.giz.de/expertise/html/4479.html.
[4]GIZ has different tools and entry points for LMM such as: a) Employment and Labour Market Analysis (ELMA), b) RLMM, and c) supporting the establishment of LMIS on the national level and d) skills needs assessment.

1.3 Methodical approach and scope of work

The following sections provide information on important developments and typical characteristics of GIZ-supported (R)LMM activities in selected developing and transition countries. The analysis is based on the following sources of information:

- Three (R)LMM case studies of selected (R)LMM initiatives (Egypt, Morocco, and Albania) elaborated by every initiative itself based on a common guideline;
- Working group discussions that took place during and after the sector network workshop *"Sustainable Economic Development in the MENA Region"* in 2016 and
- A stocktaking survey of eight GIZ-supported RLMM initiatives[5]. Intended to be the first overview on GIZ supported (R)LMM activities, it addresses the following fields of engagement:
  - The collection and analysis of data;
  - The distribution and linkage of (R)LMI to TVET and Labour Market (LM) policy-making; and
  - Institutionalisation and national and legislative framework conditions.

The first results of the stocktaking exercise were discussed during the expert round table on "How to Link Regional Labour Market Monitoring with TVET and Labour Market Policy? An International Discourse about Lessons Learned, Best Practices and Experience from the MENA Region" and a succeeding field visit on the 16-17th of November 2016 in Cairo, Egypt[6].

---

[5] See Annex GIZ supported (R)LMM projects.
[6] The Round Table brought together representatives from GIZ projects in Morocco, Egypt, Jordan, and Palestine, international development partners such as the ILO, and international experts on (R)LMM from 4 European countries, namely France, Germany, Poland and the United Kingdom.

2 (R)LMM and active labour market programme implementation in Egypt, Morocco and Albania

2.1 The case of Egypt

Basic Information

Since 2011, GIZ's Employment Promotion Project (EPP) has supported its public and private sector partners to establish structures for Regional Labour Market Monitoring (RLMM), namely the Regional Labour Market Observatories (RLMOs). Partners include the main political partner[7] of the project, the Egyptian Ministry of Education and Technical Education (MoE), in addition to the Egyptian Ministry of Manpower (MoM) and regional Investors Associations. RLMOs consist of four - eight staff, who are seconded on a part-time basis (1-2 days per week) from different Egyptian public and private sector institutions. The Steering Committees (StCs) that guide the RLMOs are composed of an assembly of local and national stakeholders involved in employment promotion. The objective of the RLMOs is to make available regional Labour Market Information (LMI), promote the implementation of evidence-based Active Labour Market Programmes (ALMPs), and initiate a stakeholder dialogue on youth employment between different public and private institutions.

The initiation of the multi-stakeholder RLMOs resulted from a GIZ planning and evaluation mission in 2011, which highlighted the need to use decentralised LMI in Egypt as a basis for policy-making and better alignment of the education system with private sector needs. In addition, the planning and evaluation mission identified the following labour market challenges to be addressed through the establishment of the RLMOs:

- A lack of trust and dialogue between public and private sector;
- Lack of data sharing; and
- Lack of awareness about the added value of designing and implementing evidence-based labour market programmes.

---

[7] GIZ projects always have one main public sector actor with whom they align project activities and with whom they jointly implement projects.

The key rationale for EPP's main partner (the MoE) to support the RLMOs was their interest in using the gained LMI to better align the TVET system with LM needs and thus enhance the employability of their TVET graduates.

In order to technically support the establishment of the RLMOs in Egypt – the first of their kind in the Middle East and North African (MENA) region – GIZ contracted the Gesellschaft for Innovative Beschäftigungsförderung (G.I.B)[8] to support knowledge transfer in implementing the PROSPECT methodology. PROSPECT is a dialogue-based, participatory method to continuously monitor regional LMs and collect LMI. It was previously applied in the Netherlands and in Germany's North-Rhine Westphalia region. The PROSPECT methodology was chosen because its survey and dialogue-based approach was considered suitable to address the identified challenges in the Egyptian Labour market. PROSPECT follows distinct methodological steps and uses qualitative and quantitative research methods to collect and analyse data about the supply, demand and matching sides of the labour market. The PROSPECT methodology does not only guide the collection and analysis of regional LMI, but also puts a strong focus on designing and implementing evidence-based ALMPs based on the collected LMI in the regions[9].

Strategy, goals and intentions

EPP's objective with regard to RLMM was stated as follows: RLMI is being used to develop and implement evidence-based ALMPs and policy recommendations by different public and private sector stakeholders. Thus, the main goal of RLMM in Egypt is geared towards employment promotion and in particular the reduction of youth unemployment. In order to achieve this goal EPP supports:

- The collection and analysis of RLMI by supporting the establishment and running of the RLMOs whose staff collects and analyses the RLMI following the PROSPECT methodology;
- The dissemination of RMLI and their linkage to TVET and LM policy-making by supporting the RLMOs in publishing and distributing the regional LM

---

8 The G.I.B. is the State Agency for Employment Promotion of NRW (G.I.B). Their aim is to support the state government of North Rhine-Westphalia in the fulfillment of its objectives of promoting employment and combating unemployment.
9 For more information on the PROSPECT methodology, please refer to http://eppegypt.net/uploads/activities/2012-09-23_C2-RLMM_mission/report_en.pdf.

analysis reports and facilitating a regular multi-stakeholder regional employment dialogue;
- The implementation of evidence-based ALMPs through own project activities and funds as well as by supporting the RLMOs to network with and reach out to other possible implementing partners (e.g. ILO, IOM, Egyptian partner institutions).
- The linkage of the regional to the national level by supporting national coordination functions such as partnerships with relevant Egyptian institutions that provide quality assurance for the regional reports, build the capacity of RLMO staff, compile and publish the regional LM analyses, and produce overarching reports (activities started in mid-2016).

Overall, the GIZ supports the RLMM process largely through capacity building and technical backstopping. This includes regular coaching visits to the different RLMOs, during which the GIZ supports the RLMO team in setting and reaching their operational plan and trains staff on topics such as questionnaire design and interviewing skills. Moreover, the project provides quality control of the LM analysis reports and supports the identification and conceptualisation of ALMPs. In terms of financial assistance, the project contributes to operational costs, such as costs for conducting employer surveys and organising dissemination events, while also (co)-financing the implementation of selected ALMPs to demonstrate the added-value of RLMI and evidence-based policy-making to regional and national stakeholders. GIZ also supports the institutionalisation of the RLMOs through developing a sustainability concept, jointly agreed upon by all stakeholders.

(R)LMM practice so far

The RLMOs' staff collects and analyses RLMI following the PROSPECT methodology. As of 2017, there are three fully functioning RLMOs in Egypt: (1) The Sixth of October City, (2) Sadat City (two major industrial zones close to Cairo) and in (3) Aswan, the most southern governorate. The opening of two additional RLMOs in industrial regions is expected in 2017. The RLMOs' staff are currently seconded in each location from the following institutions:

- Regional Investor's Associations (private sector);
- The Ministry of Education and Technical Education (public sector);
- Mistry of Manpower (Public Employment Offices) (public sector);

- Research Centres and Civil Society Representatives (e.g. Aswan University).

Data collection and analysis

The RLMOs collect and analyse supply and demand side data as well as information about relevant training and matching services in order to publish a sectoral LM analysis report. To conclude one sectoral LM analysis following PROSPECT, it takes 12-15 months. Information is collected through:

- Desk research (e.g. governorate-level data provided by the Egyptian Statistical Agency is used for the labour force analysis);
- Surveys and in-depth interviews using questionnaires (e.g. employers' survey to generate demand-side data);
- Semi-structured interviews and focus group discussions (e.g. with current employees and job seekers to gain information about working conditions and attractiveness of a sector to job seekers); and
- Field visits to acquire information about training and matching entities and their capabilities. Given the crucial importance of demand side information, a lot of time and organisational effort is devoted to conducting employer surveys.

On average, the RLMOs visit and interview 50-80 companies of different sizes, which is only possible through the active involvement of the regional Investors' Association that acts as a liaison.

The RLMI collected is sector specific and includes information about a) employment potential and working condition of specific target groups such as women or people with special needs; b) the structure of the current workforce, including levels of qualifications, age groups, and geographic origin; c) available vacancies and skills needed by employers; d) sectoral growth (estimation of current and future demand of products/ services); and e) relevant matching and training services. Since 2011, five regional LM analysis reports were published for the following sectors:

- RLMO-Sixth of October City: Engineering, Chemical, Food Processing and Textile Industry;
- RLMO-Sadat City: Engineering, Food Processing, Chemical, Building and Construction and Textile Industry; and
- RLMO-Aswan: Tourism and Mining Industry.

Governance

- ***Steering Committee:*** Each RLMO is guided by a Steering Committee (StC). The StCs are chaired by a board member of the Investors' Association in each region. The StCs comprise the supervisors of the seconded RLMO staff as well as other prominent national and regional players active in the LM. The GIZ also takes part in the StCs meetings as an advisor. On average, the StCs meet every four months to discuss the findings and status of the LM analysis reports and the suggested ALMPs. The StCs take decisions and provide guidance to the RLMO working groups.
- ***Hierarchical governance structures regarding access to data:*** Due to the lack of official data- sharing platforms and the absence of a data-sharing culture amongst ministries and between ministries and the private sector, the governance of the collection and analysis of RLMI is rather complicated and very hierarchical. In the case of the RLMOs, access to administrative data is only possible because the RLMO staff are employees of relevant entities and can access relevant data through the hierarchy in their institutions (e.g. a MoE representative provides statistical data about TVET graduates). The different RLMO members act within the hierarchical governance structures of their seconding entity to acquire the data and then share it with the other RLMO members.
- ***Network character in analysing data:*** The RLMOs have a flat hierarchy (no supervisor or director; each RLMO member is equal) and operate as a network. However, the final decision-making, such as which sectors to be analysed or the ALMPs to be implemented, takes place in the StCs. The StCs make decisions jointly and ideally after reaching an agreement through a debate.

Linkages to policy

Within the PROSPECT methodology, the regional employment dialogue (e.g. the StC meetings, or the sectoral conference where the regional LM analysis is launched) initiated through the RLMOs is designed to be the forum to ensure the linkage to policy-making. The findings of the LM analysis reports are discussed during the regional employment dialogue events and decisions about evidence-based ALMPs to be implemented (and by whom) are taken at that time. Relevant stakeholders (e.g. a representative of MoE at the regional level) are expected to take ownership in bringing up relevant evidence-based policy recommendations to the national level (e.g. central administration of MoE).

Since 2011, seven evidence-based ALMPs have been implemented with the financial support of international development partners and involve different public and private sector stakeholders. Some examples of ALMPs include:

- *Training for Employment in Sadat City.* The regional LM analysis in Sadat City showed the inability of companies to fill available blue-collar jobs with suitably skilled labour. To fill the available vacancies in the engineering and food processing sectors, a training for employment scheme was jointly implemented by Education for Employment Foundation (EFE), the International Organisation for Migration (IOM), and the Sadat City Investors Association (SCIA). Over 120 job seekers were trained and placed in jobs.

- *Female Entrepreneurship in Aswan.* The LM analysis by the RLMO in Aswan found that female graduates are disadvantaged in the LM. Given the limited number of wage employment opportunities in Aswan, the decision was made to support female employment through entrepreneurship education. In cooperation with the International Labour Organisation (ILO), local stakeholders were trained to deliver entrepreneurship education for students in Aswan. Over 250 students received entrepreneurship education so far.

- *Human Resources (HR) Club Sadat City.* The LM analysis in Sadat City showed that 69% of the interviewed enterprises do not have a functioning HR department, which has negative effects on staff turnover and productivity. Seeking to raise awareness about the importance of having an effective HR department and building HR personnel's capacities, the HR Club in Sadat City was established under the umbrella of the Sadat City Investors Association. The HR Club offers all enterprises in Sadat City an open and regular forum to learn about HR functions, international best practices on ways to increase staff retention, and how to promote productivity through better utilisation of labour. Examples of HR Clubs sessions include: *"In-Company Training and technical Education from a Practical Point of View"; "Inclusive Employment and Inclusive Hiring Practices"; "Turnover Rate and the Effect on Profitability and Productivity of Companies"; "Performance Appraisal"; "Why do you lose your best employees and how to retain them?";* and *"Optimising Work Processes".*

- *Employment Centre in Sixth of October City.* The LM analysis in Sixth of October City displayed the need to establish a matching service to fill existing vacancies. In the absence of an efficient public system, a private employment centre was established and staff was trained in partnership between the National Employment Pact (NEP), an Egyptian private sector-led recruitment service, and the Sixth of October City Investors' Association (SOCIA). GIZ provided limited financial and technical support as seed funding. As of 2017, three people are employed by the Investors Association to work as employment officers in the centre, placing about 20 people per month in mostly blue-collar jobs.

In summary, the RLMOs, with substantial support of GIZ (conceptual, organisational support etc.), act as facilitators and initiators to push the implementation of the ALMPs and the follow-up on the evidence-based recommendations. They seek to disseminate the collected LMI in different ways attractive to policy-makers and stakeholders by: a) ongoing regional employment dialogue through StC meetings; b) organisation of sectoral conference (once every 12-15 month) including thematic working groups to present the findings of the LM analysis reports and get buy-in and stakeholder commitment for the ALMPs; and c) share the ALMP proposals and policy recommendations with a broad audience by facilitating specific meetings with relevant international development actors and Egyptian private and public stakeholders.

However, linking RLMI to TVET and LM policy-making has generally been challenging, mostly due to the limited capacity of RLMO staff regarding targeted communication and networking, limited outreach to high-level decision-makers, and the lack of institutional arrangements to bring regional recommendations to the national level. Similarly, it has been difficult for the Egyptian private and public sector to take the lead in implementing ALMPs on their own. International development partners and the GIZ remain the main driving force in implementing the ALMPs jointly with national partners.

Challenges, success stories and outlook

The most significant challenges have been to institutionalise a multi-stakeholder and decentralised regional structure in a very hierarchical and centralised country and to ensure financial sustainability as well as a high quality of LM research. In this regard, one of the main advantages of the RLMO model in Egypt, namely its organisational set-up (RLMOs consisting of seconded staff from different private and public-sector institutions), is simultaneously a major obstacle. On the one hand, the RLMOs are very cost-efficient and allow for great access to data and different private and public-sector actors. On the other hand, the multi-stakeholder set-up in the absence of a national coordinating function makes institutionalisation very challenging and complicated (For example, which national entity should be the anchor in order not to lose the neutrality, regional autonomy and multi-stakeholder character of the RLMOs?). Besides, the secondment approach does currently not imply financial incentives for the RLMO staff members, leading to high fluctuation and varying degrees of staff motivation. Against this background, *GIZ will intensely support the institutionalisation of the RLMOs at the regional and national levels* over the next years while providing non-financial incentives (e.g. study visit) to RLMO members.

One methodological challenge yet to be addressed is the high informality of the Egyptian LM, which has not been taken into account by the PROSPECT methodology so far. The enterprise survey only covers formally registered companies and thus the LM analysis does not reflect specific information about the extent and characteristics of the informal economy.

On the positive side, evidence-based policymaking is experiencing growing importance in Egypt. One of the main success stories of the RLMOs has been that private and public sector stakeholders started to recognise the added value of regional LMI to inform the implementation of ALMPs. To further strengthen the awareness of national stakeholders about the benefits of decentralised LMI, EPP plans to train national entities in the future to compile the gained RLMI at a national level and produce an overarching analysis report. Besides, the plan is to use the collected LMI to feed it into a national skill needs assessment and highlight the successfully implemented ALMPs even more as a tool to increase awareness about the usefulness of LMI amongst decision-makers. Over the past years several international development actors (e.g. ILO, IOM, and EU) have also started to support the establishment of a LMIS in Egypt, which possibly could lead to better framework conditions particularly with regard to data sharing and a better understanding about the complexity and need for multi-stakeholder involvement for effective LMM.

2.2 The case of Morocco

Basic information

The Rural Youth Employment Promotion Project (PEJ) is testing a labour market monitoring approach with the aim of developing and implementing an evidence-based employment promotion programme, benefiting the rural young population of the Fez-Meknes region. Started in 2015, PEJ is financed by the Federal Ministry for Economic Cooperation and Development (BMZ) and implemented by GIZ in partnership with the Moroccan Ministry of Employment and Social Affairs and ANAPEC (Agence Nationale de Promotion de l'Emploi et des Compétences), the public employment service. PEJ falls within the framework of three key national strategies striving to decentralise employment promotion policies in Morocco:

- The "advanced regionalisation" strategy; considered Morocco's most important decentralisation policy so far and including the devolution of local employment promotion policies to the newly elected regional and provincial councils.
- The National Employment Strategy adopted in 2015; setting the framework for the regionalisation of employment policies and seeking the inclusion of new target groups as beneficiaries from employment promotion measures (incl. rural populations).
- ANAPEC's development plan 2016-2020; stressing the need for shared /participatory territorial labour market diagnosis involving local public, private and civil society stakeholders.

As a pilot experience, the project aims to improve the employability of young men and women in the Fez-Meknes region through the development and implementation of an integrated employment promotion approach, primarily in three pilot provinces (Sefrou, Taounate and Taza). Each of these largely rural provinces has between 300,000 and 650,000 inhabitants while the Fez-Meknes region is home to 13% of the Kingdom's population with a total of 4,000,000 inhabitants.

In order to implement the project, PEJ carried out an exhaustive analysis of the socio-economic situation in the three pilot provinces (notably using the Federal Ministry for Economic Cooperation and Development BMZ's Employment and Labour Market Analysis - ELMA). The analysis resulted in five main observations:

- Limited data related to local labour market is available in the provinces;
- The informal sector represents a large portion of the labour market in these rural areas;
- The available data is rarely shared amongst stakeholders;
- Functioning local labour market governance' structures and processes are absent and dialogue among local stakeholders regarding employment promotion policy is lacking;
- A significant discrepancy between available skills, locally offered TVET services and market demands.

Strategy, goals and intentions

The focus of the project's labour market monitoring approach is to provide evidence for the development and implementation of local employment promotion measures adapted to the local realities of rural youth. The framework of the approach is based on recommendations of an initial technical assistance mission[10] carried out in November 2015 by members of the European Network on Regional Market Monitoring and it obeys to three key features:

- Labour market monitoring takes place on the province level and relies on local (human) resources only;
- It does not require the establishment of a physical observatory nor a new monitoring institution;
- The monitoring approach is sector-based.

Furthermore, the approach relies on a transparent and participatory dialogue amongst local stakeholders. In each province, the work is carried out by a working group of 5 to 10 members chaired by the provincial authorities, while the local director of the public employment service carries out the role of facilitator. The other members represent the relevant local stakeholders of the public and private sector as well as civil society. The composition of the group varies between the provinces and includes TVET operators, local representatives from the employment ministry, local NGOs, private sector associations and other relevant public stakeholders (for instance local representatives of the planning authority).

---

10 The mission was carried out between the 1st and 30th of November 2015 by Dr Christa Larsen, Co-ordinator of the EN RLMM and Sigrid Rand, Manager of the EN RLMM at the Institute for Economics, Labour and Culture (IWAK)/Centre of Goethe University Frankfurt, Germany and Pierre Lorent of the Observatoire Régional des Métiers, PACA in Marseille, France.

The working groups have a large operational autonomy when it comes to planning activities and assigning workload. Therefore, the initial selection of members took into account the high level of autonomy and skills needed to carry out analysis on a "stand-alone" basis. Members were selected based on mixed and complementary sets of abilities and experiences (data gathering, management, quantitative data analysis, facilitation skills, report drafting, experience on monitoring and evaluation). The working group modality does not require any "institution building" and members are not paid to participate. Therefore, the cost of the approach is low and relies on available local stakeholders' human resources and logistical means. The working groups are reporting to provincial Steering Committees of local decision-makers of the members' organisations, chaired by the respective governors (highest authority in the Province). Being the head of the Steering Committees, the governors, ensure the linkage between the sector strategies and local policymaking. In addition, the involvement of governors insures a high recognition for the approach at the provincial level. The working groups are required to present the progress of their analysis to the Steering Committees in quarterly meetings while internal meeting of the working groups typically take place on a weekly basis.

(R)LMM practice so far

Following a sector-based approach and in concert with the provincial Steering Committee, the working groups identify and analyse key economic sectors before recommending employment promotion strategies to the Steering Committee. The working groups' tools and processes are standardised and are based on a seven-step methodology:

Step (1): Selecting an economic sector in concertation with the Steering Committee; the sectors are selected by priority following the collective rating of sectors and subsectors by the members of the working groups. The members are basing their rating on their knowledge and experience with the local labour market as well as the results of research and studies conducted by their entities.

Step (2): Sharing and analysing available sector data, after the relevant information regarding the selected sector and the province have been collected and organised in a data library (demographic data, data on the workforce in the sector, TVET offerings, etc.).

Step (3): Identifying data gaps, which are generally important due to the paucity of data in the provinces and the importance of the informal sector in rural areas.

Step (4): Mapping the relevant stakeholders of the economic sector using GIZ's Capacity Work tools[11] (private companies, business associations, public and private actors).

Step (5): Bridging information gaps with empirical data collected through focus groups, surveys and interviews.

Step (6): Developing a sector strategy, using a variety of scientific tools such as the SWOT confrontation matrix that helps draw strategic streams and proposed actions as well as the "Devising Options" tool, which is a Capacity Works instrument that helps develop strategic options.

Step (7): Monitoring and evaluating the sector strategy.

A sector analysis should usually take between nine to ten months and is presented to the Steering Committees using a standardised and brief (three to four pages) report format.

To build the capacities of the working groups the project followed a learning-by doing approach. In April 2016, the first task given to the groups was to select a priority economic sector in concertation with the steering committee. As a second step, the members benefited from a first training session in May focusing on step one to five of the sector analysis process and providing the working groups with the necessary tools to conduct their analysis. The groups, then, put the learned skills to the test by analysing the selected sector with the technical assistance of GIZ's team. A second training session was organised in December 2016 to provide members with the methodology regarding the remaining steps (step 6 and 7) of the process. Subsequently, the groups were requested to finalise their analysis and propose a sector strategy.

The retained sectors were analysed with the systematic technical assistance of GIZ in the three provinces. The technical assistance included support on processes, technical tools and instruments (on data management, empirical data

---

11 The Deutsche Gesellschaft für Internationale Zusammenarbeit (GIZ) GmbH developed Capacity WORKS, a management model for sustainable development. Today, the management model is interwoven into the structures, rules and processes of GIZ's work. Many programme managers appreciate the fact that Capacity WORKS enables them to look beyond the immediate environment of their own programmes (https://www.giz.de/expertise/html/4620.html).

collection, quantitative data analysis, strategy elaboration, etc.) as well as Capacity Works' facilitation and dialogue methods. The members relied, on standardised instruments and templates developed by GIZ.

Sefrou: In Sefrou, the working group and Steering Committee selected the quarrying sector to conduct an exhaustive analysis. The important number of sand/gravel and marble quarries in Sefrou explained the choice of this sector. Following the standard methodology, a data library was established and information gaps were identified and filled through focus groups, surveys and interviews. Subsequently, between 100 and 150 positions were identified as vacant in six professions related to the quarrying sector. The identified vacancies had never been documented by any public data prior to this analysis and the TVET operators had no information about the extent of the lack of technical skills in the province. Following the validation of the strategy by the Steering Committee, different actions are expected to be taken to respond to the current and future demand, such as providing suitable TVET offerings, supporting self-employment and strengthening employment services.

Taounate: The Taounate's working group and the steering committee's first diagnosis was related to the private pre-school education sector. The group members conducted research on regional and national studies, compared statistics regarding supply and demand for workers in the sector, and validated the results through focus groups and interviews. The group members identified a number of job profiles required to satisfy current and future demands for the workforce in the private pre-school education sector (educators, managers, cooks, drivers...) as well as potential entrepreneurial niches to expand the current offer. However, the sector is characterised by a heavy dependence on public subsidies, as well as grants from numerous foundations. Therefore, the working group is working to suggest mechanisms to support and finance the future demands and converge the current efforts deployed by the provincial stakeholders (foundations, municipality, provincial / regional council...).

Taza: The diagnosis in Taza experienced a significant delay due to difficulties in mobilising local stakeholders. Therefore, the actual implementation of the first sector diagnosis was only launched in late 2016. The working group is analysing potential labour demand in the wind energy sector to increase the benefits acquired from the upcoming investment in Taza's wind park for the local population. However, as of mid-2017, the process was still at an early stage.

Challenges, success stories and outlook

The experiment in the provinces of Sefrou, Taounate and Taza is very recent and the first sector analyses have yet to be finalised. However, two preliminary conclusions can already be drawn. First, albeit new, the multi-stakeholder dialogue and evidence-based policy-making in the field of local employment promotion sparks considerable interest from local stakeholders. Most working group members have demonstrated a high level of commitment towards the experiment by actively contributing to the monitoring approach. Moreover, the members have experienced a fruitful dialogue and collaboration between the representatives of the public, private and non-governmental sector. Second, when TVET operators are actively engaged with the working group (as in Sefrou) the entire process is more efficient and the likelihood of being able to create linkages to TVET services much higher.

PEJ will continue to assist the three working groups in their mission towards finalising their first sector strategies and reporting to their respective Steering Committees. GIZ will also be focusing on three main challenges:

- The actual implementation of the three provincial strategies elaborated by the working groups and notably the adaptation of the local TVET offering based on the conclusions;
- The linkage between the local labour market monitoring and the regional level; besides elaborating local strategies, the local labour market monitoring has a provision of information function that requires a linkage to the next level. PEJ assisted ANAPEC in elaborating and implementing a regional labour market diagnostic instrument that allows the public employment service to diagnose a number of key economic sectors of the region (yearly). The instrument is partly based on the ELMA approach and largely relies on the same tools as the working groups (minus the multi-actor dialogue/networking component of the provinces' labour market monitoring approach). The first regional diagnostics were carried out at the end of 2016 in all Moroccan regions and going forward the project will seek to link the two instruments.
- Finally, the project will endeavour to secure the sustainability of the labour market monitoring approach and its scaling up to other regions by institutionalising it within the implementation of the national employment strategy. Ideally, the implementation would be through a standardised and replicable model carried out by the ANAPEC. Therefore, to ensure the sustainability of the suggested model prior agreements between the involved entities will be needed that provide either a financial compensation for

the members of the working groups or a significantly reduced workload (less office hours, less responsibilities, integrating the analysis in their internal annual goals, etc.).

2.3 The case of Albania

Basic information

One of the strategic priorities of the National Employment and Skills strategy 2014-2020 is to *"Strengthen the governance of the labour market and qualification systems"*[12]. Based on previous experiences and lessons learned from GIZ[13] and European Union (EU)[14] supported projects, this priority area foresees the establishment of a gender-sensitive tracer system for graduates and trainees from public vocational schools and training centres to measure the impact of initial and continuous training.

In January 2014, upon the request of the Ministry of Social Welfare and Youth (MoSWY), the GIZ Vocational Education and Training Programme and a project implemented through the International Labour Organization (ILO) under the Instrument for pre-accession (IPA) of the EU (EU IPA 2010 project), elaborated a Policy Paper *"Introducing a Tracer System for Training, Vocational Education and Training (TVET) graduates in Albania: a tool for enhancing the relevance and the labour market demand responsiveness of the TVET System in Albania"*. The paper recommended actions required to establish and institutionalise a Public VET Graduates and Trainees Tracing System (GTTS). While the recommendations were focused on the public VET sector, and did not consider other segments of the educational chain, such as public and/or private general secondary schools, universities and private vocational training providers, they could also inform the

---

[12] http://www.seecel.hr/UserDocsImages/Documents/EMP-SKILLS-STRATEGY_Albania.pdf
[13] GIZ VET Programme, CARDS VET 3 "Support to Vocational Education and Training Reform", "Support to the Implementation of Albanian's National Education Strategy with special focus on Pre-University VE", funded by the European Union and implemented by a GIZ led consortium in partnership with European Profile S.A., and ILO-EU IPA 2010 Project on HRD.
[14] In 2016, GOA has signed with the EU the Budget Sector Support Contract for Employment and Skills in Albania. The contract at the amount of 30 mil EU, aims to contribute to a more inclusive and effective labour market by supporting the employment and skills development policy of the Albanian Government (National Employment and Skills Strategy 2014-2020). In this framework establishment of the tracing system for VET Graduates/Trainees is an indicator to measure achievements in the sector.

development of a tracing system across other education and training fields at the national level.

The decision to direct the intervention at the tracing system of VET graduates was based on the existing LMI data gap collected by two key stakeholders at the national and regional level, the National Statistical Agency (INSTAT) and the National Employment Office (NES), the executing agency of the MoSWY. INSTAT[15] is the main source of data that underpins labour market policy such as the Labour Force Survey (LFS) and Census of Population (CoP). Since 2012, and with support from ILO and Eurostat, the LFS is conducted on a quarterly basis and ongoing efforts are directed to increase data reliability and the level of disaggregation from the national to the regional level. On the other hand, MoSWY supported by the Swedish International Development Agency (SIDA) established a web based platform[16] at NES providing information on the registered unemployed and registered vacancies, with access to intermediaries and individual job seekers. As the institution with the overall responsibility[17] for the public VET providers, MoSWY did not have a system to collect data on student and trainee performance in the labour market. In an effort to restructure the network of public VET providers, the Ministry considered the establishment of a tracing System as a very useful instrument to evaluate the overall effectiveness and efficiency of the VET system and its alignment with labour market needs at both national and regional levels.

Against that background, a working group composed of key staff from the Ministry of Social Welfare and Youth, the National Employment Service (NES), the National Agency for Vocational Education Training and Quality (NAVETQ) and GIZ defined six steps for setting up and institutionalising the VET graduates trainees tracing system:

---

15 http://www.instat.gov.al/en/themes/labour-market/publications/books/2016/labour-force-survey-q3-2016.aspx.
16 Kerkojpune: http://www.kerkojpune.gov.al.
17 In 2013 the public VET system in Albania went under the main responsibility of the Ministry of Social Welfare and Youth (MoSWY). It consisted of 52 VET institutions, including 42 Vocational Secondary Schools (VSSs) and 10 Vocational Training Centers (VTCs), distributed in 12 regions of Albania.

Table 1   Steps to setup and institutionalise the VET graduates trainees tracing system

Step 1	Draft the relevant legal acts to officially assign the agency responsible for the management of the GTTS system.
Step 2	Build staff capacity and plan resources.
Step 3	Establish a graduates trainees tracing system through the Ministry of Social Welfare and Youth, using one centralised, web-based and integrated model for all VSSs and VTCs.
Step 4	Conduct the pilot survey through the online system in Tirana and Kamza (4,000 participants)
Step 5	Conduct the online survey for all Vocational Education and Training public providers in Albania (20,208 participants).
Step 6	Raise awareness on the availability of the tracing system and its results.

Source: own elaboration.

The close cooperation and technical support to the working group ensured an increased government commitment and ownership along the process. The support consisted in technical assistance for capacity building and purchasing the software used to conduct the tracing surveys. The activities listed in the steps above took place in the period from 2014-2016.

Strategy, goals and intentions

The assessment of key players who collect and produce LMI in the country reveals that Albania generates a wide range of LMI (quantitative & qualitative; administrative and survey based) and uses it for labour market analysis to some extent (Walsh and Muca 2012). In particular, the main sources of data such as the LFS and Census of Population are in place and, in the case of the LFS, offer the prospect of quarterly results that should underpin labour market policy. However, in comparison to the best practice in other countries, Albania still faces some major gaps in the following areas:

- Local LMI and analysis;
- Additional national surveys, such as VET students and trainees tracing survey, Job Vacancy survey, Labour Cost survey etc.;
- Forward-looking analysis (labour demand forecast by occupation and sector);
- Dissemination of acquired data.

The government that took office in 2013 set "VET and Employment" high in the political agenda and Government Programme. The MSWY decided to incorporate recommendations of the aforementioned Policy Paper (PP) in the National Strategy for Employment and Skills (NSES) 2014-2020, seeking to improve LMI in order to base policy design on good evidence. The PP recommends a 3-year short-term plan as a scenario to "close the existing data gap" (see Figure 3 for short-term interventions).

In this context, with the approval of the NSES 2014-2020, particular focus was directed to vocational student and trainee destination (tracing) data, in order to learn about students' trajectories after they leave education and training institutions (information that was not collected and analysed by any education institutions or the relevant ministries prior to 2014)[18]. The second was to improve the dissemination of information to the relevant users with simple language, different formats and communication channels. Indeed, there is a wide range of actual and potential users for LMI and student destination data, such as public and private education and training institutions, Labour Offices, career counselling centres, job seekers, students, employers, development organisations, etc., thus putting a premium on closing the data gap.

The main goal for establishing VET GTTS was to evaluate the overall effectiveness and efficiency of the VET system in Albania. Having a tracing system in place in the future would help to:

- Improve the governance, management, transparency, accountability of VET Public Providers;
- Make evidence-based policies and allocate budget to institutions based on performance criteria;
- Facilitate the matching of labour market demand with supply from the VET sector;

---

[18] Other fields of education including Primary Education, General Secondary Schools and Universities under the responsibility of Ministry of Education and Sports faced similar issues with regard to the lack of student tracking.

- Increase competition and positioning of VET institutions within the education market using the criteria of employability and relevance to the labour market;
- Inform public opinion, in particular parents and students, to choose the appropriate education and career path, and allocate the expenditures out of the family/personal budget in an appropriate direction leading to decent and beneficial employment;
- Enable career guidance and counselling by elementary schools and VSSs, VTCs, public and private employment offices, etc.;
- Help associations and individual companies to better plan future business activities in the market based on the availability or shortage of skilled labour force.

Figure 3   Short term development scenario for improving the LMIS in Albania

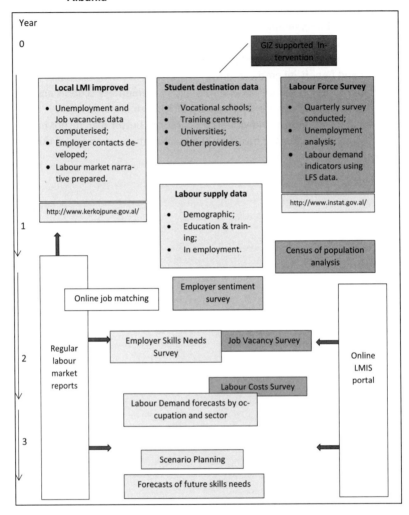

Source: Walsh, K.; Muça, Mirela (2012): Developing a Labour Market Information System in Albania.

(R)LMM practice so far

The implementation strategy and results were geared towards three key results:

Establishment and institutionalisation of VET GTTS

Step 1: The Minister of Social Welfare and Youth assigned the National Employment Service (NES) as the national authority to oversee and manage the process. A Minister's order was drafted by the Working Group. In support of the Minister's order the National Employment Service signed an internal regulation that defined roles and responsibilities of each public provider as well as the timeframe of conducting the surveys and the human and financial resources needed.

Step 2: Training staff in NES and MSWY was conducted by the GIZ and local experts. Training covered issues of LMIS, Tracing surveys approach and methodology, instruments, data analyses and use of the survey software.

Conducting the survey and producing the results

Step 3: The "Metior Solution" survey platform was identified as the appropriate online solution to conduct the tracing surveys. The software has the advantage of operating in both English and Albanian. It has an offline-solution when there is no internet. It also offers personal client manager/support, free hosting, releases, updates and data storage. GIZ VET Programme committed to ensure cost coverage for the license of this software for a limited time (purchase of the license for two - four years) and capacity building for staff in VET institutions and the MoSWY. Online surveys are widely used nowadays because they are cost effective, far cheaper compared to traditional surveys with printed questionnaires, and are very easy in terms of the data processing.

The platform operates in a very simple way. It was agreed that the administrators of the public VET providers officially submit the list of participants to the National Employment Service (NES) at the beginning of each calendar year and the survey is conducted at the end of the first semester. The lists contain contact details for all persons registered in the previous academic year for the vocational schools and calendar year for trainees of Vocational Training Centres. According to the list provided by each public VET Provider the participants invited by NES submit the information directly to the database of the platform. The online data collection is carried out over three - four weeks. The participation rate and survey results can be monitored on a continuous basis (live at any point in time) while the survey is running.

Step 4: The first testing of the system, before upscaling nationwide, was done for VET Public providers of Tirana and Kamza municipalities. There were five VSS with a total of 670 graduates for the academic year 2014-2015 and two VTCs with 3,365 registered trainees for the period January –June 2015. The survey was conducted during October 2015[19] by NES with support of the WG and GIZ. The questionnaire was developed and participants were invited to provide their responses via e-mail and mobile phone (text message). The results were analysed and shared with the Ministry, other relevant stakeholders and the wider public using different formats (leaflets, PowerPoint, press release). Other communication channels included meetings with donors, open days at the vocational and primary schools, Labour Offices, Facebook, job fairs etc.

Step 5: Following the assessment for the pilot in Tirana and Kamza, the process was extended to all public VET providers (see below). The results were shared with the MSWY.

Information and communication

Step 6: During the entire process, efforts were made to raise awareness on the institutionalisation of the GTTS as well as on the publication of results.

At the VET Skills Fair organised by MSWY in June 2016, the WG and GIZ organised a panel discussion to share information about the system and the results available from the tracing survey conducted in Tirana and Kamza. Moreover, printed leaflets and materials were available during the entire duration of VET Fair attended by about 2,000 participants and visitors from all over the country.

The Tracing System results were available and displayed in the Job Fairs organised by MSWY in 2015 and 2016. The 2016 Job Fair was visited by about 55,000 people where 11,200 job applications were posted from the companies.

The results of the tracing survey were also made available in the activities organised for primary schools at the VSS (open days), and shared with donors working in the VET sector. The information was available in printed and electronic format

---

[19] The first testing of the tracing system was conducted in October. After evaluating the situation and the work process it was agreed that surveys in the future will be conducted during the first semester of each year.

posted on the websites, in order to ensure easy accessibility. Selected data was also disseminated via Facebook and social media.

Challenges, success stories and outlook

There is already good evidence on the usefulness of the tracing system data. NAVETQ and donors including GIZ are using results of the tracing survey for improving or developing new curricula. Moreover, the Ministry reviewed the offer of Public VET providers based on a set of evaluation criteria including the level of students' employability. Thanks to the high level of enrolment and employability (increasing trend in the last three years), MSWY has decided to invest about 3 million Euros from the state budget and expand on new learning directions with high potential for employment.

It is planned to organise the tracer surveys every year based on the developed methodology and instruments via a web-based platform. Utilising web applications offers the possibility to easily reach out to all registered VET graduates and trainees in a given year, thereby eliminating the need to select a representative sample. In this case, emphasis should be placed on ensuring a good response rate, by encouraging the participants to participate and contribute. The tracing survey results provide:

- Combined quantitative and qualitative information on: activity after the completion of the education/training (in wage-employment, self-employment, working for family business, enrolment in further training, enrolment in tertiary education); level of qualification obtained; employability by region and sector; income; extent of the knowledge acquired during study programme that is used in current job; who is influencing their choices; how the graduates/trainees got their first employment; selected socioeconomic data (e.g. ethnic affiliation); factors that graduates/trainees are not in employment nor in education (unwillingness to work, financial limitations, restrictions from families etc.).
- Information on the share (%) of graduates and trainees in education, employment or not engaged in any activity (at the national level, for all public VET providers). Moreover, the system offers disaggregate data at the provider level (VS School/VTC level), which is useful for the city/regional planning. The business community can plan future economic activities based on the availability of the skilled work force, and the VET provider can anticipate skill development in line with business needs.

- The data can be disaggregated by gender, learning direction-profile etc.
- The survey data can be cross-checked and compared with LFS results in order to deepen the analysis in certain areas. The yearly database can be generated in an excel file and used for trend analysis at the national or provider level. Even though the tracing system is still at an early stage, the existence of such system and data produced by it are used by MoSWY and the EU Delegation as performance indicators for disbursements of the Sector Reform Contract for Employment and Skills Albania 2014-2020 (IPA II)[20].

As of 2017, the tracing system is only used with public VET providers. There is a need to consolidate the system and further enhance the capacities in the NES and MSWY to use the results to formulate policy and deepen the reform of the VET sector. This will likely require between one - two years, including the period for the preparation and approval of the bylaws under the new VET Law[21] which should bring institutional changes for management, financing and quality control of public VET providers.

Once the system is consolidated, it is possible to extend the tracing system as a monitoring instrument for all education providers (both public and private) at the secondary and tertiary levels. In this case, the efforts should focus on the institutional level. MWSY should cooperate with the Ministry of Education and Science (MES) and its executing agencies in order to identify the implementation steps, timeframe, institutional responsible and financial resources.

2.4 Main lessons from the stocktaking exercise

Besides the above-mentioned case studies of Egypt, Morocco and Albania, more detailed information was gathered through a stocktaking template addressed to all eight active GIZ supported (R)LMM initiatives. It addressed the following different fields of engagement through a set of questions:

- Collection and analysis of data;
- Distribution and linkage of (R)LMI to TVET and Labour Market policy-making, and;

---

20 Instrument for Pre-accession Assistance (IPA II) –Sector Reform Contract for Employment and Skills Albania 2014-2020 was signed in October 2016. The contract volume is 30 million Euros. The tracing system and results are referred to as the indicator 7. VET graduates' employment rate.
21 The Albanian Parliament approved the VET Law on February 18, 2017.

- Institutionalisation and national and legislative framework conditions.

The stocktaking form also asked about challenges, success stories and areas of further support with regard to the above-mentioned categories. The most important results are summarised below.

Collection and analysis of (R)LMI

- There is distinction between GIZ projects that support the establishment of (R)LMM structures such as providing organisational development, capacity development of personnel and supporting sustainability and institutionalisation of these (R)LMM structures (Egypt, Rwanda, Togo, and Kyrgyzstan) and GIZ projects for which (regional) LMM activities are limited to either special target groups of the project (e.g. Albania and Palestine with regard to TVET graduates), or a specific objective such as local economic development or monitoring of LM Programmes (e.g. Jordan and Morocco). Only one project (EPP in Egypt) supports the establishment of regional Labour Market Observatories as permanent entities.
- The main type of support provided by GIZ is capacity development and the provision of operational costs.
- A strong focus lies on public actors as main partners for (R)LMM, with limited inclusion of private sector actors. Only in Egypt, regional private sector associations are a key partner for RLMM. In Morocco, civil society and local NGOs play a major role.
- Governance structures for RLMM are weak in all eight countries surveyed and characterised by a hierarchical and public sector led approach to the collection and analysis of data.
- The most common challenges include access to data and a limited data sharing culture amongst different public and private sector institutions, limited information on and inclusion of rural areas and informal economy, lack of adopted and tested (R)LMM methods, and budget limitations by public and private sector partners.
- Main success factors include the involvement of multiple stakeholders, including from the private sector, a dialogue based approach, and the buy-in from policy-makers at the national level.
- Areas of further support include the usage of online surveys, ensuring demand-group orientation of collected LMI, data visualisation and management support, and advice on how to do LMM in countries with a high share of informality.

Distribution of (R)LMI and their Linkage to TVET and LM Policymaking

- There is little experience amongst GIZ projects on linking (R)LMI to policymaking. Only few success stories are available, such as in Egypt where RLMI in one region showed evidence for a high demand for a new profession (plastic technician). Based on this evidence, the Egyptian Ministry of Education and Technical Education is seeking to introduce this occupational profile as a new vocational training course.
- There is a lack of properly established channels to influence policy-making, reflecting a weak governance structure (mostly arranged in forms of networks).
- Challenges include budget limitations by partners, lack of access to decision-makers, limited partner capabilities in using evidence when designing policies and programmes, limited skills of (R)LMM practitioners with regard to moderation, mediation and communication.
- Success factors include the involvement of multiple stakeholders, including all the private sector above, a dialogues-based approach, the commitment of high-level stakeholders who act as facilitators to push recommendations to policy level, the support of entities at the national level (in case of RLMM), and awareness amongst public and private sector stakeholders of the benefits of evidence-based policies.
- Areas of further support include access to skilled experts and consultants especially with regard to "translating" the (R)LMI into special products and services which are target-group oriented and attractive to decision-makers, usage of modern means of communication and innovative distribution channels (e.g. apps and social media), as well as communication and mediation training for LMM practitioners to upgrade their skill sets.

Institutionalisation and national and legislative framework conditions

- The level of formalisation of the (R)LMM process and structures varies from loose arrangements such as a letter of secondment, to multi-stakeholder MoUs or patronage agreement of the Governor.
- None of the MENA region countries had the (R)LMM process formalised by legislation/decree or financed out of regular state budget. Only Albania and Kyrgyzstan integrated and financed the LMM within the state budget and institutionalised the process (e.g. Ministry of Labour, Kyrgyzstan). In most developing countries institutionalisation of (R)LMM structures and functions is weak and there is a high dependence on donor engagement and external financing.

- Most GIZ projects (plan to) provide support with regard to institutionalisation at national or regional level.
- Challenges include budget and capacity constraints by national partners, lack of awareness amongst decision-makers about added value for (R)LMI and evidence-based policy-making, fragmentation and overlapping responsibilities, lack of capabilities and/or political will at national level to support regional structures.
- Success factors include the involvement of multiple stakeholders, including from the private sector, a dialogues-based approach, and the commitment of a high-level stakeholder who acts as a facilitator to push institutionalisation.
- Areas of further support include strengthening knowledge about different legislative frameworks, and providing advice on financial sustainability and business models for (R)LMM structures.

General key findings

The following key findings compile both main topics and findings that originated from the stocktaking survey as well as from the discussion amongst the international experts and GIZ representatives during the Round Table in Cairo.

- The financial sustainability of (R)LMM structures is a critical issue in both developed and developing countries. In Europe, most structures do not generate sufficient income and are to a large extent dependent on state funding or on acquiring funding via EU and research grants. A few exceptions exist, such as private research companies or some private sector led RLMOs in the UK.
- As the public sector in developing countries often lacks the financial and human resources to conduct (R)LMM, donor support will remain crucial in the near future.
- The use of LMI for monitoring the effectiveness of LM programmes and policies or country development frameworks (incl. the Sustainable Development Goals) is a new field for LMM in developing countries. By taking into consideration how the collected and analysed LMI can support the governments, project partners may be more willing to mobilise resources for LMM and see its added value.
- The access to policy-makers and "translation" of evidence-based recommendations in concrete measures on the ground is a challenge in both developing and developed countries and little best practices are available so far.

- Skills of (R)LMM practitioners have changed in developed countries. To effectively support the implementation of evidence-based programmes and link LMI to policy-making, communication and moderation skills are now equally important as statistical and economic skills. This should be taken into account when designing capacity development measures for practitioners in developing countries.
- Partnerships with the private sector for (R)LMM are also rare in European RLMOs. Yet, European (R)LMOs have acquired substantial knowledge in applying for grants and selling their "individual expertise" of (R)LMO researchers/ practitioners as consultants to the private sector.
- While access to data and data validity are typically highly advanced in industrial countries, developing countries often need to invest in the collection of missing data, especially at the regional level.
- LMM approaches and methodologies need to be adapted to developing country contexts (e.g. high share of informal economy) and local specificities.

3 Conclusion and recommendations

Based on the case studies and additional country experiences discussed in this article, the following conclusions and initial recommendations emerge:

Varying degrees of (R)LMM focus

Though all (R)LMM activities can be considered an integral part of the GIZ integrated approach to employment promotion, several conceptual differences are noticeable. For instance, the extent of their regional character differs from country to country, ranging from very regional approaches (e.g. Egypt, Morocco) to more nationally orientated (R)LMM activities (e.g. Kyrgyzstan). Moreover, some projects support the establishment of structures, sustainability and even push institutionalisation (Egypt, Rwanda, Togo, and Kyrgyzstan), while some other GIZ projects' LMM activities are limited to either special target groups of the project (e.g. Albania and Palestine with regard to TVET graduates) or specific objectives, such as local economic development or monitoring of LM Programmes (e.g. Jordan and Morocco). Looking at the knowledge transfer so far, they are inspired by European models to a varying extent.

Similarities - common challenges are dominating

As discussed in the introduction of this article, LMM in developing and transition countries is influenced by a range of contextual factors and specific challenges. For instance, all of the countries analysed face a large informal economy, which makes it difficult to collect reliable labour market information. Similarly, a lack of current and regionally representative data makes it extremely difficult to obtain reliable regional labour market information. The lack of sustainable public funding by national partners also is a challenge. Moreover, unclear and mostly overlapping administrative responsibilities and weak LMIS governance structures are also common. In comparison, influencing factors with positive impact, above all new ICTs and digitalisation, are (still) of lower importance in practice, even though some projects (e.g. Rwanda) have a strong focus on it. Finally, with regard to their regional focus, it appears that most (R)LMM activities so far were starting in economically prosperous areas like industrialised capital regions and/or regions with potential in tourism.

Lack of private sector involvement

With regards to the involvement of regional stakeholders, one could see that much more emphasis is placed on the involvement of public institutions and organisations so far, while regional private sector organisations and/or companies are typically less or not involved at all. Where closer involvements of the private sector exists (e.g. Egypt), it seems to be a success factor for the whole project in general and especially for understanding the demand for workers in the region. Therefore, though mostly difficult, stronger involvement of the private sector is a clear potential for further (R)LMM and should be much stronger on the agenda of development cooperation and local partners.

Need for more demand side RLMI

Data collection in most of the eight cases appears to be largely focused on the supply-side, such as different target groups of the labour market, different professions, and levels of qualification. In comparison, data collection related to demand-side issues and specific political objectives, such as structural change or promoting local and regional development is much less common. Clearly, reliable information on regional labour demand can only be provided in cooperation with the private sector (being single enterprises, chambers or sector associations). Hence, in order to strengthen private sector involvement, it is necessary that (R)LMM products and services are targeted at regional actors and regional companies.

Development status - mostly still captured in the "information stage"

In view of the rather short period during which the eight GIZ supported (R)LMM activities have been implemented, it is useful to consider the (R)LMM's general development stage (see Figure 4). Based on European LMM developments to-date, Larsen et al. identified three distinct stages of (R)LMM activities (Larsen et al. 2013) which can serve as a blueprint for (R)LMM developments in general.

Figure 4   Typical development stages of (R)LMM activities

Phases	Provision of information	Information + Communication	Information + Communication + Action
Main Users	Traditional stakeholders Administrations	+ Regional and local decision-makers TVET actors, universities Business associations	+ Companies Regional networks
Activities	Research Detailed Reports	+ Targeted data presentation Dissemination activities Forms of dialogue be-	+ Targeted activities in cooperation with regional/local actors Regional networking

Source: based on Larsen et al. 2013: 29.

- ***Provision of information.*** In their beginnings, regional and local labour market monitoring functions are mainly limited to provision of information on labour market supply. Structural data from public employment services and statistical offices are used for analysis. Some cases use primary data for sectors, fields of professions, and target groups, often documented in long reports. Traditional stakeholders are the main recipients for this information and no special communication components exist.

- *Information plus communication.* Especially since 2008/09, activities involve more and more communication, such as targeting specific presentations of data and customised information. There is a trend away from only supply-orientated outputs and a stronger focus on regional and local decision-makers with their concrete information needs. This leads to a stronger focus on dissemination carried out by customised communication activities and enhanced dialogue formats towards stakeholders. In turn, more attention is paid to enhancing the availability of ICTs Evidence-based policy-making in regional contexts is increasingly becoming an important issue, and RLMM are responsible for interpreting the data and support and advise local decision-makers. Moreover, further user groups become more important than before: stakeholders of the TVET system, other stakeholders such as schools, businesses and business associations, universities and their students. There is increasing pressure towards more comprehensive data collection and use.
- *Information plus communication plus action.* Derived from the information and communication stage, the next step includes more and more concrete activities. Especially small and medium-sized companies are hard to reach and engage, as well as other potential (R)LMM users like schools and parents. This shows that good "interpretation of (R)LMM data" must include activities specifically targeted at specific groups. In this stage, (R)LMM increasingly becomes an engine of regional networking. Mostly recognised as neutral agents without pursuing own economic interests, (R)LMM are now central for communication, cooperation, coordination and coordinated decisions on the regional or local level (Larsen et al. 2013).

Against the background of the above-mentioned 3-phase-model, it is clear to see that

- Egypt, as "oldest" of the GIZ supported (R)LMM projects, is the only case study that can be rated as having reached phase two and partly even phase three due to focus on designing and implementing evidence-based ALMPs based on collected RLMI.
- Morocco, from the beginning, has a strong conceptual focus on regional labour market information and a strong link to decentralisation policy and dialogue formats as well, but remains in phase one after starting with trainings and first sector analyses in the spring of 2016;

- Albania, from the beginning, has had a very specific focus on tracing graduates for better placement results. After expanding its scope to all TVET providers and beyond the two pilot regions, as well as creating linkages to more non-public stakeholders, it has the potential to become more influential on policymaking and programming. At the time of consideration here, the activities conducted so far seem to be mainly located in phase one, too.[22]

Many (R)LMM governance experiences still have to take shape

Matters of governance, defined as the *"directing, guiding or regulating individuals, organizations, nations (...) in conduct or actions"* (Lynn 2010: 2), are always linked with structures of decision-making and policy implementation. They may appear through different types and forms, such as hierarchy, markets, and networks. As the stocktaking made clear, governance structures for (R)LMM are weak in all surveyed eight countries, and characterised by a hierarchical and public sector led approach to the collection and analysis of data, a lack of data sharing culture and, if available, a mostly inefficient Labour Market Information System (LMIS). Faced with an overriding lack of non-public partners and users so far, these (R)LMM activities, often in the middle of their institutionalisation process, are still more or less fully embedded in a circle of dominating administrative actors.

While these are governance issues of an early stage, all real governance related activities surface at a later stage when (R)LMM activities reach at least the second stage of communication, when creating active linkages to different political actors and policy fields, and becoming an integral part of customised regional strategies (Larsen et al. 2013)[23]. Looking at the GIZ supported (R)LMM activities from this point of view, it becomes clear that only the case of Egypt has reached a state of development where governance issues related to (R)LMM products and services, the involvement of non-public partners, users etc. start playing a

---

22 With regard to this "soft classification", the following aspects of all eight stocktaking responses can be regarded as indications, too. When asked about all three main areas, the field of data collection/analysis and the field of institutionalization seemed to be the most challenging at the moment. In contrast, the important area of distribution and linkages to policies got much lower attention as a challenge. One explanation might be that currently not all projects were explicitly focused (yet) on such "bridges" to policies, especially if (R)LMM is not a rather dominant element of their whole development project.

23 See EN RLMM Anthology 2017: The Importance of Governance in Regional and Labour Market Monitoring for Evidence-Based Policy-Making. Call for Papers.

bigger role. As a result, real differentiated governance issues for GIZ supported (R)LMM activities will take shape in the upcoming years when more and stronger bridges to other actors will be built.

Selected inputs from European models are helpful

The results of the stocktaking as well as discussions during the sector network workshop *"Sustainable Economic Development in the MENA Region"* in November 2016 showed that there remains a gap in experience and practice between many European (R)LMM activities and (R)LMM in developing and transition countries. If well-adapted to the national and regional needs and based on the needs of the regional stakeholders (demand-driven approach), selected inputs from European models can continue to prove useful for (R)LMM in developing and transition countries. The case of Egypt in particular shows that, European inputs can be successfully adapted for a very different labour market.

Returning back to the question raised in the title, are there shortcuts to building strong (R)LMM? Looking at GIZ supported (R)LMM, at least some of them, above all Egypt, were able to benefit from knowledge transfer in the form of such a "shortcut" and implement development steps faster. On the other hand, the European experience also shows that many (R)LMM developments needed enormous social interaction and came in consecutive steps over decades before having reached the more advanced stages of communication and action. Against this background, while a certain catching up is certainly possible, institutionalisation and reaching more mature systems will most likely take time.

References

Brzozowski, Jan/Rand, Sigrid/Surdej, Aleksander (2013): Changing framework conditions for operating and developing regional and local labour market observatories in Europe. In: Larsen, Christa/Rand, Sigrid/Schmid, Alfons/Atin, Eugenia/Serrano, Raquel (Eds.): Shifting roles and functions of regional and local labour market observatories across Europe, München: Rainer Hampp Verlag, pp. 11-25

Larsen, Christa/Rand, Sigrid/Lorent, Pierre/Baruffini, Moreno (2013): Shifting roles of regional and local labour market observatories, in: Larsen, Christa/Rand, Sigrid/Schmid, Alfons et al. (Eds.): Shifting roles and functions of regional and local labour market observatories across Europe, München: Rainer Hampp Verlag, pp. 26-38

Larsen, Christa/Rand, Sigrid/Schmid, Alfons/ Holopainen, Päivi/Jokikaarre, Pirita/Kuusela, Katrin/Alapuranen, Nina (2016): Digital (R)evolution and its effects on labour. Opportunities and challenges for regional and local labour market monitoring, München: Rainer Hampp Verlag

Lynn Jr., Laurence E. (2010): Adaptation? Transformation? Both? Neither? The Many Faces of Governance, Jerusalem: Jerusalem Papers in Regulation and Governance. Working Paper No. 20

Walsh, Kenneth/Muça, Mirela (2012): Developing a Labour Market Information System in Albania, GIZ and MoSWY, Working Paper

Vertopi, Etleva/Gomes, Maria/Hartig, Sabine (2014): Introducing a Tracer System for TVET graduates in Albania: a tool for enhancing the relevance and the labour market demand responsiveness of the TVET System

Websites

Deutsche Gesellschaft für Internationale Zusammenarbeit: https://www.giz.de/ expertise /html/ 447 9.html (accessed on 29 June2017)

Deutsche Gesellschaft für Internationale Zusammenarbeit: https://www.giz.de/expertise/ html/ 462 0.html (accessed on 29 June 2017)

Deutsche Gesellschaft für Internationale Zusammenarbeit: http://eppegypt.net/uploads/activities/ 2012-09-23_C2-RLMM_mission/report_en.pdf (accessed on 29 June 2017)

Instat: http://www.instat.gov.al/en/themes/labour-market/publications/books/2016/labour-force-survey-q3-2016.aspx (accessed on 29 June 2017)

ANNEX: GIZ SUPPORTED (R)LMM PROJECTS

The following eight GIZ projects took part in the stocktaking exercise.

GIZ projects from MENA region countries:

- *Employment Promotion Project in Egypt* (phase 1: 2011 - 2015, and phase 2: 2016 - 2020), funded by Federal Ministry for Economic Cooperation and Development (BMZ), Germany,
- *Employment Promotion in Jordan* (duration 01/2016 - 09/2020), funded by Federal Ministry for Economic Cooperation and Development (BMZ), Germany,
- *TVET and Employment Promotion Programme (TEP) in Palestine* (duration 07/2015 - 06/2018), funded by Federal Ministry for Economic Cooperation and Development (BMZ), Germany, and Swiss Agency for Development and Cooperation (SDC),
- *Promotion de l'Emploi des Jeunes en Milieu Rural (PEJ) in Morocco* (duration 01/2012 - 12/2017), funded by Federal Ministry for Economic Cooperation and Development (BMZ), Germany.

GIZ projects from Africa outside MENA region:

- *Promotion of Economy and Employment (Eco-Emploi) in Rwanda* (duration 06/2016 - 05/2019), funded by Federal Ministry for Economic Cooperation and Development (BMZ), Germany,
- *Programme for Vocational Educational Training and Youth Employment (ProFoPEJ) in Togo* (duration 11/2016 - 10/2018, with 2 previous phases), funded by Federal Ministry for Economic Cooperation and Development (BMZ), Germany.

GIZ project in Central Asia:

- *Vocational Education & Training and Employment Promotion in Kyrgyzstan* (duration 01/2014 - 12/2016), funded by Federal Ministry for Economic Cooperation and Development (BMZ), Germany

GIZ project in South-Eastern Europe:

- *Vocational Education and Training Programme Albania* (duration 01/2015 - 12/2016, with 2 previous phases since 2010), funded by Federal Ministry for Economic Cooperation and Development (BMZ), Germany.

4. PERSPECTIVES

The Labour Market's Regulation and the Transition from Government to Governance

Marco Ricceri

> *"We cannot solve our problems with the same thinking we used when we created them"*
>
> Albert Einstein

1. Introduction

"New Challenges, New Approaches": with these words, Angel Gurria, OECD Secretary-General, has introduced a new initiative launched in 2016 in order to better understand the nature and implications of the ongoing structural changes in the economic sphere. It deals with the initiative called *New Approaches to Economic Challenges* (NAEC). "The goal – Gurria explained - is to develop a better sense of how economies really work and to articulate strategies which reflect this understanding. A fundamental reflection is required on the changing nature of the economy which conventional analyses struggle to explain. This is why we launched the New Approaches to Economic Challenges (NAEC) exercise. With NAEC, we are asking hard questions and challenging our assumptions and our understanding about the workings of the economy. We are transforming our ways of thinking and acting with respect to the economy, the environment and society as a whole system".

The basic document discussed at the *OECD Council at Ministerial level* on 7-8 June 2017 in Paris clearly highlights the positive and negative aspects of current global development processes and the risks of a world-wide open economy not supported and driven by adequate governance. Specifically, that *"the uptake of new technologies has been found to have been a core factor in the profound transformations in the occupational and industrial structures of OECD markets. Like every industrial revolution which has involved a process of creation-destruction, it is difficult to predict what will be the outcome of the process for workers.*

Nonetheless, with better tools for analysis and the sharing of experiences with different policies, it is hoped that the process will be better handled for people's wellbeing. The extent to which the current production revolution will involve larger traditional costs and both a faster and larger change of the world of work is still being debated". In any case, according to the OECD, it is sure that *"increased technology adoption displays the strongest association with labour market polarization and de-industrialization"*.

"Transforming our way of thinking", "industrial revolution": these are the key words of the binomial to which the governance open issue refers. Indeed, all economic systems and, consequently, all labour markets in the industrialised areas of the world, with reference to their mission, facilities, organisational models, operational mechanisms, are subject to continuous and increasing pressure by the changes linked to the globalisation processes and its positive and negative effects, such as: the emergence of new forms of competitiveness, the pursuit of new profit conditions, industrial restructuring, transfer of production units, labour mobility, migration flows, the formation of new communities, social networks, and, often, of unprecedented cultural relations.

The management of such situations, which also have substantial geo-political and geo-economic implications, requires governments, regional authorities and managers of public services, on the one hand, to develop sufficient knowledge both of the economic system (the values of the production factors) and of the territorial system (the values of the area of reference), to understand how these processes can be translated into opportunities for a peaceful progress of the communities involved; and, on the other hand, this situation requires public decision-makers to express remarkable capability to address the structural change of the society with the courage of proper policies: "go structural", "go social", "go green", "go institutional", following the indications of the specific OECD guidelines.

To this aim, public decision-makers are required specifically to adapt laws, rules, procedures, industrial relations (the quality of the regulatory systems); to modernise the facilities (in terms of efficiency); to strengthen the incentive actions (in terms of effectiveness). In other words, public decision-makers are required to have a remarkable capability to manage the change processes related to the international competition, by improving and innovating profoundly the services' performances and identifying points of advanced balance between the actions dealing with the *government* of such processes (set of rules that refer to an institutional body with executive power) and those dealing with the *governance* (web of rules of different origins, including for example the autonomous initiatives taken by private operators), so as to promote a more fruitful collaboration between public and private actors, in the common interest.

The new processes started in the economy as well as in the world of work, Angel Gurria stressed on another occasion (2014), require a change of orientation to evaluate, certainly, "what needs to be done" but also to pay special attention to "how it can be done", what governance mechanism are needed, how responses can be tailored to local conditions; and how the various stakeholders can be brought together.

2. Some open questions dealing with the global processes

To adequately address the open problems of the labour markets governance, it is necessary to clarify some fundamental issues related to the nature of the globalisation processes. They concern mostly:

- The asymmetry in the conditions in which the development actors operate: institutions, capital, labour;
- The key role of the institutional economy.

2.1 The asymmetry between the development actors

Globalisation's phenomenon is very different from the previous one of the internationalisation, which was identified with the increasing dimension of the international trade. Globalisation is a process of much broader scope, which invests the set-up of the society as well as the life of individuals and their communities. In this regard, the basic question is the following: this process reflects an "order" or a "disorder"? Constantly, for example, this question arises in occasion of the international summits of the heads of states and governments, as the G20 summits, together with the need to give an order to the world development's process: it deals with the idea of a "big correction" of such a process (see the UN Agenda 2030 for a Sustainable Growth), with the issue of the new governance.

In fact, what we are experiencing currently is rather a period at least of great disorder. Globalisation, in short, reflects a chaos - a chaos that can be also creative, not just destructive – based on a continuous change of the traditional terms of reference of human life and activity: new dimension of space (the nonsense of the traditional state borders for some social categories as the global élite or, for instance, the migrants), and new dimension of time (the prevailing "culture of the present' over any reference to the value of the past as well as to any hypothesis of possible future. In this respect, the Italian scholar Remo Bodei (2010) highlights that contemporary society *"is drastically reducing the ability to imagine a collective future, to imagine it beyond the private expectations ... We are facing the desertification of the future"*.

Herein lies the main source of the labour and social tensions that prevail in contemporary society; in the large asymmetry between capital, that is increasingly global, and labour and politics which remain bounded to the local scale. An employee is tied to his local community, the company for which he works always less. A public authority is bound by definition to the service of its territory, but, on the contrary, the economic actors whom it faces have a very different and wider scope for their action. Therefore, the conditioning capacity of the economic players over public institutions is much stronger today than ever before.

This asymmetry, typical of our times, is the first element that labour market organisations have to consider very carefully; and in order to maintain the efficiency of their services, policy-makers are called to overcome some "institutional inertia" (OECD 2014), promote new organisational models, incorporate labour market activities into comprehensive economic development projects. In other words, global competition requires labour market structures as an extension of their traditional functions and interventions; an extension of their mission, to meet the real needs both of businesses and workers. To this aim, labour market structures are required, in particular, to act on the basis of an adequate system of economic and territorial intelligence (" l'intelligence des territoires", according to the French experience), primarily by promoting adequate analysis of the quality of the production factors (business and labour) and the real values of a territory; then, to connect the collection of data and information (description of the phenomena and trends) to the subsequent moments of knowledge (assessment of the phenomena), decisions and actions (active participation in the choices concerning planning and monitoring activity).

In essence, labour market structures are increasingly required to strengthen their theoretical knowledge heritage; to make it functional for the correction of imperfections that limit the matching of supply and demand; to develop and use tools to assess functional activity (as descriptive indicators) and programming activity (as planning indicators); in essence, to know how to connect the past, the present and the future.

These new tasks of the labour market structures – from economic and territorial intelligence to an active participation to planning activities - require a strict cooperation between the main public and private development's actors, a shared vision of the economic and social processes and their interconnections, the implementation of horizontal and vertical institutional coordination. In other words, an appropriate governance mechanism to assure the effectiveness of the labour market policies.

2.2 The quality of the regulatory system

Global competition highlights the growing importance of the institutional factors, namely the set of laws and rules governing the behaviour of the most important development actors: governments, businesses and business systems, workers and trade unions. In fact, experience has shown that improving economy and social welfare as well as promoting a sustainable growth depends, ultimately, on the capability to adapt institutions, norms and behaviours. Here are the problems which refer to the governance-government of such processes. This approach is used not only to analyse the present situation but also to drive its evolution.

Competition needs regulation: this is a necessity for the economic players, only in a fair and transparent environment do they have the possibility and the opportunity to verify and eventually affirm the real value of their own ideas, projects and initiative. Starting from this assumption we arrive to address the issue - very topical today - of the relationship between the quality of regulatory system (not necessarily identified in the law) and social and economic performances (since the eighties of the last century a group of economists, for instance, the British economist John Williamson and the economist and politician Padro Paul Kuczynski (currently president of the Republic of Perù) based their studies on an essentially experimental approach, highlighting the fundamental role of the institutional economics for good development).

3. Global government – global governance

In this regard, in order to proceed further in our reflection, it is useful to recall the terms of the clear distinction between government and governance, two concepts that are often inappropriately used and interchanged.

Global Government is the set of international standards that are based on an implementing agency which is responsible for supervising their application. Examples are the IMF-International Monetary Fund, the World Bank or the UN agencies. More widely, government is the set of rules that refer to an institutional body – international, national or regional – with executive power, responsible for overseeing their implementation.

Global Governance, on the contrary, is a set of rules that are enforceable without the intervention of a national or supranational executive structure (Cassese 2002). Governance - ultimately - is provided by a network of standards and rules (Web of Rules) of different kinds and origins (including for example collective agreements made by trade unions and managerial associations) which converge in the solution of practical problems. Their application results both by judicial decisions from multiple sources that are part of the net of standards, and from autonomous initiatives taken by private operators.

It is noted that, in the globalisation process, legal decisions can be requested by a state, as is the case during competition. These trends, which are the result of history, have a growing cultural importance for the purpose of the regulatory reform, both inside and outside the borders of a state. It is a common opinion, we may add, that in the current European system the regulatory reform necessary to build a new economic governance, should aim at enhancing just the autonomous contribution of the main private economic and social actors.

To achieve this goal, for example, the European Economic and Social Committee EESC repeatedly calls the EU Commission on the importance of giving broad scope to social dialogue in order to address issues such as "the impact of digitization on the services industry and the employment - which has - an impact on the entire society" (see Opinion CCMI/136 of 16 September 2016).

4. The regulatory reform: towards a governance without government?

The growing interdependence between human activities affects the legal system more and more, their nature, their hierarchical structure and their adaptability, in view of certain needs and goals.

When the boundaries are expanded, as in the case of supranational institutions (EU, Eurasian Economic Union, NAFTA, or similar bodies related to the integration processes), this gives space to vertical subsidiarity. But also, the need for a horizontal adjustment occurs when the regulation or the self-regulation replaces the state rules and institutions which are no longer suited to the new spatial dimension of the sector economy.

This has already happened, for example, in sectors as telecommunications, energy, maritime and air transport, banking and insurance, in which, beside the national constraints, many other rules came out directly by the agreements between private or public operators, active in the international space. Last, in order of time, the definition of a new architecture of the international finance. Let's take, for instance, the IATA agreements for air transport, or the agreements between national systems to manage their activities on the matter of railway or postal services, and more. The same remarks may be done about the self-regulative standards applied in the sport activities, mostly promoted by international institutions with private status. Regulatory reform has paved the way to liberalisation and privatisation in many sectors: energy, air transport, telecommunications and banking services, as well as in many agreements related to the best management of the new situations. All these are striking cases of adaptations by the sector markets to the new spatial dimension.

These facts highlight the direct relationship existing between expansion of globalisation processes and governance systems, understanding, the latest, as the convergence of norms or networks of norms by various sources as well as by various hierarchical ranges. In fact, experience clearly shows:

- That we must overcome the idea that only the state and national laws are the sources of regulations;
- That globalisation is creating an increasingly fragmented international legal space;
- At the same time, the nation-state has not disappeared with globalisation and liberalisation; rather globalisation is forcing nation-states into a vast process of transformation, adjustment and reorganisation to adapt their

structures and functions to new situations and overcome their own weaknesses;
- The nation-state loses power when it grants part of its sovereignty to international institutions, but gains power when these institutions support the nation-states in implementing their policies.

In this regard, although we do not talk very much about it, all the new standards of governance at the political-legal level suggest a shift from rigid to flexible regulations. That is, a shift from legislative rules adopted by the parliaments having their reference into the jurisdiction of the ordinary courts, to more flexible rules originated in the free bargaining, both collective and individual. With the result that the jurisdiction may be relieved by the use of conciliation and arbitration.

Globalisation is implying, in short, a different relationship between the nation-state and non-state actors, which in our case play a key role in the labour market's functioning.

It is a fact that in the international arena, numerous other organisations operate alongside the states, and their number has grown a lot, especially from the second half of the twentieth century. It deals with governmental or non-governmental organisations, business associations, trade unions, multinational companies: all structures that largely end up limiting the role of the states. This applies in particular also to intergovernmental organisations which are constituted by the national governments of the states, but that ultimately take increasingly higher degrees of autonomy, going so far as to sign treaties, make rules and regulations, as well as to extend their competences, and also to multiply autonomously their numbers. Here some data to give a precise idea of what we are talking about: *Intergovernmental organisations* were 37 in 1906, 123 in 1951, 1,039 in 1981 and 7,608 in 2011. *Non-governmental organisations* were 176 in 1909, 832 in 1951, 13,232 in 1981 and 56,834 in 2011.

Some examples to clarify the situation: an example of multiplication comes from the *Codex Alimentarius Commission*, established in 1963 by the FAO (the UN organisation for food and agriculture) and WHO (World Health Organization). An example of an intergovernmental network is *the Basel Committee on Banking Supervision*, consisting of representatives of the 28 EU member states. An example of a hybrid public-private organisation is the ISO (*International Organization for Standardization*). An example of a global regulator completely private entity is the IIC (*International Chamber of Commerce*).

All of these organisations participate together with the states, or without them, to construct the international regulations (the *globalised administrative regulation*, Kingsbury et al. 2005). In total, we're talking about *2.000* regulatory regimes.

In practice, all human activity is now governed by regulations of different nature and sources that go beyond the rules of a nation-state, and this has happened because in the contemporary world many issues relating to human progress could no longer be resolved at the state level. Hence the emergence of a global governance that cannot be referred to a single government, as a state institution, but to a new global governance system. Hence the question: where are we going? The global government is still a general idea, far to be a reality. In the same time, the global regulatory regimes are a very complex, hybrid, system, in permanent evolution towards a situation, which some scholars call a "governance without government".

5. The Labour Market Information System in the framework of the new governance

The challenges of the ongoing industrial revolution, as we have seen it were underlined by the OECD secretary, and require a profound change in the way of thinking as well as in the operational way. In coherence with what is underway with the construction of the new governance system, the functioning of labour market services and, in particular, the management of the specific issue of the information and communication system, this requires the organisation of a different relationship between public and private, between state laws and private acts, as the agreements among social partners, which are increasingly taking on a decisive strategic value.

A new labour market governance requires, in essence, the definition of a regulatory system under which public institutions define and guarantee to non-state actors a well-defined, autonomous decision-making space that is functional in solving new problems; creating moments of sharing with the public authority, but leaving the same information exchanges on which the actual adjustments are made, which are organised and managed directly by the main players of development.

The nature of ongoing changes, their speed, intensity and complexity, do not only require the involvement of private stakeholders in public decisions; but something more and very different. Such changes require that public authorities limit their interventions to strategic guidelines and support actions, but leave private operators the responsibility both of building information systems and the adjustments to be pursued.

By now, too many variables are out of control at public institutions; too many constraints that the development processes impose on the macro and micro economic level. Under these conditions, politics and public institutions can hardly give assurances of results in terms of employment and work. Rather, the action of public institutions can have an effective impact on current reality insofar as it is capable of interpreting the current dynamics, of orienting them along a shared objective axis, by organising forums for permanent dialogue with non-public actors aimed at promoting convergence between labour policies, industrial relations policies and social policies; and to this end assuring that the administrative machine will operate as an efficient supporting tool. This is the essence of the transition from government to governance in the labour market, also with regard to production and management of information flows.

References

Bodei, Remo (2010): The Shared Future or Global Uncertainty, in: International Letter, No. 106, online: www.letterainternazionale.it

Cassese, Sabino (2002): The Crisis of the State, Yale: University Press

Czempiel, Ernst-Otto (2005): The CSCE-Process: Stabilization of the Blocks through Cooperation?, in: Hoppenstedt, Wolfram/Pruessen, Ron/Rathkolb, Oliver (Eds.): Global Management, Wien: LIT Verlag

European Economic and Social Committee EESC (2016): The Impact of Digitalization on the Service Industry and Employment, Opinion n. CCM/136, Bruessels

Gurría, Angel (2016): New Challenges, New Approaches, in: Love, Patrick (Eds.): Debate the Issues: New Approaches to Economic Challenges, Paris: OECD Publishing

Kingsbury, Benedict/ Krisch, Nico/Stewart, Richard B. (2005): The Emergence of Global Administrative Law, 68 Law and Contemporary Problems 15

OECD (2014): Report on Effective Approaches to Support Implementation of the G20/OECD High-Level Principles on Long-Term Investment Financing by Institutional Investors, Paris

OECD (2017): Meeting of the OECD Council at Ministerial Level, Basic Document, Paris

UN (2015): 2030 Agenda for Sustainable Development, New York

INFORMATION ON AUTHORS

Dr Moreno Baruffini has been a post doc researcher at the Institute for Economic Research – IRE – (Università della Svizzera italiana, USI) since June 2014. He works in the fields of regional sciences and statistics. Moreno Baruffini graduated with honours from the Politecnico di Milano (Italy) with a dissertation in regional sciences. He worked at the METID Centre (Metodi E Tecnologie Innovative per la Didattica) at the Politecnico di Milano and at the Institute of Earth Sciences of the University of Applied Sciences of Southern Switzerland (SUPSI). In his PhD dissertation at the Faculty of Economics of the Università della Svizzera italiana (USI) he analysed labour market flexibility, security and complexity in the Swiss context. He is currently a senior researcher at the Observatory for Economic Dynamics (O-De) and his academic work concerns the analysis of European cross-border labour markets and economics of border regions, specifically focusing on trans-border mobility and "flexicurity".

Dr Moreno Baruffini
Institute for Economic Research (IRE)
Via Maderno 24
CP 4361
6904 Lugano
Phone: + 41-(0) 58 666 41 16, Fax: + 41-(0) 58 666 46 62
E-Mail: moreno.baruffini@usi.ch
Homepage: www.ire.eco.usi.ch

Prof Vyacheslav Bobkov is an honoured science worker of the Russian Federation. He is founder and General Director of the All-Russia Centre of Living Standards since 1991. He is also a Chief Research Worker at the School of Science for "Human Resource Management" at Plekhanov Russian University of Economics (Moscow) since 2016. He has long-standing experience in researching political economy, labour economics, manpower market and employment, quality of life and living standards of population. Over 300 scientific and applied projects have been carried out under his guidance in more than 50 Russian regions. In addition, he contributes to the quarterly monitoring of incomes and living standards in the country. Vyacheslav is a member of both the European Network – SUPI (Social

Uncertainty, Precarity and Inequality) as well as EURISPES - Institute of Political, Economic and Social Studies (Rome).

Prof Vyacheslav Bobkov
School of Science "Human Resource Management"
Plekhanov Russian University of Economics
Stryemyanniy Per., 36
115093 Moscow
Russia
Phone: +7(499)1649964
E-mail: bobkovvn@mail.ru
Homepage:www.rea.ru

Dr Claudiu Brândaș is an Associate Professor at the West University of Timisoara, Faculty of Economics and Business Administration, Department of Business Information Systems. He obtained his PhD from Babes-Bolyai University of Cluj-Napoca (Romania), the Faculty of Economics in Decision Support Systems conception and design. Currently, his research interests include DSS (Decision Support Systems), Business Intelligence, Web Mining, Ontologies and Web Semantics, Agent Based-Modelling and Corporate Governance Support Systems. Since 2015 he is affiliated with the research group on Social and Economic Complexity from the West University of Timisoara.

Dr Claudiu Brândaș
The West University of Timisoara
Business Information Systems Department
Research Group on Social and Economic Complexity
Blvd. V. Parvan 4, 300223 Timisoara
Phone: +40 256 592 551, Fax +40 256 592 551
E-mail: claudiu.brandas@e-uvt.ro
Homepage: www.feaa.uvt.ro; www.claudiubrandas.ro

Melanie Castello is a social scientist. Her research focus lies on regional labour markets, sustainable development and demographic change. She studied sociology and political sciences at the University of Magdeburg (Germany). In her master thesis, she analysed the impacts of increased fuel prices on the elderly population. From 2015 to 2017 she has worked at the Institute for Economics, Labour and Culture (IWAK) at the Goethe-University, Frankfurt/Main with a focus on long-term unemployment and labour markets of the healthcare system.

In 2017 she transferred to the University of Magdeburg, commencing her PhD there.

Melanie Castello
Otto-von-Guericke University Magdeburg (OVGU)
Department Political Sciences
Zschokkestraße 32
39104 Magdeburg
Germany
E-mail: Melanie.Castello@ovgu.de

Dr Vera D'Antonio has a PhD in Communication Technology and Society from the Department of Communication and Social Research – Sapienza University of Rome, Italy, and a Master's Degree in History and Digital Humanities from the Univeristy Pablo de Olavide, Seville, Spain. Her studies focus on the effects of Big Data on society and on privacy and reputation management on social network sites. Currently, her research interests include digital communication, computational social science, online identity management and personal privacy. She is part of the Editorial Board of the Scientific Journal Comunicazionepuntodoc (Fausto Lupetti Editore, Bologna).

Dr Vera D'Antonio
Sapienza University of Rome
Department of Communication and Social Research
Via Salaria 113
00198 Roma
Phone: +39 06 499 18 448, Fax +39 06 499 18 403
E-mail: vera.dantonio@uniroma1.it
Homepage: www.coris.uniroma1.it

Dr Andrew Dean is a British researcher and writer on the topics of employment, skills and the labour market. He works at the University of Exeter's Marchmont Observatory, a research centre dedicated to supporting real-world interventions in local and regional labour markets. His main interests include regional and local labour market monitoring, achieving impact through research, the role of social partners in employment policy, European Union employment programmes, vocational education and training and linking policy with practice.

Dr Andrew Dean
Senior Impact and Partnership Development Manager
Marchmont Observatory, IIB
University of Exeter
Innovation Centre
Rennes Drive
Exeter, EX4 4RN
United Kingdom
Phone: +44-(0)1392 724925, Mobile: +44-(0)7900692593
Twitter: @AndrewDean20
E-mail: a.dean@exeter.ac.uk
Homepage: www.exeter.ac.uk/business/marchmont/

Prof Patrizio Di Nicola is a sociologist and works at ISTAT, the Italian National Institute of Statistics, where he is responsible for organisational well-being, telework and smart working. He is also a Professor of Advanced Organisational Systems at the University of Rome "La Sapienza", where in the past he was also a Professor of Sociology of Organisation and Sociology of Work & Economic Processes. He was scientific director or national coordinator for many researches, and was a managing consultant for national and international government bodies and top enterprises. He is author or contributor of many books and a member of the Scientific Committee of Eurispes and of the Editorial Board of the International Journal of Work Innovation. His current research activity concerns the analysis of precarity and unemployment in the international labour market, with a special focus on youths.

Prof Patrizio Di Nicola
ISTAT – Italian National Institute of Statistics
Direction of Human Resource
Via Cesare Balbo 39
00184 Rome
Italy
Phone: +39-(0) 6 46 73 42 26, Fax: +39-(0) 6 46 73 43 69
E-mail: dinicola@istat.it
Homepage Istat: www.istat.it
Homepage (personal): www.dinicola.it

Prof Alessandra Fasano is a researcher of the sociology of economic processes and works at the "Department of History, Society and Human Studies', at the University of Salento. She has collaborated with "Sapienza" University of Rome and with different research institutes, such as the Italian National Institute of Statistics (ISTAT) and the Institute for Research on Population and Social Policies (IRPPS - CNR). Her research interests include: labour markets in Italy and in Europe; social systems, organisation and public policy analysis; social policies; healthcare, health and social protection; policies of work life balance in Europe, equal opportunities and gender differences.

Prof Alessandra Fasano
Department of History, Society and Human Studies
University of Salento
Studium 2000, Edificio 5, Stanza 29
73100, Lecce
Italy
Phone: +39-(0)832294854
E-mail: alessandra.fasano@unisalento.it

Heike Hoess is an advisor in the Competence Centre Education, VET and Labour Markets at GIZ. The Competence Centre has expertise in the areas of education systems strengthening, basic education, higher education, technical vocational education and training as well as labour market policy.

She has seven years of work experience in development cooperation in research and with GIZ headquarters and at the country level. She started her career in the German Development Institute in Bonn where she did research on donor coordination (Paris Declaration, Accra, Busan). She worked as a TVET and Labour Market advisor in the GIZ employment promotion programme in Rwanda. Since 2013 she is the technical backstopper of different GIZ TVET and Labour Market projects in the MENA region an Africa.

She holds a Bachelor in Political Science from the Institute d'études politique in Lille/France and a Master in Political Science from the University of Potsdam/Germany.

Heike Hoess
Deutsche Gesellschaft für Internationale Zusammenarbeit (GIZ) GmbH
Germany
E-mail: produkt-beschaeftigung@giz.de

Zvjezdana Jelić is a senior specialist for Data Collection and Processing in the Labour and Employment Agency of Bosnia and Herzegovina. She has been working at the agency since 2008. She is engaged in the collection and processing of statistical data concerning employment and unemployment. She prepares information on the basis of results gained from collected and processed data and participates in the preparation of reports on employment and unemployment and publications for the agency. She participated in the analyses and implementation of the EC funded CARDS Project "Employment Policy Reform and Establishment of Labour Market Information System".

Zvjezdana Jelić
Labour and Employment Agency of BiH
Đoke Mazalića 3
71000 Sarajevo
Bosnia and Herzegovina
Phone: +387 (0)33 560 356, Fax: +387 (0)33 209 475
E-mail: zvjezdana.jelic@arz.gov.ba

Dr Uwe Kühnert holds a PhD in economics. He has been working at Personaltransfer GmbH in Berlin as a consultant since 2009. Previously he worked for 18 years as a consultant, researcher and head of division at the former Brandenburg State Agency for Structure and Labour (LASA). He has more than 25 years of experience in the fields of employment, labour market policy, labour market monitoring, training and vocational education, in particular regarding economic transition, structural change and regional development. During his time at LASA, he was actively involved in establishing the Labour Market Information System in Brandenburg. Working several times for GIZ projects as consultant, he is a member of the GIZ German Expert Forum "Human Resources Development and Labour Market".

Dr Uwe Kühnert
PersonalTransfer GmbH
Am Borsigturm 9
13507 Berlin, Germany
Phone: +49 30 330 99 76 80, Fax: +49 30 330 99 76 89
Email: uwe.kuehnert@personaltransfer-gmbh.de
Homepage: www.personaltransfer-gmbh.de

Vadim Kvachev is a senior lecturer in the Human Resources Management Department at Plekhanov Russian University of Economics (Moscow). His fields of scientific interests are precarious employment, social-labour relations, social classes and inequality, social structure and stratification.

Vadim Kvachev
Human Resource Management Department
Plekhanov Russian University of Economics
Stryemyanniy Per., 36
115093 Moscow
Russia
Phone: +79652700769
E-mail: kvachevvg@mail.ru

Dr Christa Larsen is a social scientist. She works in the fields of labour markets, regional development and empirical methods. Christa Larsen studied sociology, political sciences and economics at the Universities of Duisburg and Bielefeld (Germany) and at the University of Oregon (United States). In her dissertation at the University of Essen (Germany), she applied multi-level models in the field of socialisation. She has research experience in the fields of methods and statistics with a focus on quantitative network analyses, as well as in education and professional training, labour markets, socialisation and gender relations. Since 2002 she has been based at the Institute for Economics, Labour and Culture in Frankfurt am Main and has been acting as managing director of the institute since 2008. Her current scientific work concentrates on regional labour market monitoring, regionalised analyses of labour markets for health workers, setting up labour market information systems and conducting regional forecasts.

Dr Christa Larsen
Institute for Economics, Labour and Culture (IWAK)
Centre of Goethe University Frankfurt am Main
Senckenberganlage 31
D-60325 Frankfurt am Main
Phone: +49-(0) 69 79 82 21 52, Fax: +49-(0) 69 79 82 82 33
E-mail: c.larsen@em.uni-frankfurt.de
Homepage IWAK: www.iwak-frankfurt.de
Homepage EN RLMM: www.regionallabourmarketmonitoring.net

Oliver Lauxen is a nursing scientist. He has worked as an elderly care nurse and as a charge nurse in nursing homes and home healthcare services. He studied nursing and health sciences at the Protestant University of Applied Sciences in Darmstadt (Germany) and graduated with a master's degree. Since 2010 he has been a researcher at the Institute for Economics, Labour and Culture (IWAK) at the Goethe-University, Frankfurt/Main. His current scholarship focuses on regionalised analyses of labour markets for healthcare workers and operational competence management in home healthcare.

Oliver Lauxen
Institute for Economics, Labour and Culture (IWAK)
Centre of Goethe University Frankfurt am Main
Senckenberganlage 31
60325 Frankfurt am Main
Germany
Phone: +49-(0) 69 79 82 54 57, Fax: +49-(0) 69 79 82 82 33
E-mail: lauxen@em.uni-frankfurt.de
Homepage IWAK: www.iwak-frankfurt.de

Pierre Lucante is in charge of the "Rural Youth Employment Promotion" Project implemented by GIZ in partnership with the Moroccan Ministry for Labour and financed by BMZ. He has been working for GIZ since 2009. He has experience in the fields of employment promotion, private sector promotion, ICT for development, competition policy, telecommunication regulation and European affairs. He holds Master's degrees in Law from the University of Pau, in Utilities Regulation from the London School of Economics and Political Science and in Management for the MENA Region from the School of Oriental and African Studies, University of London.

Pierre Lucante
Deutsche Gesellschaft für Internationale Zusammenarbeit (GIZ) GmbH
Morocco
E-mail: produkt-beschaeftigung@giz.de

Prof Ronald McQuaid is Professor of Work and Employment at the University of Stirling. He has degrees from Lancaster University and the London School of Economics and a PhD from Harvard University. He has carried out work for many regional, national and supra-national bodies such as the European Commission, UK, Scottish and Northern Ireland Governments, UK Commission for Employment and Skills, Joseph Rowntree Foundation, the Asian Development Bank Institute and various agencies and employers in the fields of employment, unemployment, partnerships and economic development. He has written over 100 academic publications as well as many reports on employment and related issues.

Prof Ronald McQuaid
Management, Work and Organisation Division
Stirling Management School University of Stirling
Stirling FK9 4LA
Scotland, UK
Phone: +44-(0) 1786 467323
E-mail: ronald.mcquaid@stir.ac.uk
Homepages: www.stir.ac.uk/management; rms.stir.ac.uk/converis-stirling/person/22715

Tilman Nagel is the head of the GIZ Competence Centre of Education, Vocational Education and Training and Labour Markets. The Competence Centre covers the sectors of primary and secondary education, technical and vocational education and training (TVET), university education as well as labour market policy.

Tilman Nagel holds a Master in Economics from the University of Bamberg/Germany and Charles University in Prague/Czech Republic. He has 13 years working experience at GIZ, both at head quarter and at the country level. Tilman combines expertise in planning, monitoring and evaluation of TVET and employment projects, moderation of stakeholder dialogues as well as policy advice and leading teams in complex development projects. Prior to his current position, he served as manager of a TVET and employment promotion programme in Egypt.

Tilman Nagel
Deutsche Gesellschaft für Internationale Zusammenarbeit (GIZ) GmbH
Germany
E-mail: produkt-beschaeftigung@giz.de

Prof Irina Novikova is an Associate Professor at Plekhanov Russian University of Economics. She carries out research dedicated to regional labour markets, employment of various population groups, remote employment and information economics. Irina is developing a proposal in order to regulate employment in the Russian Far East.

Prof Irina Novikova
Plekhanov Russian University of Economics
Oktyabrskaya str. 162-27
675000 Blagoveschensk, Amur region
Russia
Phone: +7962293309
E-mail: irakrasa@mail.ru

Dr Nina Oding is senior researcher and the Head of the Research department at the International Centre for Social and Economic Research "Leontief Centre" in St Petersburg, Russia. As an expert and project coordinator, she has built up a vast experience in developing and managing research programs, policy advice projects, in research of urban economics and regional development. She conducts studies regarding the transit economy issues, budgetary federalism, public sector reform and spatial planning. Nina Oding is a team leader and deputy of the director in the international projects commissioned by WB, TACIS, EU, USAID, DFID. Her current scientific work is on regional development issues and regional labour markets.

Dr Nina Oding
International Centre for Social and Economic Research "Leontief Centre"
25,7ya Krasnoarmeyskaya 190005
St .Petersburg
Russia
Phone: +79812-746 8830
E-mail: oding@leontief.ru
Homepage: www.leontief.ru

Dr Ciprian Pânzaru studied sociology and economy at the West University of Timisoara. Currently, he works as a researcher and teacher at the Sociology Department coordinating disciplines such as Sociology of Migration, Labour Economics, Social Mobility and Economic Sociology. His areas of interest include computational sociology, international migration, labour market issues and population forecasting. Since 2015 he leads a research group on Social and Economic Complexity at the West University of Timisoara.

Dr Ciprian Pânzaru
The West University of Timisoara
Sociology Department
Research Group on Social and Economic Complexity
Blvd. V. Parvan 4
300223 Timisoara
Romania
Phone: +40-256 592 148, Fax +40-256 592 182
E-mail: ciprian.panzaru@e-uvt.ro
Homepage: www.cpanzaru.socio.uvt.ro

Dr Carmine Piscopo, PhD, is a Fellowship Researcher at the Department of Communication and Social Research – Sapienza University of Rome, where he is working on cultural heritage and digital strategies. Currently, his research interests include territorial development, mobility media, digital communication and sociology of consumption.

Carmine Piscopo
Sapienza University of Rome
Department of Communication and Social Research
Via Salaria 113
00198 Roma
Italy
Phone: +39 3295457214, Fax +39 06 499 18 403
E-mail: carmine.piscopo@uniroma1.it
Homepage: www.coris.uniroma1.it

Sigrid Rand studied political science, economics and Slavonic studies at Goethe University Frankfurt, Germany. Since 2010, she has been working as a senior researcher at the Institute for Economics, Labour and Culture (IWAK)/Centre of Goethe University Frankfurt. Sigrid Rand carries out research in the fields of employment and social policy with a particular focus on skills systems, migration, social care and long-term care. Since 2013, Sigrid Rand manages the European Network on Regional Labour Market Monitoring (EN RLMM).

Sigrid Rand
Institute for Economics, Labour and Culture (IWAK)
Centre of Goethe University Frankfurt am Main
Senckenberganlage 31
60325 Frankfurt am Main
Germany
Phone: +49-(0) 69 79 82 54 74, Fax: +49-(0) 69 79 82 82 33
E-mail: s.rand@em.uni-frankfurt.de
Homepage IWAK: www.iwak-frankfurt.de
Homepage EN RLMM: www.regionallabourmarketmonitoring.net

Prof Piera Rella is a sociologist. She is Associate Professor at the Faculty of Political Sciences, Sociology, Communication at the Department of Social and Economic Sciences - "Sapienza" University of Rome, where she teaches "Economic Sociology of Welfare" and "Sociology of Work and Organisation".

She is member of AIS (Italian association of sociology); was a member of an international group of researchers, promoted by Denki Rengo (Japanese Trade Union), which conducted three surveys (1985, 1994, 2000) on industrial workers in the electronics' sector. She was scientific coordinator for many researchers in the field of underdevelopment and emigration and in gender differences and empowerment related with unemployment, work, social stratification and integration, especially in the city of Rome.

Prof Piera Rella
Department of Social and Economic Sciences
Faculty of Political Science, Sociology, Communication
Sapienza – University of Rome
Via Salaria 113,
00198 Roma
Italy
Phone: +39-(0) 6 49918446
E-mail: piera.rella@uniroma1.it

Prof Marco Ricceri acts as the Secretary General of the EURISPES, a primary Italian research institute in the economic and social sectors, mostly engaged in building and reinforcing a network of excellence with other European research institutes. Marco Ricceri is also Professor at the Link Campus University of Malta in Rome, coordinator of the Ethic Committee of the European Agency of Investments (AEI), enrolled in the special list of experts of the EU-Commission, DG Research, CORDIS Research Programme dealing with the issues: European Social Policy and Industrial Relations. After the degree in Political Science, University of Florence, Marco Ricceri worked at the National Study Office of the CISL (Free Italian Trade Union) dealing with the questions of the technological processes and their contribution to the economic development and social changes, at the Parliamentary Groups of the Italian Chamber of Deputies as Chief Officer for the Economic Policies. He acted also as substitute member of the European Social Committee (CES), advisor of the Italian Ministry for Scientific Research, and member of the National Council of the Italian journalist association.

Prof Marco Ricceri
EURISPES
via Cagliari 14
00198 Rome
Italy
Phone: +39-06 68 21 02 05, Fax +39-06 68 92 898
E-mail: eurispes.intl-dept@libero.it
Homepage: www.eurispes.it

Prof Ludovica Rossotti is Professor of Labour Organisation at the University of Perugia. Since 2014, she has a PhD in "Applied Research in Social Sciences" from the Department of Social and Economic Sciences, at Sapienza- University of Rome. During her PhD, she developed a parallel analysis on European and Latin America policies, in particularly in Brazil, where she conducted a period of study and research. She is currently engaged in the following researches: youth and illegality, public and private employment office, policies to combat poverty at European and international level focused on basic income.

Prof Ludovica Rossotti
Department of Experimental Medicine
Faculty of Medicine, University of Perugia
Via Bambagioni 4,
06126 Perugia
Italy
Phone: +39-(0) 6 49918446
E-mail: ludovica.rossotti @uniroma1.it

Javier Ramos Salazar is responsible for the Technical Office of the Basque Employment Service LANBIDE. He works in the field of information systems for the labour market, the evaluation of employment policies and the definition of employment strategies. He studied economics at the University of the Basque Country UPV/EHU and his work experience has been linked to both education and local development, as well as to the employment services. Regarding employment, he has been responsible for projects such as the Basque Placement Service (LANGAI), the institutional employment web (www.lanbide.net) and the Basque Employment Service (LANBIDE), of which he has been its first General Director. His current professional activity focuses on the development of information systems for the labour market and its relationship with the educational system, identification of needs of skills and qualification in the production structure and the evaluation and monitoring of employment policies.

Javier Ramos Salazar
LANBIDE – Basque Public Employment Service
C/ José Atxotegi 1
01009 Vitoria-Gasteiz, Alava
Spain
Phone: + 34 945181300, Fax: + 34 945017751
E-mail: javier.ramos@lanbide.eus
Homepage: www.lanbide.eus

Lisa Schäfer is a social scientist. She works in the field of labour markets, regional developments in the healthcare sector and empirical methods. She earned her bachelor's degree in sociology and educational science at the University of Trier (Germany) and a master's degree in sociology at the University of Frankfurt (Germany). Since 2015 she has been a researcher at the Institute for Economics, Labour and Culture (IWAK) at the Goethe-University, Frankfurt/Main. Her current scholarly work concentrates on regionalised analyses of labour markets and the usage of e-recruiting in Germany.

Lisa Schäfer
Institute for Economics, Labour and Culture (IWAK)
Centre of Goethe University Frankfurt am Main
Senckenberganlage 31
60325 Frankfurt am Main
Germany
Phone: +49-(0) 69 79 82 36 11, Fax: +49-(0) 69 79 87 63 23 61 1
E-mail: lisa.schaefer@em.uni-frankfurt.de
Homepage IWAK: www.iwak-frankfurt.de

Prof Alfons Schmid is a Professor of Economics at the Johann Wolfgang Goethe University in Frankfurt am Main. His main areas of research are regional developments of employment and labour market, new information technology and its impacts on employment situation, regional competitiveness and attitudes in the context of welfare state.

Prof Alfons Schmid
Institute for Economics, Labour and Culture (IWAK)
Centre of Goethe University Frankfurt am Main
Senckenberganlage 31
D-60325 Frankfurt am Main
Germany
Phone: +49-(0) 69 79 82 82 29, Fax: +49-(0) 69 79 82 82 33
E-mail: alfons.schmid@em.uni-frankfurt.de

Laura Schmid is currently working as an Advisor for the Gesellschaft für Internationale Zusammenarbeit (GIZ) GmbH in the Employment Promotion Project (EPP) in Egypt. Her work in EPP focuses on supporting the promotion of evidence-based Active Labour Market Programmes (ALMPs) for youth employment and the establishment of regional labour market monitoring systems.

Her main areas of expertise are youth employment, labour market policies and, technical vocational education and training. Prior to working for GIZ, she was a research officer for the International Labour Organization's (ILO) Employment Department in Geneva. At the ILO her main focus of work was on the transition to formal employment and research about macroeconomic and fiscal policies.

Laura received her Master of Science in International Relations at the School of Oriental and African Studies (SOAS) in London, UK. and she holds a BA. Sc. in International Economics and Development from Bayreuth University in Germany.

Laura Schmid
Deutsche Gesellschaft für Internationale Zusammenarbeit (GIZ) GmbH
Egypt
E-mail: produkt-beschaeftigung@giz.de

Luzius Stricker is a PhD student in Economics. He received his Bachelor's and Master's degrees in Economics at the Università della Svizzera italiana, USI and since 2014 is a collaborator at the Observatory for Economic Dynamics (O-De). His research focuses on wage policies. In the past he collaborated in projects dedicated to policies for improving regional economic attractiveness.

Luzius Stricker
Institute for Economic Research (IRE)
Via Maderno 24
CP 4361
6904 Lugano
Switzerland
Phone: + 41-(0) 58 666 41 66, Fax: + 41-(0) 58 666 46 62
E-mail: luzius.stricker@usi.ch
Homepage: www.ire.eco.usi.ch

Željko Tepavčević is Deputy Director of the Labour and Employment Agency of Bosnia and Herzegovina. In 2012-2015 he served as Head of the Department for Economy and Social Activities at the municipal administration of East Ilidža. He also headed a team for local economic development and a centre for investment attraction. In addition, he performed the role of project manager in the projects of the BiH Ministry of Human Rights and Refugees that were implemented in the municipality of East Ilidža. He attended training courses, workshops and seminars on public procurement, development of strategic documents, project cycle management, energy efficiency and nomination of projects for the EU pre-accession funds. He participated in the drafting of the Development Strategy of the municipality of East Ilidža, as well as in the preparation of procedures in accordance with the ISO 9001:2008 standard regarding the quality management in the municipality. He was also the President of the Commission for Award of Municipal Incentives and the Commission for the Drafting of the Social Welfare Development Strategy for the municipality of East Ilidža.

Željko Tepavčević
Labour and Employment Agency of BiH
Đoke Mazalića 3
71000 Sarajevo
Bosnia and Herzegovina
Tel: +387 (0)33 560 340, Fax: +387 (0)33 209 475
E-mail: zeljko.tepavcevic@arz.gov.ba
Homepage: www.arz.gov.ba

Etleva Vertopi is the head of the Vocational Education and Training department of the GIZ Programme on Sustainable Economic and Regional Development, Promoting Employment, Vocational Education and Training in Albania (ProSEED). She studied civil engineering at the Polytechnic University, and has a Master's Degree in European Studies from the University of Tirana, Albania. In the last 22 years Etleva Vertopi worked for international organisations such as UNDP, WB, ILO and GIZ on development programmes in the Social, Economic and Human Development area with a focus on vocational education, training and labour markets.

Etleva Vertopi
Deutsche Gesellschaft für Internationale Zusammenarbeit (GIZ) GmbH
Albania
E-mail: produkt-beschaeftigung@giz.de

Siniša Veselinović is the Head of the Domestic Labour Market Department in the Labour and Employment Agency of Bosnia and Herzegovina. He has been working at the agency for seven years on duties which include coordination in employment and harmonisation of labour market policies across Bosnia and Herzegovina. He has relevant experience in the fields of employment, implementation of active and passive labour market policies and coordination of activities in the labour market of Bosnia and Herzegovina. He participated, in the capacity of an expert, in analyses, preparation and implementation of the EC funded labour market projects (CARDS, IPA).

Siniša Veselinović, Head of Domestic Labour Market Department
Labour and Employment Agency of BiH
Đoke Mazalića 3
71000 Sarajevo
Bosnia and Herzegowina
Tel: +387 (0)33 560 355, Fax: +387 (0)33 209 475
E-mail: sinisa.veselinovic@arz.gov.ba
Homepage: www.arz.gov.ba

Neshat Zeneli is a researcher in employment policy at the Faculty of Social Sciences at the University of Tirana. His thesis title was "Alignment of Albanian employment policy with the European Union Standards". He has been working in the fields of labour market policy and vocational education and training for more than 17 years at the National Employment Service of the Republic of Albania. He is under process of graduating with a PhD and has completed a post university graduate program (Master) at the Ferrara University, in Italy in 1998-1999, after graduating from the University of Tirana, at the Faculty of History and Philology, Department of Foreign Languages. Besides the academic studies he has completed in the framework of lifelong learning a lot of vocational training on labour market policy and vocational education and training in France for six months during 2003-3004, and more than 60 weeks of training/ study visits in different European countries, such as Germany, United Kingdom, Austria, Swiss, Denmark, Netherland, Italy, Sweden, Belgium, Romania, Bulgaria, Montenegro, Kosovo, Serbia, Bosnia and Herzegovina, and in International training institutions like the European Training Foundation and at the International training Center of Turin (International Labour Organization). His current position is director of employment service and migration directorate at the National Employment Service and the finalisation of his PhD thesis after the completion of all other obligations (publication of three papers through peer review in scientific journals and three presentations in international scientific conferences).

Neshat Zeneli
Employment Service and Migration Directorate
National Employment Service
B. B. Curri
1001, Tirana
Albania
Phone: +355 44 538807, Mobile: +355672009608
E-mail:zenelineshat@gmail.com; neshat.zeneli@shkp.gov.al
Homepage: www.shkp.gov.al